Connections: A Lifetime Journey

Through the World of Celebrity

By Gordon Lore

Connections: A Lifetime Journey
© 2017. Gordon Lore. All rights reserved.

All illustrations are copyright of their respective owners, and are also reproduced here in the spirit of publicity. Whilst we have made every effort to acknowledge specific credits whenever possible, we apologize for any omissions, and will undertake every effort to make any appropriate changes in future editions of this book if necessary.

No part of this book may be reproduced in any form or by any means, electronic, mechanical, digital, photocopying or recording, except for the inclusion in a review, without permission in writing from the publisher.

Published in the USA by:
BearManor Media
P O Box 71426
Albany, Georgia 31708
www.bearmanormedia.com

Printed in the United States of America
ISBN   978-1-62933-177-5 (paperback)

Book & cover design and layout by Darlene Swanson • www.van-garde.com
Cover photo courtesy of the Calvert Marine Museum, Solomons, Maryland

Dedication

To **Neil and Susan Earle** and **Alan Doshna** for their enduring friendship, encouragement and support, my stepsons **Junius Adam ("Jay") Triche III and his wife Carol, James Lloyd ("Jim") Triche and his wife Beverly and son Justin Bright, and Louis ("Lou") Triche**—whose unfailing love, patience, generosity and giving nature have made my life and journey through this world an unmitigated pleasure—and to the memory of my late wife, **Marty Lore**, the love of my life.

Contents

Introduction:	An Odyssey to the Chesapeake Bay and Beyond	ix
Chapter One	The Boggs Dynasty	1
Chapter Two	Stars Sailing the Chesapeake Bay	21
Chapter Three	Burl Ives	45
Chapter Four	The UFO Connection	61
Chapter Five	Chaco Canyon High: Ecstasy in New Mexico	93
Chapter Six	The Psychic Connection	125
Chapter Seven	Beverly Hot Springs	135
Chapter Eight	Frank Gehry and the Walt Disney Concert Hall	157
Chapter Nine	Kidney Kill	169
Chapter Ten	Quick Takes: From Baltimore to Stockholm	179
	References	217
	Index	237
	About the Author	245

Acknowledgements

A very special thanks goes to my stepson, Jay Triche, for his expert technical help in preparing this manuscript for publication.

Special thanks also to Neil and Susan Earle, Duarte, California, and Alan Doshna, Syracuse, New York, for their friendship and support and their reading of the manuscript and offering helpful suggestions.

Thanks also to my grand niece, Jessica Lore-Lawshe, Sterling, Virginia, for her generous help with the photos.

Thanks are also extended to Jon Shaw and Faye Lore, Baywood on the Patuxent, St. Leonard, Maryland, for providing photos and other family-related information.

A special appreciation is extended to my editor, Robben Barquist, who is every author's dream. Except for a few minor changes conforming to publishing style, he has left my manuscript virtually intact. I am also grateful to my publisher, Ben Ohmart, an unusually industrious young man who has built BearManor Media into a major celebrity-based publishing firm. Ben is to be commended for trying to bring an old manual/electric typewriter author into the 21st Century of publishing. Their patience and understanding is greatly appreciated.

Introduction:

An Odyssey to the Chesapeake Bay and Beyond

Early Memories

I will start this odyssey with the first three words of Charles Dickens' immortal classic, *David Copperfield* (1850): "I am born." On March 15, 1936. The Ides of March. The day Julius Caesar was assassinated in 44 B.C. One hundred years and nine days after the Battle of the Alamo (March 6, 1836). The old income tax day.

The first thing I remember was being caught with my parents and grandparents in a violent hurricane in the summer of 1938 in the middle of the Chesapeake Bay in Southern Maryland when the storm hit in all its fury. We were in dad's race-cruiser *Penguin*.

Grandfather and Grandmother Frank and Annie DeBoy were on the floor of the rocking-and-rolling boat praying for deliverance. Dad, G.I. Rupert ("Dick") Lore, came to the rescue. He knew the bay and its eccentricities like he knew his homeport. While Frank and Annie were wailing like banshees, Dick steered the storm-lashed *Penguin* to port. It was reminiscent of Captain Guy Earle, skipper of the vessel that fought its way into the harbor at Oporto, Spain, during a violent North Atlantic snow-and-rain storm during World War II. This incident is depicted in my book *The Earle Family of Newfoundland and Labrador* (2015).

During the summer of 1938 or 1939 (I was two or three then), dad took my infant brother, Jon Shaw, Mom Dora and me for an outing on the bay. The *Penguin* stopped at a spot near Drum Point Lighthouse where many thousands of sea nettles were waiting for human flesh to sting on.

Even at that young age, I knew mom was an excellent swimmer. Therefore, I would show her that I was as good. While she wasn't looking, I dove into the water and quickly sank down through the sea nettles to the bottom. I had done it now! A very short life in the offing... The sea nettles might be happy, though....

Mom was alert. She jumped in like Esther Williams, grabbed me from the bottom and dragged me by the neck to the surface. Life could now go on and I could grow up to be a bane to my parents. Still, as the title of the most popular Christmas film of all suggests, it's been *A Wonderful Life* (1946).

World War II on Solomons Island

One of my earliest memories involved the sudden influx of military personnel that swarmed over Solomons Island and the entire Chesapeake Bay area of Calvert County, Maryland, shortly after war was declared against Japan and the Axis following the bombing of Pearl Harbor on December 7, 1941. Nearly 68,000 soldiers and sailors stormed the beaches of the Chesapeake Bay. About one third of these men would go on to join the millions of other service personnel fighting the war upon beaches around the world from the Pacific to Europe and North Africa.

In 1942 and 1943, Army personnel were in training at Solomons and on the beaches of nearby Cove Point, Maryland. It was at Cove Point that dad had a summer cottage. It was also directly in front of our cottage that

Army-Navy soldiers surged ashore in their amphibious vessels as I watched fascinated.

Dad hated this intrusion on the beach in front of our cottage. As he tried to shoo off the soldiers, whose vessels dug large trenches in the sand, he was met with more than a few derogatory comments and more than one middle finger in the air from the training seamen.

As dad returned to the cabin fuming, the soldiers and sailors accepted me as their mascot. I was given rides in some of the amphibious landing craft, including one that traveled under the water of the Chesapeake, then rolled ashore on the sand as one of the young soldiers held me tight and tried to assure me that I would live through it all. Actually, I loved it! The soldiers also seemed to love me. Meanwhile, dad tried to lure me away from them, but I stood my ground and the men on the landing craft cheered me on for it!

It wasn't until after the war that I learned the men who accepted me as their mascot were training for the fighting in Morocco and Algeria in North Africa with the feisty General George Patton. Some of the soldiers were also part of history's largest amphibious assault on the Normandy beachhead in France on D-Day, June 6, 1944. Other Army and Navy personnel who trained on the beaches of Calvert County found their experience to be invaluable during the assaults on Guadalcanal, Tarawa and other military operations in the South Pacific.

At the start of World War II, Solomons Island was a small village of fewer than 300 residents. Following the sudden influx of military personnel intent on ridding the world of the Axis warmongers, however, its population (including many service personnel who rented rooms and houses) swelled to more than 2,600 in only a few short months. Two of these personnel were Navy Lieutenant Commander Joseph ("Joe") Leary and his wife, Anne, who rented a room in our home and remained good friends long after the war ended. Joe and Anne also accepted me as their personal "mascot" and were quick to grab and hug me whenever they visited us in the decade or so following the end of the global conflict.

During the beginning of America's war against the Axis, an amphibious training base quickly sprung up as part of three military bases attracted to Calvert County by Solomons Island's deep, protected harbor. In 1942, the Patuxent Naval Air Station (still in existence today) was rapidly built to aid in the war effort. The small island also hosted the U.S. Navy's amphibious training base, the dispensary, and the mine warfare test and experimental stations.

During this long and frenetic period, the Chesapeake watermen saw their population dwindle as many of them took much higher paying jobs at the bases. Much of the oyster, fish, crab and clam population in the bay and the Patuxent River was nearly decimated by exploding bombs and underwater detonations. I remember that the seafood kill stench was so strong from the explosives that it could be smelled from as far away as the county seat in Prince Frederick more than twenty miles to the north!

Jonathan Livingston Seagull

One of my earliest memories growing up on Solomons Island—where the Patuxent River meets the Chesapeake Bay at the tail end of Calvert County in Southern Maryland—was being awakened every morning by the caw-caw-cawing of seagulls from my second-story bedroom window. I watched as they swarmed over the harbor beneath my window and felt an immediate attraction to them. It was better than any alarm clock. If I didn't hear and see them gracefully winging their way over the harbor, I would think the world had come to an end. I even dreamt that end-of-the-world scenario once or twice.

Decades later, in the early 1980s, I spent three years living in a whaling captain's house complete with widow's walk on the shore of the Chesapeake

Bay in Holland Point, Maryland, about thirty-five miles north of Solomons. A small pier jutted out into the bay. A beautiful bird I named Jonathan Livingston Seagull after the book and later movie sat on a piling of the pier every day for a full year or more. The first thing I saw when I awoke every morning was Jonathan, who never disappointed me.

Then, one day when I looked outside, my feathered friend wasn't there anymore. I never saw him again . . . but I have always remembered him. Today, I have a statue of a seagull I named Jonathan sitting among the many ship models and nautical photographs in my apartment in Santa Clarita, California.

The Oyster House

Growing up working in my father's oyster house, J.C. Lore & Sons, on Solomons Island, was special to me. Tied to the wharf were several oyster dredge boats, including the *William B. Tennison*. This majestic Chesapeake workhorse is still regarded as the vessel holding the oldest or second oldest (sources differ) Coast Guard license (1899-to-date) in North America. The refurbished vessel continues to ply the waters of the Cheapeake Bay and the Patuxent River by taking visitors to the Calvert Marine Museum on regularly scheduled cruises.

I spent many days and a few nights with dad on board the *Tennison* as he planted and harvested his oyster beds from the Chesapeake to one of the bay's main tributaries, the James River in Virginia. One of his beds was near the historic remnants of North America's oldest colonies in Jamestown and Roanoke, Virginia.

During the cold fall-winter nights on the *Tennison*, Dad would cook up a large pot of a soup-stew he called "slumgullion." This consisted of boiling water from the Chesapeake in a large black pot. Then slowly boil a bag of

Navy beans. Add strips of thick bacon and a potato and onion or two. Throw in handfulls of chunky ham. As a final touch, dad would expertly shuck a pint or so of freshly caught oysters and carefully spread them into the boiling stew. This was followed by a slow stirring with a large wooden spoon (that was my job). After adding a liberal amount of Old Bay seasoning from Baltimore and letting it slowly simmer on the makeshift stove in the captain's cabin, it was a meal worth writing home about. It might even qualify for a spot on the menu at Antoine's in New Orleans.

Arriving at the oyster house pier with the *Tennison* or another oyster dredge boat loaded to the point that it might sink if a fierce storm or hefty waves confronted it made me hold my breath. Dad wasn't worried, however. He had done it many times before . . . and after.

We nearly lost dad one day in 1946. I had just seen a movie on the old theater-over-water Evans Pavilion. Mother and I were slated to be at the oyster house late at night to welcome dad and the *Tennison* loaded with oysters home.

The lights at the oyster house were on. The headlight on the *Tennison* shone bright as the boat sped through the harbor. This was unusual. Dad always slowed down to the regulated speed after entering the harbor. We immediately knew something was wrong. The old hooker was coming in full throttle, churning the placid water under its bow.

Dad was at the wheel feeling weak, ready to pass out. The worker who was helping him steer the boat to its dock lay dead at his feet. Dad had tried to revive him, but was unsuccessful. He also knew he had to keep himself alive if he were to arrive home.

The dredge boat slammed into the wharf with a thud that seemed to rock the entire oyster house. This knocked my mother and I down. What the hell was happening? Where is dad? Is he dead or alive?

Father slowly opened the cabin door and stumbled onto the dock. He was oviously weak and barely able to step ashore when he quickly passed out and fell at our feet. He had been overcome in the shut-up wheelhouse as deadly carbon monoxide fumes penetrated his space in the shuttered cabin.

After dad fell at her feet, mom Dora screamed for my Uncle Joe to call the paramedics from the Prince Frederick county seat twenty-one miles away. Luckily, an ambulance was already in the vicinity. It had responded to another local emergency call and was able to arrive at the oyster house in only a few minutes.

Dad was revived as we stood by terrified. Mom joined him in the ambulance as they sped north to the Calvert County Hospital. It all scared the hell out of me and I never fogot the day dad almost lost it all.

Bookworm Heaven

In 1942, World War II was raging in the Pacific and European theaters. We moved into a Victorian-style three-story home overlooking the Solomons harbor. The property had a large lawn, a huge garden area leading down to the town swamp, and even an outhouse.

Dad was the local Air Raid Warden. At night, the island turned black as a defense against a possible Nazi submarine attack. There had been at least one report of what some residents believed to have been a sighting of an enemy submarine plying the waters of the Chesapeake.

I drew my bedroom curtains and turned my clothes chest light on to read. Even then I was a voracious reader. Dad would shine his powerful flashlight into my room while yelling for me to turn the light off during those long required blackout evenings. For several years, those were long, black, dusk-to-dawn nights.

Our home attic was filled with books from the previous owner, the town doctor and his daughter. These inlcuded a complete set of the Household Editions of the works of Charles Dickens, old medical books and journals from the nineteenth century, and a number of Tarzan books by Edgar Rice Burroughs.

I was in bookworm heaven. As the years sped by, I added many volumes of my own. I spent many hours in the attic and on the screen porch of our home reading. The world was coming home to me as I felt confined to my small spot on our small island with the Chesapeake Bay on one side and the Patuxent River on the other.

Having my eyes glued to a good book became my passion. Not so with my parents, particularly my mother. She thought I was mostly wasting my time by preferring to read and learn rather than actively seeking employment at the oyster house or elsewhere.

Shortly before entering my three-year stint at the private McDonogh School for Boys with a military regimen in Baltimore (see Chapter One), my mother decided that the only way to get me away from the books was to get the books away from me. Maybe mom took a leaf from the book burning in Nazi Germany. Crammed into our attic and my bedroom was a virtual library of works by William Shakespeare, Bertrand Russell, Henry David Thoreau, Herman Melville, Socrates, Plato, Robert Louis Stevenson, Franz Kafka, Aldous Huxley, Leo Tolstoy, Sigmund Freud, Margaret Mitchell, Jane Austen, Oscar Wilde, Fyodor Dostoevsky, William Faulkner, Ernest Hemingway, John Steinbeck, Charles Dickens, James Joyce, George Orwell and many other practitioners of the writing pen. What did they have to do with getting a job? Earning a living? Nothing. Worthless.

Meanwhile, dad had pyromanic tendencies. He maintained a wide area under a large tree in our backyard where he regularly burned trash. He almost lovingly tended to those fires. Pages of burned paper floating into the air excited him. There was even talk around town that he may have burned down the old ice house he owned in order to collect the insurance. Mom apparently took her cue from that.

One day, while I was away from home, mother cornered father and persuaded him to haul box-after-box of books from the attic and my bedroom out onto the burning spot in the backyard. Father stood by with the matches as mother threw the books into a huge pile. As dad was ready to stike the match, I returned home.

I couldn't believe what I was seeing. I was about fifteen at the time, but thoughts of matricide and patricide quickly entered my too-learned brain. I grabbed mom's arm and swung her around.

"Goddammit, Mom! What are you doing?!" I screamed. "I swear to God, if you burn those books, I will throw you on top of the fire!"

My scream was a howl of freedom. Freedom to read the books I loved. To learn. To be who I was and wanted to be. I would be goddamned if I was going to allow this assault on literary freedom to succeed.

My forceful outburst was enough. With stunned looks, mom and dad allowed me to rebox the books and return them to their resting places. They never interfered with my desire to read again. Nor did they encourage it.

James A. Michener

My high school years were spent in a strictly regimented military style at the McDonogh School near Baltimore, about eighty-five miles north and slightly east of Solomons. I hated the military regimen, but did find it to be a good learning experience.

My English teacher was Justin Williams. Being a real film lover who, even then, spent as much time in a darkened movie theater as he could, I was intrigued to learn that Justin's brother was Rhys Williams, who I knew was one of Hollywood's most respected supporting actors.

It was 1953 and, already, Rhys had an impressive and long list of credits. These included his first film, *How Green Was My Valley* (1941), followed by

Mrs. Miniver (1942), *The Bells of St. Mary's* (1945), *The Farmer's Daughter* (1947) and *The World in His Arms* (1952). I had seen all of these films and would have loved to have met Rhys Williams.

I had to settle for James A. Michener instead. Not a bad substitute.

I don't know how Justin Williams was able to persuade Michener to give a talk at our small English class, but he did. Perhaps the hook was that the author loved sailing on the Chesapeake Bay (see Chapter Two.)

It was a quickly put together event. Michener wanted a relatively short visit with only a few students. There was no announcement in the school paper. We only knew that our teacher had great respect for Michener and his love of all things Chesapeake.

Michener joined our early afternoon English class with a dozen or so students. He was quickly introduced by Justin Williams.

The author was still riding high on his being awarded the Pulitzer Prize for fiction in 1948 for *Tales of the South Pacific* (1947). The book was partly based on his own experiences during World War II. It was quickly adapted by Richard Rodgers and Oscar Hammerstein II for their highly successful Broadway musical *South Pacific* (1947) starring Mary Martin and Ezio Pinza. The movie version with Rossano Brazzi, Mitzi Gaynor and John Kerr followed in 1958.

At the time of our meeting, Justin Williams said that his favorite Mitchener book was the novel *The Fires of Spring* (1949). During our visit with the author, however, it was *Tales of the South Pacific* that the general public really knew about. Michener would go on to write mammoth, epic-sized novels such as *Hawaii* (1959), *Centennial* (1974), *Poland* (1983), *Texas* (1985) *Alaska* (1988), and *Mexico* (1997). From 1939 to 1997, he also tapped out a long list of non-fiction workls.

James Michener was noted for working at his manual typewriter twelve- to-fifteen hours a day seven days a week for months on end to type out his epic novels. Even when the computer age was coming to full flower in the 1990s, Michener held steady to his typewriter. Later, however, as the twentieth century faded into history, he apprehensively turned to a computer keyboard and found it to be a real writing boon.

At the time I met Michener with the rest of our small class, all of that was in the future. Instead of standing up and lecturing before the class, he pulled up a desk and sat down next to me. Our teacher asked him a few introductory questions. Then I piped in.

"What would you consider the great American novel to be?" I asked.

"If I had to pick one, I suppose it would be *The Adventures of Hucklebury Finn* [1884] by Mark Twain," he responded. "Twain knew the people he wrote about and brought them alive like no other author. You really knew about the people he wrote about, the places they inhabited, and the adventures they shared."

"Would you tell us a little about your early life and how you came to be a successful writer?" one of the student cadets asked.

Michener's response was a real education in itself:

My clearest memory goes back to about, when I was only five years old. I was surrounded by wonderful women, particularly my mother. My father was nowhere around. Mom took in stray children in and around my hometown, Doylestown, Pennsylvania. She worked for a real estate man who would move us from house to house to clean and renovate them for sale.

Mother began my education by reading to me the works of Charles Dickens, Emile Zola, and other classic authors. There was a pretty good library near where we lived and I read nearly every book on its shelves. I was also fortunate to have good school teachers dedicated to helping students learn.

My real-life education came when I was a young teenager. I hitchhiked with little more than my two feet, a handful of change, and a small sack of clothes, heading for Florida. The police in Georgia took me in, fed me, let me sleep in one of the jail cells, then gave me a little money and sent me home.

I didn't stay home for long. The urge to keep taveling continued. I was a young hobo on the road. People were good to me. They sometimes took me in and fed me. It was a good education. Courage and a resolve to do my best in life were the lessons I learned. It instilled in me a real love of traveling and what I would call strength of character.

"Would you tell us a little about your tour of duty in the Pacific during the war?" I asked.

Michener elicited a gentle smile and looked up at the ceiling for a moment. Then he slowly looked around the room and spoke:

When we entered the war, I was a thirty six year-old Quaker, which made me exempt from the draft. I decided to enlist, however. I believed that, if we didn't get in there and win the war in both Europe and the Pacific, we would be in real trouble under the thumbs of dictatorial rulers.

I was assigned to duty in the U.S. Navy as an aviator. I remember that, one night, we were flying into Caledonia, where Admiral "Bull" Halsey had his fleet headquarters. The weather was really bad and we had to make a careful pass over a mountain. Then we flew out to sea and carefully made a complete turn around to come home safely. I was really worried that we wouldn't make it, but we did. It was incidents like that that made me appreciate the wonderful guys around me. They played a big role in my continued education and my journey around the South Pacific.

After that, I began concentrating on the wonderful natives, particularly the women and children. Then I started thinking about putting all this down on paper. The seeds had been sown for Tales of the South Pacific. After that book was published, the Broadway muscial quickly began to take shape. It dealt with some wonderful natives of the islands, including the lovely Polynesian children. Also, Richard Rodgers and Oscar Hammerstein II provided some great songs.

Mitchener then told us how much he enjoyed sailing on the Chesapeake Bay.

"Would you consider writing a novel about the Chesapeake?" I asked.

"You know, young man, I have thought about that," he answered. "Someday, I may well write a novel about that beautiful body of water and the people who live on its shores."

That "someday" came a quarter of a century later when his epic *Chesapeake* was published in 1978. It was another of his thousand-plus-page efforts.

Nearly twenty years later, in 1997, I was the Editor of *Contemporary Dialysis & Nephrology* and *For Patients Only* magazines. I was approached by my colleague and friend Kris Robinson, President of the American Association of Kidney Patients, to join with her in interviewing James A. Michener.

The author was suffering from kidney failure and had been on dialysis for the past four years. He agreed to the interview, but soon cancelled out. He was quickly failing. The prolific author said he had accomplished everything he wanted to in his life and was ready to call it quits. He refused further treatment and died about two weeks later on October 16, 1997, at the age of ninety in Austin, Texas. America and the world had lost a literary giant.

My Life With Marty

I met my future wife, Martha ("Marty") Degroat Triche, on my first day as a staff member at the National Investigations Committee on Aerial Phenomena (NICAP) in 1965 (see Chapter Four.) She was there as a volunteer worker, but she immediately found a place in my heart and mind.

Marty was unhappily married then to Junius Triche, an IBM computer researcher. I immediately fell in love with Marty and her sons, Jay, Jim, and Lou Triche. During my tenure at NICAP, she divorced Triche and married Richard ("Dick") Hall (see Chapter Four) in 1967. They divorced three years later and Marty and I were wed when we moved to Albuquerque, New Mexico, in June 1974.

Whew! It was a struggle. My wife, Marty, and mother, Dora, didn't get along at all. Both were strong-willed, independent women who wanted things their way and to hell with the world and whoever didn't agree with them. That division became one of the most difficult and painful drawn-out events of my life.

As I was living with Marty in our woods-strewn home in the Carderock Springs section of Bethesda, Maryland, a suburb of Washington, D.C., Marty and mom had a knock-down, drag-out telephone argument that put me firmly on the family shit list. Mom was determined to squire me away from Marty, even going to the extent of purposefully introducing me to other women at events with Marty present. She also saw to it that I was effectively cut out of dad's estate as long as I was with "that woman."

The bitter conflict between mother and wife came to a sad culmination in December 1976, when mother laid in her hospital room at St. Mary's County Hospital in Southern Maryland. I was there to see her the day before her heart surgery, which she was expected to survive. When I bent down to kiss her, however, she turned away and abruptly said: "I don't want to kiss you. I don't love you anymore!"

Her comment cut through my heart like a dagger. The next day, after I returned to California, mother unexpectedly died on the operating table at Johns Hopkins University Hospital in Baltimore, Maryland, in December 1976 at the age of sixty-eight. I had been left with the lifelong knowledge that she had rejected me as her first-born son on her deathbed. She was determined that I could never be happy or satisfied as long as I was with "that woman."

As it turned out, mom was partially correct. Marty and I had our fair share of marital ups-and-downs. We separated for three years (1981-1984) as I moved back to Maryland to be with dad, who was slowly dying from the effects of diabetes. It was during that separation, however, that Marty and I exchanged the most loving letters and phone conversations of our years together. We had truly missed each other and longed to be together again.

Soon after dad passed away on Halloween night of 1982 and his estate was settled a year later, Marty came to visit at my home on the Chesapeake Bay early in 1984. A few weeks later, I moved with her to Taos, New Mexico, where we participated in the clinical trials for MDMA, later known as the "love drug" Ecstasy (see Chapter Five).

Stars Over Hollywood

Nearly four years after moving back to Los Angeles and later to Burbank, California, I joined the staff as the General Manager at Beverly Hot Springs in Los Angeles. This is where I met and interacted with such celebrities as Tom Hanks, Jodie Foster, the main *Star Trek: The Next Generation* cast (Patrick Stewart, Jonathan Frakes, LeVar Burton, Brent Spiner), Oliver Stone, Frank Langella, Sam Neill, William ("Billy") McNamara, Nick Mancuso, Matthew Modine, Joe DiMaggio, Jean-Claude van Damme, Daryl Hannah, Lesley Ann Warner, Tina Louise and many others. (Chapter Five.)

The Fisher and Saugus Café Experiences

After leaving Beverly Hot Springs in 1992, I began a fifteen-year stint as the Associate Editor and Editor of *Contemporary Dialysis & Nephrology, For Patients Only, Dimensional Stone* and *Tile & Decorative Surfaces* magazines for Publisher Jerry Fisher. Mainly from my headquarters office in Southern California, I interviewed, wrote and published articles about world-famous architect Frank Gehry (Chapter Eight), Human Rights advocate Harry Wu (Chapter Nine) and actor and Screen Actors Guild/American Federation of Television and Radio Artists (SAG/AFTRA) President Ken Norton (Chapter Ten) and many others.

Since the turn of the twenty-first century, I have not had the opportunity to meet many celebrities. I currently live in a seniors' apartment building in Santa Clarita, California, an easy two-block walk to the Saugus Café, the oldest restaurant in Los Angeles County and, possibly, the entire state of California. It is an historic greasy-spoon-type eatery frequented by my colleague and friend, Neil Earle, and me. Neil and his family are the subjects of a chapter in my book *The Earle Family of Newfoundland and Labrador* (2015) and he has been a great help to me in researching and writing this book. We are both history and film buffs and the Saugus Café is the perfect place for our frequent ruminations on these topics and others such as a draft on a book about the history of ice hockey and its rough-and-tumble players on which we are collaborating.

The café has been in continuous operation since 1886. It is situated across the street from the railroad tracks, where the screeching roar of the train whistles seem to shatter the window panes. During the early years, at least two presidents, Benjamin Harrison and Theodore Roosevelt, ate at the restaurant. As he and his entourage waited for the arrival of the connecting train across the street from the café, Roosevelt reportedly said that the Saugus had the best steak he had ever eaten. This opened the door for a countless number of local celebrities to break bread and drink at the café. These included such actors, actresses, directors and other film crew members from both the silent and talkie eras as (in alphabetical order): Harry Carey, Charlie Chaplin, Gary Cooper, Marlene Dietrich, Douglas Fairbanks, John Ford, Hoot Gibson, Cary Grant, D.W. Griffith, William S. Hart, Tom Mix, Mary Pickford, Frank Sinatra, and John Wayne, among many others. Even famed cowboy movie stars Roy Rogers and Gene Autry were believed to have eaten there.

Perhaps the most remembered guest to have eaten at the Saugus Café was the late actor James Dean. On the afternoon of September 30, 1955, the brilliant young actor had his last meal at the eatery on his way to a racing event nearby. After his short lunch, he hopped into his swanky Porsche sports car and sped off. On his way to the race, as he crossed an intersection, he was hit head-on by another car and lost his life in a horrific crash on that tragic day. Only two weeks earlier, he had completed his last scenes opposite Elizabeth Taylor and Rock Hudson in George Stevens' epic masterpiece *Giant* (1956).

Shock waves were sent around the globe. At that time, Dean had starred in only two films: *East of Eden* and *Rebel Without a Cause*, both released in 1955. The two movies had quickly made him a star on the same level as the late silent film actor Rudolf Valentino, who also died at much-too-young an age. Among the café's many photographs of major stars is one of Dean with a rifle cradled over his shoulder standing above Elizabeth Taylor in a scene from *Giant*.

Conclusion

In 1989, my wife Marty was diagnosed with breast cancer. I immediately went into high gear taking care of her with daily, weekly and monthly visits to the doctor and hospitals for three breast surgeries and numerous chemotherapy and radiation treatments.

Marty, a fiercely independent soul, was hardly the easiest person in the world to care for, but I managed. I never knew how really deeply I loved her before she became sick and I became her caretaker. In retrospect, I regard those two and a half years taking care of her as my finest hours. I loved her and missed her terribly when she finally passed away at a nursing home on March 22, 2002. She had died less than thirty-six hours after I told her how much I loved her and she had my permission to pass on to the other side of life into a new beginning at the Right Hand of God.

Rest in peace, dear Marty.

Author's Note

One drawback I had in writing this biographical-style narrative and meeting the many fascinating celebrities involved my not keeping a diary or journal. Nor did I take photographs, mainly out of respect for the privacy of those with whom I interacted. Therefore, I cannot guarantee with complete accuracy what was discussed. I have had to invent most of the actual dialogue based upon what was and may have been said relating to the subjects of the conversations. Memory fades in a number of areas as I enter my ninth decade of life, but my remembrance of the wonderful people and celebrities I have met and the general subject matters I discussed with them remain clear. It is in the exact accuracy of some of the details of these subjects that I do not fully remember.

It was Dr. Allan Nevins, a long-time Professor of American History at Columbia University, who said that while history and "imaginative reconstruction" have their individual places in any historical, biographical, or genealogical book, "the two are not necessarily irreconcilable." He added that it is permissible to use a "controlled imagination" to fill in some of the narrative gaps as long as the author "is careful not to go beyond the reasonably conjectural or to alter the spirit of historical truth."

The same could be said about this journey through the world of celebrity.

Chapter One

The Boggs Dynasty

I first met the political dynamic duo Hale and Lindy Boggs and their children Barbara, Cokie and Tommy on the shores of the Chesapeake Bay at Cove Point, Maryland, in June 1951. My parents had met and become good friends with Hale and Lindy about a year before. A framed signed photo of the family (above) had been sitting on a desk in the entranceway to our home in Solomons Island, Maryland, at the tip end of Calvert County, where the Chesapeake Bay meets the Patuxent River. I was only fifteen at the time, but I had wondered who this distinguished, happy-looking family framed by the U.S. Capitol building in the background was. I was about to find out.

I remember hearing the soft lapping of the waters from the Chesapeake on the shore a short walk from our summer cabin. The moon was visible, shining a dim light on the surface of the water while a soft wind caressed the area. It was the perfect setting.

I knew that the Boggses were a prominent family in the political arenas of Washington, D.C., and they were good friends of Charlie and Elizabeth Coulon, whose cottage was next door to ours. I was eager to meet them after admiring their photo for close to a year.

The first member of the family to charge through the screen door of our cabin porch was Barbara Boggs, who immediately lit up the area like a penetrating searchlight in her gleaming white dress. She was only twelve years old and I was fifteen, but my hormones quickly kicked in and I fell in love. I remembered having seen Ava Gardner and James Mason in *Pandora and the Flying Dutchman* (1951) earlier that same year and, to me, Barbara immediately became the perfect Pandora. I would have sailed across the oceans of the world with her.

"Hello," she said, flashing a smile that entered my heart. "I'm Barbara."

And I'm in love, I silently responded. Her eyes seemed to twinkle a golden glow as my heart soared.

The Surrogate Daughter

Cokie Boggs scurried in next. At the age of seven, she was a little dynamo in a black dress. She literally danced around the room. Without a word, she grabbed Barbara in one hand and me in another and led us both outside. Our hands linked, we ran down to the water's edge as the evening moon shone a wavy line on the waters of the Chesapeake.

Cokie quickly became a matchmaker as she led us in a circular dance. Like her sister, she also quickly found a place in my heart. Today, at the age of eighty, I still remember her words: "If you and Barbara get married, can I be your daughter?"

"Yes! Yes!" I quickly replied.

We removed our shoes and sped around the shoreline with Cokie leading the race. I could have continued like that forever, but the voice of their mother, Lindy Boggs, drew us back to the Coulon cottage. There I also first met Democratic Congressman Hale Boggs, his wife Lindy, and son, Tommy.

In only a few minutes, I had fallen in love with an entire family. It was the start of a twenty-five-year-long friendship that I still cherish. I quickly yearned to find out more about these remarkable people.

Chapter One: The Boggs Dynasty

Hale Boggs

Thomas Hale Boggs, Sr., was born on February 15, 1914, in Long Beach on the Mississippi Gulf Coast. He received a law degree from Tulane University in New Orleans in 1937 and began his practice there.

In 1940, Boggs was elected to the U.S. House of Representatives from the Second District of Louisiana. At the time, he became, at the age of twenty-six, the youngest member of Congress. He served out his first term (1941-1943), but lost a reelection bid in 1942. Then he joined the U.S. Navy as an ensign and served for the remainder of World War II.

After the war, Hale quickly began chartering out his political comeback. In 1946, he was again elected to Congress and reelected thirteen times until his ill-fated death in 1972.

Picking Crabs and Huey Long

During one of my first meetings with Hale, Lindy and their offspring, my parents and I were sitting in the Coulon cottage enjoying drinks. I was alone with Hale for a while. My father had brought along a basket of delicious Chesapeake Bay steamed hard crabs and Boggs was doing his best trying to elicit the flaky meat from the shell. He knew that restaurants on the banks of the Potomac River in Washington served hammer-like mallets with the steamed crabs. He had a small hammer, which he smashed onto the crab shell, splattering the delicate meat along with the prickly shells all over the table and onto the floor. Uttering an expletive, he began trying to pick the meat from the little shattered pieces of shell.

"Would you like me to show you a much easier way?" I politely asked.

"I wish you would," he grimaced. "Forgive my language, but I'll be damned if I can figure it out!"

As Hale watched attentively, I picked up one of the crabs and gently pulled its top shell from the body. With a sharp, slender kitchen knife, I sliced off the legs, then cut through the two body cavities, exposing most of the flaky white meat. A small cut into the two claws enabled the meat to be extracted.

Boggs then dipped the claw and body meat into a pool of butter slightly salted with Old Bay seasoning and enjoyed what he called one of the tastiest meals he ever had.

That summer, Hale had decided he would run for Governor of Louisiana in an attempt to break the stranglehold that the political machine of Governor and U.S. Senator Huey Long and his family had on the state. Even though Long was assassinated in 1935, his brother Earl and other members of his family still held the primary positions of power in the state. Long's story was superbly told in fiction form in Robert Penn Warren's Pulitzer Prize-winning novel, *All the King's Men* (1946). Hale, however, lost his bid for Governor even though, surprisingly, U.S. Senator Russell B. Long, Huey's son, had supported Boggs.

Party of the Year

In what was then described as the "Party of the Year" in our weekly newspaper, *The Calvert Independent,* my parents pulled out the stops and created a festive event the likes of which few people in the county had seen. The big yard of our Victorian-style home was filled with tables of steamed hard crabs, fish, fried chicken from Grandmother Annie DeBoy's well-used iron stove, all kinds of snacks, homemade ice cream, and drinks to suit every taste.

The Boggs family also came and spent the weekend. Barbara and Cokie climbed the spiral stairway to my bedroom and we spent an hour talking while viewing the party beneath my window. The sisters were still excited about Hale's run for governor as I turned on the radio and heard the lilting sounds of Patti Page singing *The Tennessee Waltz* (1951), then the number one song on the hit parade. Barbara remarked that it was her father's favorite song. We also discussed a new film we both had recently seen: *Showboat* (1951), starring Kathryn Grayson, Ava Gardner, and Howard Keel, based on the novel by Edna Ferber and the Broadway musical.

Guy Lombardo and *Slo-Mo-Shun*

A major part of that weekend's festivities involved the annual Formula One speedboat regatta race. Dad was Commodore of the Solomons Island Yacht Club and was responsible for refereeing the event in which prominent speedboat racers from around the country participated. One of these was famed bandleader Guy Lombardo, racing his speedster inappropriately named *Slo-Mo-Shun*, which already had won a number of Formula One races.

With the Boggses and other family friends—including the Coulons, Murtos, Richwines, Keaveneys and others—we boarded Dad's boat the *Penguin* and took our place at the starting line on the Patuxent River. Dad raised the yacht club flag in one hand while he shot off the pistol starting the race in the other.

The race was on as the sound of the boat motors shattered the silence. Guy Lombardo was expected to win the race, but, as he approached the final buoy, *Slo-Mo-Shun* struck the buoy, nearly throwing him into the water. He did manage to slowly steer his racer to the finish line. Guy Lombardo and his orchestra were then well-known for hosting the annual New Year's Eve Times Square celebrations in New York City.

The Warren Commission

My visits with the Boggs family continued through the 1950s and 1960s. In 1964, Hale put his own career on the line by being one of only seven southern Congressmen to support the Voting Rights Act of 1965. Meanwhile,

Lindy Boggs was quickly becoming a trusted aide to President Lyndon B. Johnson. I had briefly met Johnson in early 1963 when he was vice president at the fiftieth anniversary celebration of the Capitol Radio Engineering Institute (CREI) at a swanky hotel in Washington, D.C. I was working at CREI assigning field agents to prospective students. I did not realize at the time that the institute was a C.I.A. front.

Shortly after the assassination of President John F. Kennedy on November 22, 1963, Johnson appointed Hale as a member of the controversial Warren Commission. In a 1966 appearance on *Face the Nation*, Boggs defended the finding that Lee Harvey Oswald was the only one involved in the murder of Kennedy and that only one bullet had killed the president and wounded Texas Governor John Connally. During one of our many visits at the Cove Point cottage, however, Hale told Dad and I that he thought there may have been a "rush to judgment" (a phrase later used as the title of a popular book on the subject) in the commission's haste to quickly get the report out. Boggs told us that he may be having second thoughts about the single bullet theory. This came as somewhat of a shock since all the news reports had the congressman sticking strongly to the single-bullet-lone-gunman commission finding.

Alcohol and the FBI

Early during the month of April 1971, Boggs strongly attacked decades-long Federal Bureau of Investigation Director J. Edgar Hoover for leading the organization into a near-dictatorial entity beyond the reach of even the Commander-in-Chief. Hale's speech in the halls of Congress reportedly led to a meeting on April 6 between Congressman Gerald Ford (R-MI), the Republican Minority Leader (Hale was then the Majority Leader), and President Richard M. Nixon.

The President asked Ford to scratch Boggs' name from those top Congressional members from whom he could elicit counsel. In a secret White House recording, Nixon asked Ford to persuade a House delegation to include an alternate to Boggs. The recording also had Ford telling Nixon that Boggs was an alcoholic as well as a pill-popper.

I also knew that Hale had a drinking problem. That was obvious in the way he could down the John Barleycorn during his visits with us at Cove Point. It was also clear in 1953 when he and Lindy drove me to Baltimore dressed in my McDonogh School uniform. Hale was still reeling from the effects of alcohol and was driving the car over the speed limit. Lindy sternly told him to slow down mainly in deference to my being in the car. I wasn't worried, however. I trusted Hale to get me safely to my destination.

A few weeks, later, Hale and Lindy invited me for a weekend visit at their home in Bethesda, Maryland. I was hoping that Barbara would be there since I was so in love with her, but I was not so lucky.

Lost in Alaska

After becoming House Majority Leader, Hale often campaigned for other Democrats. This led to one of the saddest periods of my life.

On October 16, 1972, Hale Boggs was aboard a twin engine Cessna 301 on a campaign trip on behalf of Alaska's only Congressman Nick Begich. Also aboard the flight were Russell Brown, Begich's aide, and the pilot, Don Jonz. They were on their way from Anchorage to Juneau for a Begich fundraiser during the night when the plane disappeared as it approached the Chugach mountain range in the southeastern part of the state.

A Sad Visit With Lindy

The missing flight quickly sent shock waves through the halls of Congress. Hale Boggs, the person who was slated to become the next Speaker of the House and who would have been second-in-line to the presidency was missing. Early the next morning, I learned that Hale's plane was reported missing and immediately called Lindy, saying that I was coming to her home to offer whatever help and comfort I could.

I quickly drove from my apartment in Washington, D.C., to the Boggs home on Bradley Boulevard. Lindy greeted me at the door and led me into her spacious kitchen, where I sat with her at a gleaming silver-topped table. For a full hour, she managed to comfort me instead of my consoling her.

It was typical of that wonderful woman. At this early time during Hale's disappearance, there was still some hope he would be found alive. Over coffee, I did what I could to offer support to Lindy. She thanked me and later called my parents to express her appreciation for my visit.

"My Heart is Filled With Gratitude"

As the days passed and hope began to fade that her husband and the others would be found "alive and well," the eternally optimistic Lindy wrote me the following letter (I was known as "Dick" rather than "Gordon" then in deference to my father) on her husband's official Congressional letterhead dated November 8, 1972:

> *Dear Dick:*
>
> *My heart is filled with gratitude for your thoughtful concerns for Hale's safe return and for my consolation. Thank you so much.*
>
> *Our family had the gratifying experience of being in Alaska with the dedicated experts who are conducting the search and rescue mission.*

We want to share with you our encouragement from the magnitude of the search and the kindly attitude of those involved in its direction and operation, and also from the numerous accounts of long-term survival and miraculous rescues.

We have great hope that Hale and the others will be found alive and well soon. In the meantime, we are sustained by the prayers and loving messages of our wonderful friends.

My warmest good wishes.

Gratefully and Affectionately,

(s) Lindy

Mrs. Hale Boggs

The Long Search

The hunt for Hale Boggs and Nick Begich had quickly become the biggest such search in U.S. history. It included around twenty civilian aircraft along with about forty Air Force, Navy and Coast Guard planes. Daily reports were sent back to Lindy Boggs, who kept praying that Hale would be found alive. My prayers joined hers.

After thirty-nine days of intensive hunting for the downed plane, it had become obvious that there was scant hope that the Congressmen would be found alive. The massive search was suspended. As of this writing nearly half-a-century later, neither the plane nor its occupants have been found.

Lindy Boggs

Following her husband's loss in Alaska, I didn't see much of Lindy Boggs, but stayed in touch with her. Sadly, the visits to our home on Solomons Island and cabin on the Chesapeake Bay ceased. The last time I saw her was early in 1973 after, in a special election, she succeeded her husband as the U.S. Representative from the second district of Louisiana. As a member of the National Press Club, I invited my parents, Dick and Dora Lore, as my guests to the club where Lindy was to announce her election and outline her agenda. Following her well-reported speech, we approached her.

"What are you two doing here?" Lindy asked, glaring at my parents.

I noticed her icy tone. It was something new to me.

"I'm a member of the Press Club, Lindy," I responded for them. "I invited them to honor a friend."

Lindy wasn't one to hold a grudge for long. She graciously hugged my parents and me. It wasn't until many years later that I discovered what may have been the cause of her initially cold greeting.

Dad had been courted by Hale Boggs and other prominent politicians, including John and Robert Kennedy—who visited our marina on Solomons Island during John's run for President in 1960—in an effort to persuade dad to run for a seat in Congress. He apparently had a private meeting with President Johnson at Hale and Lindy's behest.

While Johnson was in office, Lindy had become what dad called "the president's right-hand gal." In what may have been another attempt to persuade my father to run for a Congressional seat in order to bolster the Democratic ticket in Maryland, Hale and Lindy had persuaded the President to meet dad in a private audience in the White House. My father reluctantly agreed. He was not a Johnson supporter. Still, it wasn't everyone who could have a one-on-one meeting with the nation's Commander-In-Chief.

Dad never talked much about his own accomplishments, the celebrities he had met, or those with whom he had interacted. Although he was a sought-after candidate by Democratic members of Congress, what they didn't know was that he was a life-long registered Democrat who voted the straight Republican ticket. He also never shied away from expressing his own opinions about most politicians, calling them "liars and thieves."

Although I suspected dad may have met with Johnson, I didn't know for sure until about fifty years later when my first cousin (the son of dad's sister), John Malone of Paradise, California, confirmed the meeting. John was living with his parents at the time in Washington, D.C. He told me that, one day in 1964 or 1965, dad had shown up at their home and announced he had just met with the President. John doesn't remember much, but did tell me that dad remarked: "I'll never set foot inside the White House again as long as that man is President!"

An Historic Perspective

With the rather bulky name of Marie Corinne Morrison Claiborne Boggs, Lindy was born on March 13, 1916 (she always got a kick out of the fact that her birthday and mine were only twenty years and two days apart, mine being on March 15, 1936), at Brunswick Plantation near New Roads, Pointe Coupee Parish, Louisiana. She was a descendant of hardy historical southern stock. This included being a direct descendant of William Charles Cole Claiborne, the first territorial governor of the Louisiana Territory and the first elected governor of the State of Louisiana. Claiborne had been in direct conflict with the Barataria Bay pirate Jean Lafitte at the time that Lafitte was considering joining General Andrew Jackson in his fight against the British during the Battle of New Orleans in January 1815. The battle was fought less than a month after the Treaty of Ghent was signed on Christmas Eve, 1814, officially ending the War of 1812. Lindy also had some original letters from Jackson which I had the privilege of seeing while visiting her in the Boggs' Garden District home in New Orleans during the Mardi Gras festivities in February 1955.

During this visit, I also had the privilege of seeing the actress Sarah Churchill star in the lead role of the play *Tea and Sympathy* (1953). Sarah—who starred and co-starred in many plays, TV shows, and movie films—was the second daughter of British Prime Minister Sir Winston Churchill. I went backstage and briefly met her. I congratulated her on what I thought was a fine performance. She thanked me with a winning smile and I quickly left, making way for the short line of admirers waiting behind me.

My Main Mentor

The same summer I met her, Lindy Boggs became my main mentor. I remember her sitting in my mother's kitchen on Solomons Island in 1951 sketching out a plan for me to attend the McDonogh School for Boys in Baltimore. The school was a spin-off of the McDonogh School group in New Orleans, which then had a 100-year history. The campus in Baltimore was home to a strict military-style institution, which I hated, but I did manage to graduate in 1954. Lindy was also instrumental in sending me to college at Louisiana State University (LSU) in Baton Rouge, where I majored in journalism.

Vice President Alben Barkley

Lindy Boggs was kind enough to take me under her wing, especially during the 1950s. She taught me a lot about U.S. and Louisiana history. Sometime in 1952, during a break from my schooling at McDonogh, she spent an entire day with me as we toured the halls of Congress. We had lunch at one of the House buildings where a special bayou-style gumbo dish Lindy created was named in her honor.

Chapter One: The Boggs Dynasty

We also visited a House meeting where Lindy gave me a history lesson on the intricacies of how Congress functioned. During a lull in the proceedings, she pointed out to me where Vice President Alben W. Barkley was standing alone. She said that the Vice President (VP) was also the President of the Senate. Like other novices, I was puzzled as to how a VP could also be a President. She clued me in that the only constitutional duty of the VP was to be the President of the U.S. Senate. But, Lindy pointed out, the Senate President was not allowed to cast a vote unless there was a tie. It took a while for that to settle in.

"Would it be possible for me to meet him?" I asked. We were only a few yards away from Mr. Barkley.

"Sure, why not?" Lindy responded, grabbing my hand and leading me forward.

As we approached the Vice President, he turned around and said: "Hello, Lindy. So nice to see you."

"Thank you, Mr. Vice President," she responded. "I have here a young family friend who would love to shake your hand."

"Hello, young man," Barkley said, extending his hand.

I was surprised by how gentle, almost feminine, his handshake was. He smiled and seemed ready to say something, but someone had signaled to him and he had to quickly excuse himself.

I later discovered that Alben W. Barkley was both a lawyer and a politician from McCracken County, Kentucky, and at the time was serving as Vice President during President Harry Truman's final term in office. Born in Lowes, Kentucky, on November 24, 1877, he died in Lexington, Virginia, on April 30, 1956, only a little more than three years after serving as Vice President.

Anita Morrison

While at LSU majoring in journalism, I often visited with Lindy Boggs' aunt, Anita Morrison, the mother of New Orleans Mayor DeLesseps ("Chep") Morrison, who was Lindy's second cousin. I had earlier met Chep in 1953 and again in 1955 with my father who was twice presented with the Keys to the City of New Orleans from Chep in recognition of dad's work in helping to preserve the oyster and crabbing industry in the Chesapeake Bay and the Gulf of Mexico. Dad later became the President of both the Oyster Institute of North America and the National Shellfisheries Association.

Tragically, in 1964, Chep Morrison was killed with his son in a small plane crash, devastating his mother and the entire Boggs family. Chep had also been the U.S. Ambassador to the Organization of American States.

Maven of the French House

Anita Morrison was the head of the French House at L.S.U. where only female students lived. My Saturday evening visits with her became a regular occurrence, which were enlivened by frequent pop-in visits from the girls who appeared to be drawn to Anita like a magnet. I wanted to ask a few of the girls out for a date, but they popped in and out so quickly, I didn't get a chance.

My visits with Aunt Anita were mainly leisurely. She told me a little more about the history of the Morrison and Boggs family. One tidbit that piqued my interest was the fact that the Morrison family line descended from Ferdinand DeLesseps, the architect of the Suez Canal. I remembered seeing the film, *Suez* (1938) starring Tyrone Power as DeLesseps. Most of our time together, however, involved watching television. She deferred to me watching my favorite series, *Gunsmoke* (1955-1975), while I joined her in viewing *The George Gobel Show* (1954-1960) and the *Lawrence Welk Show* (1951-1971) with the famed bandleader's champagne music.

During the summer of 1956, after I left L.S.U., Lindy surprised me by bringing Aunt Anita for a weekend visit to our home on Solomons Island. It was the last time I saw Anita, but I still remember her with deep affection.

A "First" Lady

My visits with Lindy continued through the next several years. While she told me a lot about Louisiana history, there was still much I didn't know then about her own impact on both politics and countless other individuals who, like me, considered her as both a friend and a mentor.

Lindy was truly a "first" lady, something her daughter, Cokie, was particularly proud of and wrote about. She was the first woman from Louisiana to be elected to the U.S. Congress. She was also the first chairwoman of a major party convention, the 1976 Democratic National Convention, which nominated the Jimmy Carter-Walter Mondale ticket. Lindy was the first woman to have a federal building named after her. She was also appointed by President William ("Bill") J. Clinton as the first female and fifth U.S. Ambassador to the Holy See. Lindy later said that her position representing the United States in the Vatican was one of the highlights of her life. Vice President Al Gore also credited Lindy with being one of his mentors. It was Gore who announced her appointment to the Vatican and praised her for her service to the country.

Lindy also chaired the Inaugural Ball committees of both Presidents John F. Kennedy and Lyndon B. Johnson.

There were other honors along the way, starting with her Congressional election. Following Hale's presumed death, she was elected to a full term in Congress in 1974 with a whopping eighty-two percent of the vote. Lindy was reelected seven times until she voluntarily left her seat in January 1991 to be with her daughter, Barbara (see following section), who was seriously ill with cancer. Along the way, Lindy polled more than eighty percent of the votes. Following the restructuring of her district in 1984, she became the only white member of Congress representing a majority constituency of African Americans. In 1994, Lindy published her own book entitled *Washington Through a Purple Veil: Memoirs of a Southern Woman.*

In 2006, Boggs was honored for her time in the House of Representatives with the Congressional Distinguished Service Award. The Boggs Center for Energy and Biotechnology Building on the Tulane University campus is named in her honor. Lindy was also proud of the fact that she and her historic family name boasted more members in both houses of Congress than any other family in U.S. history.

Following a long and superbly fruitful life during which her son Tommy Boggs (see section below) remarked that he never heard his mother utter a negative remark about anyone, Lindy Boggs died on July 27, 2013, at the age of ninety-seven. Like Tommy and the rest of her family and innumerable friends, I will always remember her illuminating presence in my life.

Barbara Boggs-Sigmund

The last time I saw Barbara was ca. 1970 at a reception line with her mother at the wedding of Candy Coulon, the daughter of Charlie and Elizabeth Coulon, long-time family friends. I was with my fiancée, Martha DeGroat, whom I later married. The love flame I had for Barbara, however, had not yet been completely extinguished.

Even then, I remembered having sat with her and her sister, Cokie, on at least two occasions in the movie theater at Evans Pavilion on Solomons Island during the summer months of the early 1950s. We could hear the gentle lapping of the waves against the wharf pilings. I held Barbara's hand as we watched *Follow the Sun* (1951) with Glenn Ford as golf great Ben Hogan and Anne Baxter as his wife and Gary Cooper and Walter Brennan in *Task Force* (1949).

By 1970, Barbara had already begun to distinguish herself in a big way. She had worked as a letter writer for President John F. Kennedy in 1962. Two years later, she married Paul E. Sigmund, who was a professor of Political Science at Princeton University in New Jersey.

Like the rest of her family, politics and public service had been undeniable ways of life for Barbara. She founded an agency named Womanspace that provided emergency and other vital services to victims and survivors of sexual and domestic abuse.

The last seven years of Barbara's life were apparently her most productive. This followed the discovery in 1982 of a melanoma behind her left eye. The eye was removed and she wore an eye patch, which she regarded as a badge of honor. That same year, she made an unsuccessful run for the U.S. Senate.

In 1983, Barbara was elected as the first female Mayor of Princeton, New Jersey, a position she held until the day of her death at fifty-one on October 10, 1990. I had read that, as sick as she must have been, she spent part of the last day of her life at the Mayor's office signing some bills. Then she came home and wrote farewell letters to her husband and three sons as if she knew this would be her last day on earth. Barbara, the love of my young life, quietly passed away a few hours later. I have not been able to confirm this story of her last day, but, if true, her passing from this world was a true class act.

Cokie Boggs-Roberts

Cokie was a real charmer as a child. I loved my interactions with her almost as much as I did with her sister, Barbara. With the hefty full name of Mary Martha Corinne Morrison Claiborne Boggs-Roberts, she remains better known as Cokie Roberts, a senior news analyst for National Public Radio and a roundtable analyst for *This Week with George Stephanopoulos* (1981). She is also a political commentator for ABC News.

With her husband, Steven V. Roberts, Cokie writes a weekly column for United Media that is distributed to newspapers throughout the United States. She was appointed by President George W. Bush to his Council on Service and Civic Participation. She also distinguished herself as the co-anchor of ABC News TV's *This Week With Sam Donaldson and Cokie Roberts* from 1996 to 2002.

Along the way, Cokie won a number of prestigious awards and honors, including the Edward R. Morrow and the Everett McKinley Dirksen Awards as well as an Emmy. She also wrote several books about the contributions women have made to American history and its heritage.

Thomas Hale Boggs, Jr.

I haven't seen Tommy Boggs for nearly half a century but remember him as a sharp, smart, gregarious individual who was destined to go far. He seemed to be a little withdrawn and serious as a boy, but I had the feeling that he would eventually become an integral member of his extended and very successful family.

Born on September 18, 1940, in New Orleans, Tommy received his law degree and joined the law/lobby firm of James R. Patton, Jr., now known as Squire Patton Boggs. Tommy became the law firm's senior partner and was recognized by many as the top lobbyist in the nation's capital.

The last time I saw Tommy Boggs was briefly in 1970 when he ran for Congress in Maryland's eighth district. I remember his father, Hale, saying that he was definitely going to uphold the Boggs tradition of winning big. The opposite was the case, however. Tommy lost big, but he did continue to hit long-distance home runs as a lobbyist.

Chapter One: The Boggs Dynasty

As Tommy's career and life were winding down, the *National Law Journal* praised him as "one of the most influential lawyers in the nation." In 2013, he was named one of the "Top Innovators in Big Law in the Last 50 Years."

On September 15, 2014, Tommy Boggs suddenly died of an apparent heart attack in Chevy Chase, Maryland. Words of praise and condolences came from around the nation, with former U.S. Senator John Breaux of Louisiana calling him "one of the smartest men I've ever known and one who had an abiding commitment to seeing how government works and explaining it to others."

Chapter Two

Stars Sailing the Chesapeake Bay

In 1950, in the flush of post-World War II expansion, my father, G.I. Rupert ("Dick") Lore, a prominent seafood (oysters and blue crabs) planter and packer (see Introduction), decided to expand his horizon by building a yacht marina in the harbor at Solomons Island, Maryland, close to the mouth of the Chesapeake Bay.

By June 1, the marina, connected to a large white house containing a spacious screened-in porch with tables and chairs for occasional dining, was open for business. A 150-foot-long central pier with several smaller adjacent docks flanked the area. There was a lift for boats that needed to be beached for repairs and painting along with a machine shop.

For more than a decade, the Lore marina became a favorite stopping spot for boatmen, including numerous celebrities, along the eastern Atlantic coast. In 1958, the prestigious *Inland Waterway Guide* awarded the G.I. Rupert Lore & Sons Marina as the best U.S. Atlantic Coast marina from northern Maine to Norfolk, Virginia.

Following are some of the author's interactions with celebrated visitors at the marina, in Cove Point, Maryland, and Washington, D.C., during the 1950s, 1960 and 1982.

The Hand of Harry S. Truman

Around the end of March 1951, my dad and I made our regular morning tour of the marina. As we approached the end of the long main pier to the crackling-cawing sounds of the seagulls, we saw a huge vessel rounding the harbor bend. It was heading straight for the pier.

The sleek vessel was a U.S. Coast Guard boat assigned to Harry S. Truman, the thirty-fifth President of the United States.. As dad and I watched intently, the long boat slowly pulled into the pier. We helped secure it to the dock as a ladder was lowered from the deck.

"Can we get some gas?" someone yelled from the deck.

"Sure, absolutely!" Dad yelled back.

A crewmember scurried down the wooden ladder, grabbed the long gasoline hose and pulled it back on board. A second crewmember stepped down to the dock.

While Dad, a staunch conservative, was no fan of Harry Truman, he still couldn't resist asking the sailor if the President was aboard.

"Yes, he is," the young man answered.

His response surprised both dad and I. We knew that only a few months had passed following a failed assassination attempt on the life of Harry Truman.

During the autumn of 1950, the White House was being renovated while the President and his family took up residence across Pennsylvania Avenue at Blair House. On the afternoon of November 1, Truman and his wife, Bess, were upstairs when they heard the sound of gunshots and yelling coming from the front steps.

Two members of the extremist Puerto Rican Nationalist Party were resorting to violence in an attempt to gain full independence from the United States. The party members were called the *Independistas*. Two of its members, Griselio Torresola and Oscar Collazo, were intent upon killing the President.

Chapter Two: Stars Sailing the Chesapeake Bay

The two men were unchallenged as they quietly strolled up to the front door of Blair House and began firing. Some reports said they never got past the front steps while others related that one of the assassins had actually made it to the second floor open door of the room where the President was sitting at his desk.

During the quick firefight, Secret Service Agent Leslie Coffelt was mortally wounded, but he managed to kill Torresola. Later, Collazo admitted that the assassination attempt was poorly planned. The two assassins were even unsure that Truman would be in Blair House when they attacked the residence at 2 p.m. The irony was that Truman had been targeted in spite of his support for greater Puerto Rican autonomy.

In typical Missouri style, Truman appeared unfazed by the attempt on his life. He even kept his scheduled appointments for the day.

Oscar Collazo was sentenced to death, but the President, in an admirable gesture of forgiveness, commuted the would-be assassin's sentence to life imprisonment.

Despite the recent attempt on Truman's life, dad still wanted to see if we could meet the President. He asked the Secret Service agent if Truman would come out on deck.

"Yes, he's aboard," the agent surprisingly said, "but I'm sure you know there was an attempt to kill him just a couple of months ago."

"Yes, we know," Dad said, "but my son and I would still like to shake his hand, if he is willing."

"All right, I'll ask him," the agent remarked.

The agent climbed back up the ladder and returned a few minutes later.

"The President says he will shake your hand," he stated. "Come aboard."

Dad and I eagerly climbed the ladder. We were on deck of the mammoth yacht, but there was no sign of Harry Truman.

"Come on over here," the agent instructed.

We were led to a closed porthole.

"Because of security reasons, the President can't come out on deck," the agent instructed, "but he'll shake your hands through this porthole."

Dad couldn't stifle a laugh and I was astonished. The porthole opened and a hand appeared through it. I was the first to shake the hand of President Harry S. Truman.

"Hello, there, young fella!" Truman said, firmly squeezing my hand. "Don't forget to vote Democrat when you get old enough."

"Thank you, Mr. President," I remarked, astonished. "It was a pleasure shaking your hand."

"It's boys like you who will grow into the men we need to keep this country alive and well," the President remarked.

Following dad's turn at the porthole, we were escorted off the vessel. We watched as it left the wharf and disappeared from sight into the broad expanse of the Chesapeake Bay.

Dad never changed his opinion of Truman, but I have always remembered that unusual and very brief meeting. It was one for the memoir books.

Governor Theodore Roosevelt McKeldin

On or about the morning of July 15, 1952, my dad, Dick Lore, and I met with Maryland Governor Theodore Roosevelt ("Teddy") McKeldin at his office in Annapolis, the Maryland state capitol. Dad was excited about the meeting because, just a few days before our meeting, in Chicago, Illinois, McKeldin—in a fiery, rousing speech worthy of the President for whom he was named—placed in nomination General of the Army Dwight David Eisenhower on the Republican ticket as President of the United States. Dad, a lifelong registered Democrat who always voted the straight Republican ticket, considered Eisenhower to be one of his heroes.

Chapter Two: Stars Sailing the Chesapeake Bay

Hearing the Republican National Convention on our radio at home on Solomons Island only a few days before our meeting with the Governor, Dad exulted in McKeldin's speech. It was the linchpin in switching convention delegates from the front-runner Senator Robert A. Taft (R-Ohio) to the popular five-star General who had been the Supreme Allied Commander on the European front during World War II.

McKeldin's powerful speech was so rousing that the Governor was seriously being considered as Eisenhower's vice presidential running mate. It was the future President Richard M. Nixon (see Chapter Ten), however, who received that honor.

"Congratulations, Governor, on your great speech nominating General Eisenhower as our next President, I hope," Dad remarked with a smile as he firmly shook McKeldin's hand.

"Thanks very much," the Governor responded while extending his hand to me for a firm handshake. "It was, indeed, an honor. The General will make a great President."

The Governor reached into the drawer of his desk and pulled out a large mounted oyster shell with his name scrawled in black across the open shell and handed it to me. (I still have that oyster shell displayed among the other nautical memorabilia in my apartment in Southern California.)

"Here, young man," the Governor said, grabbing my shoulder with a firm grip. "A symbol of your dad's business ... Please have a seat while your father and I get down to our business of the day."

Dad remained in his chair in front of the Governor's desk while I sat back on a large yellow couch nearby fondling my oyster shell. I also looked out of the large Governor's office window at a marina loaded with an assortment of pleasure yachts and Chesapeake Bay workboats.

"Well, Dick," McKeldin began, "my people have told me that it was time you and I met, that you are one of the best men in the state to consult about the health of our beautiful Chesapeake Bay. As I am sure you are aware, the Chesapeake, considered possibly the most valuable estuary in the world due to its quantity and quality of seafood, is in ill health. Pollution from various sources has nearly destroyed it.

"As Governor of this state, I want to create a commission that will explore and detail the health of the bay and submit a report to me. I would like to appoint you as an integral part of that committee. It would involve studying the health of the bay while being in close proximity to it. What can, should, and must be done to save the Chesapeake? It will probably take more than one commission or the lifetime of one man, but it *must* be done. My God, Dick, the bay is over 200 miles long and touches a total of six states! Thousands of watermen and millions of Americans depend upon its resources. *Goddammit*! Our precious Chesapeake must be saved!"

"I definitely agree, Governor," Dad piped in. "A lot of livelihoods depend upon it. A complete cleanup of the bay probably won't happen in your or my lifetime, but we can sure as hell start on it. There's a lot of bad stuff to contend with, including all sorts of toxic runoffs that have to eventually be contained and controlled. Oysters, crabs, fish, clams, and other vital bay resources are being poisoned."

"You agree, then, to be one of the heads of this proposed commission?" McKeldin asked.

"Absolutely, Governor," Dad quickly replied.

"Good," McKeldin retorted. "I'll ask my people to draw up a proposal and you can get to work on it right away. I would like to have an initial report by sometime early next year. I look forward to working with you on this important project, Dick, so please call me if you have any questions."

"I'll get right on it," Dad remarked.

The visit with the Maryland Governor was over. Dad quickly began working on his new project to help save the Chesapeake Bay. Little did he

Chapter Two: Stars Sailing the Chesapeake Bay

know then that this endeavor would take long beyond his allotted time on earth. (Dad passed away on Halloween night in 1982.)

As of this writing in 2016, the health of the world's most valuable estuary remains threatened while the Chesapeake Bay Foundation and others continue the fight that McKeldin, dad, and a few others began. Fortunately, the supplies of fish, crabs and clams continue to thrive. It is the oysters, once the seafood king on the bay, that have been nearly completely depleted due to both over-harvesting and pollution.

Six months or so after our visit with McKeldin, Dad turned in an initial report saying it would cost at least $10 billion to get the bay back to its more or less pristine condition. Back in 1953, that was news! *Ten billion dollars?!* Dad's report was picked up by United Press (UP), UP International and other news outlets. It was simply unbelievable. Nothing could cost that much, not back in the early 1950s. . . .

Years after our meeting with the Governor, I wanted to find out more about him. I learned that the Baltimore native was born on November 20, 1900, to a stonecutter turned policeman. The first job Teddy (as he was known) had was as an office boy in a bank earning the munificent sum of $20 a month. During that five-year stint, he met and married Honolulu Manzer and the couple bore two children.

McKeldin received his law degree from the University of Maryland in 1925. From there, it was nowhere to go but up for him. He served two times as the Mayor of Baltimore and two more as Governor of the State of Maryland. He began his second term as Governor early in 1955 by affirming his effort to build up the state's tradition of "tolerance, brotherhood and human freedom." He also became a strong civil rights leader and led in the passage of a bill aimed at "insuring equal opportunities in employment, education, accommodations, housing and welfare." Many believe that this bill was instrumental in Baltimore escaping "the bulk of the racial disorders which swept the larger cities of the nation between 1964 and 1967." The laws became known as "the most sweeping package of civil rights legislation enacted at one time by any major municipality within this nation."

Theodore Roosevelt McKeldin died on August 10, 1974, and was buried in Baltimore's Greenmount Cemetery.

James Cagney

The years 1955 and 1956 brought other distinguished visitors into the marina. These included the great actor and hoofer James Cagney. He arrived one sunny spring day from his home on Martha's Vineyard aboard, I believe, the *Mary Ann*, his forty-three-foot Chesapeake Bay bugeye ketch.

I helped Cagney tie up his boat. He quickly told me that he hoped it would be quieter here. He said he had to leave the marina in Oxford, Maryland, because so many people discovered he was there that "kids started climbing all over my boat."

It was a quiet arrival. After his vessel was secured, he headed for the screen porch of the marina home. He and I sat down. I asked him if he would mind if I visited with him for a little while.

"No, go ahead," he replied. "I get this all the time, but you seem like a nice young man."

I told him I had recently seen him play opposite Doris Day in *Love Me or Leave Me* (1955), the biopic about 1920s songbird Ruth Etting. Cagney played Marty ("The Gimp") Snyder, a gangster. He was even nominated for a Best Actor Oscar for the part.

"You were great as The Gimp," I said.

"I enjoyed working with Doris," he replied. "She's quite a gal and knows how to belt out a song, too."

Chapter Two: Stars Sailing the Chesapeake Bay

"Do you have a favorite actress you really enjoyed working with?" I asked.

"That's a tough one, young fella," the tough guy remarked with a slight grin. "I have had the good fortune of working with a number of lovely ladies. My friend and fellow New Yorker Joan Blondell was right up there at the top of the list. She's a lovely person and fine actress. She has striking, bulging eyes that are so big I thought they would pop out of her head. I love her."

Blondell was well on her way to a seventy-year career as an actress. She starred with her friend in seven films, including *Blonde Crazy* (1931). Blondell also acted opposite such major Hollywood stars as Clark Gable, Errol Flynn, John Wayne, Steve McQueen, Edward G. Robinson, Greer Garson, Rock Hudson, and Dick Powell. Her co-star, Cagney, of course, is best known for his tough-guy roles, beginning with *The Public Enemy* (1931) and continuing with the sizzling *White Heat* (1949).

"I loved your 'Top o' the world, Ma' performance in *White Heat*," I told him.

"Thanks," he said, smiling. "A lot of people loved that one."

Cagney won an Oscar for his rousing song-and-dance portrayal of George M. Cohen in *Yankee Doodle Dandy* (1942). The picture highlighted his great ability as a dancer, something not too many people knew about at the time. He reprised this talent the same year I met him by teaching Bob Hope how to dance in *The Seven Little Foys* (1955).

"I'm surprised that Bob Hope didn't know how to dance," I remarked. "He seemed to do OK in the road movies with Bing Crosby and Dorothy Lamour."

"That was a slow, comedic style," Cagney replied. "I taught him how to *really* dance, to fly off the floor and soar like a swan. Real tabletop hoofing. I told Bob he had to halt his part in the film for three weeks. We must have practiced twelve hours a day, but, in the end, Bob nailed it."

"It showed," I responded.

"What are your aims in life, young man?" Jimmy asked.

"I want to be a published writer," I answered. "I also love classical and folk music."

"Well, I'm sure you will make it," Cagney said. "Good luck and keep truckin.'"

"A Beautiful Whore"

"I recently read that you live on Martha's Vineyard in Massachusetts," I remarked. "How do you like it there?"

"I love it," the actor replied. "I can get away from the hustle-and-bustle of making a movie there. It's quiet, peaceful, and the wonderful people there accept me as one of their own."

Cagney did confide, however, that, when he first arrived on the Vineyard looking for a house to rent or buy, he noticed a feeling of resentment among those who lived on the island. At first, there was what he described as a "deep freeze" toward outsiders, which inspired him to write a short protest poem:

When you give your heart to fair Martha's Isle,
That Queen of insular sluts,
It's like falling in love with a beautiful whore,
Who hates your goddamned guts.

Cagney soon realized that, if he were to win the trust of the standoffish islanders, he would have to quickly begin acting like one of them. The actor's warm, earthy personality soon won them over, however. He was soon eating lobster at the Home Port restaurant with them and became one of their social circle. He even did some tabletop dancing at one of the local watering holes.

It was 1936, the year I was born, and Cagney felt that the Vineyard was where he wanted to be. He quickly purchased a large vintage house originally built on more than 200 acres in 1728 in Chilmark, where he and his wife and two children lived until a couple of years before his death in 1986 at the age of eighty-six. He quickly fell in love with his spacious farm with outbuildings, cows, and chickens, where he spent many summers.

"I love it more than I can say," Cagney told me.

The actor was also an amateur painter and joined a local artists' group. Among those he drank, smoked, and caroused with was the celebrated painter and Chilmark summer resident, Thomas Hart Benton.

The actor extolled the virtues of living on Martha's Vineyard in his autobiography *Cagney by Cagney* (1976). He said he loved the farm "beyond words" and described it as a true fantasy that provided refuge from the hustle-and-bustle of Hollywood. Besides, he wrote, "the taxes were $39 a year, which made it an ideal place to land if the movie business ever dropped me." After he completed filming in Hollywood, California, he couldn't wait to jump into his drawing room on the earliest eastbound train.

"I couldn't think of anything more satisfying, more life-fulfilling, than living on a farm surrounded by salt water," Cagney wrote. "That is what Martha's Vineyard allowed me to do . . . I loved it beyond words."

At that point, I shook the tough guy's hand. He wished me well and I never saw him again. I will, however, always remember my visit with him as I continue to watch his films. I also remember the words of the late great Orson Welles, who called Cagney "maybe the greatest actor who ever appeared in front of a camera."

Richard Matheson

Perhaps the most prolific and well-regarded writer in the fantasy, horror, and science fiction genres with occasional touches of spiritual wisdom was Richard Matheson. Even such better-known writers and filmmakers as Stephen

King, Anne Rice, Steven Spielberg, George A. Romero, and Roger Corman have credited him with much of the inspiration for their own works.

I had the privilege of meeting this remarkable writer less than a year after his first major work, *I Am Legend* (1954), was published. This novel has been translated to film several times. My favorite is the latest version with Will Smith, released in 2007.

After he jumped from his boat and sat down at one of the tables on the screen porch at the marina, Matheson invited me to sit with him. I had not heard of him, but he soon learned of my desire to be a writer.

"It can be a tough go," he told me, "but it can be enormously satisfying and rewarding if you stick with it. You must know your subject, draw out your characters as if you own them and want your readers to truly know them, and create a rollicking good story in the bargain. Horror and science fiction are the rage these days. Also, get to know and talk with others in the field you choose. For instance, I am a member of the Southern California Sorcerers Society, which includes such writers as Ray Bradbury. Get to know them. They can teach you much."

Excellent advice. I only had a short visit with Matheson, but I continued to follow his career. He went on to write the book that the movie *Somewhere In Time* (1980) with Christopher Reeve and Jane Seymour was based on. There was also *The Incredible Shrinking Man* (1957), *The Legend of Hell House* (1973), *What Dreams May Come* (1998) and many more that were also translated to film.

Richard wrote the short story *Duel* in 1971 and adapted it as a teleplay directed by Stephen Spielberg. The TV version was long regarded as the best made-for-TV movie.

Stephen King tagged Matheson as one of his major creative influences and dedicated his novel *Cell* (2006) to him and filmmaker George A. Romero. Romero also regarded Matheson as an influence for his zombie ghouls in *Night of the Living Dead* (1968). Even vampire queen Anne Rice said that, when she was a mere child, Matheson's "A Dress of White Silk" (1951), a short story, was an early influence on her later writings in the vampire and fantasy genres.

After a lifetime of success and being regarded as a true innovator in several genres of the literary field, Matheson died at his home in Los Angeles on June 7, 2013, at the age of eighty-seven.

Rita Hayworth

Another celebrity who graced the marina with her presence was the lovely, sexy Rita Hayworth. I recognized her immediately as she stepped off a sleek, sparkling white, eighty-foot yacht and strutted her way to the marina porch. I held the door open for her.

"Welcome, Miss Hayworth, to the G.I. Rupert Lore & Sons Marina," I greeted.

"Thanks, young man," she replied. "I've heard this is the place to stop all along the Atlantic coast."

Rita sat at one of the tables as I got her a coke with ice.

"Would you like some lunch?" I asked.

"I am a bit hungry," she answered. "What do you suggest?"

"My grandma makes the best crabcakes in the world," I replied. "They melt in your mouth."

"Sounds good," she replied.

"I'm what you would call a real fan," I began. "Do you mind if I talk with you for a little while?"

"No, not at all," she responded.

"I recently saw you in *Miss Sadie Thompson* [1955] with Jose Ferrer," I related. "A great performance. The best you ever gave, I thought. I also saw the old Joan Crawford-Walter Huston version of the Somerset Maugham story under the name *Rain* [1932]. However, I thought your performance was the best. You can also belt out a song with the best of them."

"Thanks again," she said.

"I know you hit it big about ten years ago starring with Glenn Ford in *Gilda* [1946]," I continued. "Your performance as the *femme fatale* was really something. Didn't Fred Astaire also say you were his favorite dancing partner, Ginger Rogers notwithstanding?"

"Yes, he did, bless him," Hayworth acknowledged. "Dear Fred. . . ."

"I also saw you in the Orson Welles film, *The Lady From Shanghai* [1947]," I continued. "That was another fine performance."

As Grandma DeBoy brought Rita a plate piled high with crabcakes, I excused myself. She left the marina early the next morning.

Rita Hayworth went on to receive good reviews for her performance in *Separate Tables* (1958) with Burt Lancaster and David Niven (who received the Best Actor Oscar for his performance). She continued making films through the 1960s and early 1970s.

Hayworth married the great Orson Welles in September 1943, at the height of her career. Joseph Cotten (see Chapter Ten) was the Best Man.

In 1981, Rita announced that she had contracted Alzheimer's disease. She quickly became the number one public face of the disease and was influential in ensuring that "future patients did not go undiagnosed."

Rita Hayworth died on May 14, 1987, in Manhattan, New York, at the age of sixty-eight. Tributes poured in from around the world. Hayworth had called Orson Welles "the great love of her life." Welles, on the evening before his death in 1985, said Rita was "one of the dearest and sweetest women that ever lived."

Chapter Two: Stars Sailing the Chesapeake Bay

Robert Mitchum

One bright and sunny summer day in 1959, veteran actor Robert Mitchum made a short visit to the marina. I knew that he and his wife, Dorothy, had purchased a farm directly across the Chesapeake Bay in Trappe, Maryland, where they lived until 1965.

My sister-in-law, Faye Lore, and I were in the small check-in cabin at the end of the main wharf when we saw Mitchum walking toward us with his trademark gait. He was there to fill his small motorboat with gasoline and buy some cigarettes. In the cramped cabin, he quickly lit a cigarette. As someone was servicing his boat where Dorothy remained, I had a few minutes to talk to him. I got straight to the point.

"Hello, Mr. Mitchum," I greeted. "It is a pleasure to see you."

"Yeah, thanks," he responded somewhat gruffly.

I had heard he could be difficult, but I was determined to have a brief talk with him about his films.

"I was most impressed with your performance as Reverend Harry Powell in *The Night of the Hunter* [1955], directed by the great Charles Laughton," I remarked. "It was a wonderful, menacing performance, your best yet. I've seen it about twenty times so far. No doubt, Mr. Laughton played no small role in drawing such great acting from you and the rest of the impressive cast, including the great Lillian Gish."

"There's something to be said for that," Mitchum responded with a slight laugh. "Charlie Laughton may have drawn a good performance from me, but I still don't know how people can say I'm a good actor. To me, it's only a job. They pay me well, that's for sure. But, mainly, I just want to collect my paycheck and get back to my farm."

"Burl Ives told me much the same thing about wanting to get away from the Hollywood studio hoopla when he was here two years ago in his little sailboat, *Sparrow*," I remarked (see Chapter Three).

"Oh, yeah?" Mitchum retorted. "So, Burl was here, too?"

"Yes, he was sailing with his wife, Helen, to Florida to make *Wind Across the Everglades* [1958]," I remarked. "He also said he wanted to get away from Hollywood as quickly as he could when he could."

"There ya go," Mitchum rather flippantly remarked.

The actor quickly boarded his small craft and sped away from the marina.

A Master of Menace

I had previously seen Mitchum in a number of films, including *The Story of G.I. Joe* (1945), the only movie for which he received an Academy Award nomination as Best Supporting Actor. I never really considered him a great actor, however, until *The Night of the Hunter.* Another menacing role for which he gained fame was in *Cape Fear* (1962) with Gregory Peck. His slithering snake performance as he crawled through the swamp of the Cape Fear River in North Carolina culminating with his squishing a grapefruit into the face of co-star Polly Bergen was one for the celluloid fan magazines.

I later discovered that the young Mitchum was a rebel who was involved in fistfights and other mischief. During the 1930s, he traveled around the country hobo-hopping on railroad cars. He worked at various jobs as a coal miner, boxer, aircraft assembler, and laborer. At only fourteen years of age, he was arrested for vagrancy and was confined for a while on a local chain gang. He soon escaped and eventually rode the rails to Hollywood, California, where he was signed to a seven-year contract with RKO Radio Pictures.

The Pot Bust

On September 1, 1948, Robert and actress Lila Leeds were reportedly arrested for possessing marijuana as the result of a sting operation. He was said to have spent two months at a prison farm in Castaic, California (only about twenty miles from where I now live). It was there that *Life* Magazine photographers took pictures of him mopping up his prison cell. There were also reports that, in January 1951, the actor's case was reviewed following a probation period. Following an investigation, his conviction was erased from the official record.

Many years later—during a segment of one of Turner Classic Movies' Private Screenings—I saw Mitchum tell host Robert Osborne that his marijuana arrest "never happened." He said it had been staged by his studio's publicity department. Osborne was not only just surprised. He had a totally stunned look on his face.

It was likely that the actor was having a little sadistic fun with Osborne, who may (or not) have believed him, particularly since there was a record of his arrest, imprisonment and eventual exoneration.

Robert Mitchum continued to build on his acting resume with the 1970 David Lean epic film *Ryan's Daughter* and was considered for a Best Actor Oscar nomination, but didn't make it. The irony was that George C. Scott won the Best Actor award for *Patton*, a project that Mitchum had turned down so he could take the lead role in *Ryan's Daughter*. Years later, the actor expressed regret for not taking the Patton role.

Many years after I met him, I learned that the tough-guy actor wasn't really the rough-hewn cynic about his craft that he seemed to evoke. While he enjoyed torturing newspaper, magazine, radio, and television reporters and hosts with his flippant remarks about acting, he was really regarded by his peers as a fully dedicated colleague who took his profession seriously. He was described as a talented, dedicated craftsman who was always on time, knew his lines perfectly, and used his clout for striving to make top-quality films. This included butting heads with more than one lackluster director.

Movie critics were also catching on to Mitchum's bad-boy act and were rejecting it. In his review of *Going Home* (1971), *The New York Times* critic Vincent Canby said that the actor had "reached that point in his career where he doesn't seem to act as much as inhabit whatever film he's in, whatever role he's playing, whether it's an Irish schoolmaster, an Australian sheepherder, or, as here, a nice, well-meaning garage mechanic with a talent for bowling."

Academy Award-winning actress Shirley MacLaine saw a simpler side of Robert Mitchum. In *Lucky Stars*, her 1995 autobiography, she wrote about her affair with the actor when they were filming *Two for the Seesaw* (1962) and added: "He saw himself as a common stiff, born to be lonely, who should expect nothing from life except that the roof doesn't leak."

In early July 1997, I was saddened to learn that, like Burl Ives (see Chapter Three), Mitchum, at the age of seventy-nine, had paid dearly for being a lifelong heavy smoker. He died from lung cancer and emphysema. He was cremated and his ashes were scattered over the Pacific Ocean near his home in Santa Barbara, California. He had been married to Dorothy Mitchum for fifty-seven years. She passed away in April 2014 at the age of ninety-four.

The people in Trappe, Maryland, still remember Robert Mitchum by keeping Mitchum's Steakhouse there on Maryland's Eastern shore open for business.

Madam Illarion V. Mishtowt

During the summer of 1960, at the Cove Point, Maryland, home of my friend Jessie Koushnareff, facing the Chesapeake Bay, I spent an evening with Jessie and her friend, Madam Illarion V. Mishtowt, the niece of famed and beloved composer Pyotr Ilyich Tchaikovsky.

Madam Mishtowt was a delightful person. I was particularly interested in meeting her since I had just finished writing the first draft of an unpublished novel based on the life and work of her Uncle Peter. She quickly perused what I had written and said it showed promise, urging me to continue with it.

Mishtowt told us that, as a young girl, she had been at her uncle's deathbed in St. Petersburg shortly before he died on November 6, 1893. This was not long after the composer had conducted one of his seminal works, the *Sixth Symphony ("Pathetique")* in New York that same year.

The official cause of the composer's death was from drinking tainted water, but Madam Mishtowt said it was no secret to the family even then that the composer died from the effects of syphilis as a result of his homosexuality. The family believed he may have contracted the disease from a Russian prince with whom he was in love.

"A prophet is without honor in his own land," Madam Mishtowt told me. "He was just 'Uncle Peter' to us even though we knew he was famous."

Tchaikovsky was not only one of the most beloved of all classical composers, he was also one of the most prolific. His lifetime output included seven symphonies, eleven operas, twenty choral works, three piano concertos, three ballets, five suites, a violin concerto, eleven overtures, and more than 100 songs and piano compositions.

From Russia With Pathos

The composer's niece, Madam Mishtowt, was the wife of a former naval attache at the Imperial Russian Embassy in Washington, D.C. She had been living there for forty years at the time I met her. Her mind, however, was as sharp as a tack as she recalled long-ago details of her life and her visit with Uncle Peter as a young girl. She was only eleven when Tchaikovsy died, which would make her sixty-seven when she visited Cove Point.

Mishtowt also clearly remembered her uncle's many visits to her home in St. Petersburg. He was staying with her grandparents following successful concert engagements in Europe and the United States. She described her time with the famed composer as "wonderful visits never to be forgotten."

This lovely woman told me she had been a Lady-in-Waiting to Czarina Alexandria. She was fond of the Czarina and was greatly saddened when the Czarina, Czar Alexander and their children were assassinated following the Russian Revolution in 1917. The Czarina gave her an Imperial pin, but she only wore it on very special occasions such as royal weddings or visits to the White House.

"I knew and loved the royal family," Madam Mishtowt told us. "At the time, however, we were all unaware of the real danger of a revolution."

During World War I, Mishtowt lived in New York, but moved to Washington shortly after the global conflict. After her first husband died, she married his successor, a naval attache, at the Imperial Russian Embassy in the District of Columbia.

Madam Mishtowt, Jessie and I listened to a recording of the *Pathetique Symphony* (1893).

"This was Uncle Peter's favorite work," she told us. "I am sure he would have wished to hear it on his death bed."

The wonderful but mounfrul sounds of the recording by Pierre Monteux and the Boston Symphony Orchestra resounded through the beach cottage out into the warm summer air. Outside, the waves from the Chesapeake gently lapping the shoreline and the mournful sounds of the foghorn of the nightly Norfolk-to-Baltimore ferry seemed to add a special accompaniment.

As I was about to leave following an evening with two extraordinary women, Mrs. Mishtowt said that she and her husband were greatly looking forward to attending a very special event on Friday, Ocober 21, 1960. On that evening, they would attend a performance by the Opera Society of

Washingon of her uncle's opera *Queen of Spades* [1890] in the Lisner Auditorium. She said that work had a special significance for her.

"Why is that?" I asked.

"Because my Uncle Modest Tchaikovsky, Uncle Peter's brother, wrote the libretto," she quickly responded while holding out her arms for a quick hug.

My friend, Jessie Kousnnareff, was also no stranger to great classical music. Her late husband, Sergei, was a famed classical pianist in Russia and a student of Sergei Rachmaninoff, composer of the beloved *Piano Concerto Number 2* (1900) and *Rhapsody on a Theme of Paganini* (1934).

Not long after my visit, Jessie moved to Sarasota, Florida. I visited her there once in 1966. We remembered our evening with Madam Mishtowt with special fondness.

It had been a great evening for me with two extraordinary women.

Reverend Sun Myung Moon and *The Washington Times*

In 1982, while I was living back in Southern Maryland to be with my ailing father, I contacted the first editor of Washington, D.C.'s new daily newspaper, *The Washington Times*. Even before its first issue was coming off the presses, it was gaining notoriety because of its founder, the controversial Reverend Sun Myung Moon.

Moon was the founder of the Unification Church and its members were labeled "Moonies." Moon himself was an ardent anti-communist and had already gained notoriety for leading mass wedding ceremonies at such venues as Madison Square Garden. His critics labeled him as a cult leader who kept a tight rein on his followers.

In 1974, after he moved to the United States, Moon urged that his church members support President Richard M. Nixon during the Watergate scandal. Nixon publicly thanked Moon and his followers for their support and invited him to the White House.

I told the *Times* editor that I was interested in writing an article for the prototype issue about the Chesapeake Bay oysterman as a tribute to my ailing father. He agreed and assigned several members of his Moonie staff to accompany me aboard the *Miss Faye*, an oyster dredge boat owned by my brother, Jon Shaw Lore, and his son, Jon, Jr.

It was a cold winter day as we left the harbor in St. Jerome's Creek in Ridge, Maryland. The Moonie staff members snapped the photos while I took notes.

The result was an article titled "Grueling Winter tested mettle of Chesapeake Bay Oystermen" that was published in the prototype issue of the *Times* dated April 13, 1982.

The article was apparently well-received because I was invited to the lavish party inaugurating the *Times* at the beautiful, elaborate Corcoran Gallery of Art in Washington, D.C.

Reverend Moon knew how to throw a party. The first floor of the gallery was laden with marble tables full of lavish food bowls and plates, including Chesapeake Bay oysters, blue crab meat, shrimp, and Oriental food. The drinks were plentiful and exotic. Moon even hired members of the string section of the National Symphony Orchestra to serenade the attendees.

Moon, his editor, and main staff were seated on an elevated marble stand where they greeted the attendees. It reminded me of an emperor receiving his subjects. I approached Moon and shook his hand.

"Ah, you wrote the article on the Chesapeake Bay oystermen," he remarked. "Good job. I would like to have my editor talk to you about more articles."

"Thank you," I responded. "I look forward to it."

Overall, the event was a rigid affair. Moonies hovered over the guests with expressionless, stoic looks. I felt uneasy, as if I had stumbled into a conclave where I was not welcome. After gorging myself on the elaborately and beautifully prepared Chesapeake Bay seafood and Oriental delicacies, I quietly left the Corcoran to the lilting sounds of the National Symphony's string section.

I never heard back from Reverend Moon or his editor. The *Times* went on to have a big effect on conservative politics in the nation's capitol. President Ronald Reagan was said to have read the paper every day during his two terms as the nation's chief executive.

The *Times* operated in the red financially during its first thirty-three years. It wasn't until 2015 that it had its first profitable year. By 2012, the Unification Church had spent nearly $2 billion subsidizing it.

Conclusion

There were many other celebrities who also showed up at the G.I. Rupert Lore & Sons Marina. These included such prominent politicians as Senators John and Robert F. Kennedy, Senator Joseph Tydings, Congressman Hale Boggs (see Chapter One), Maryland Governor Millard Tawes, and long-time Maryland State Comptroller Louis Goldstein. I had brief interactions with each of them. They were trying to persuade dad to run for Congress in order to strengthen the state Democratic ticket, particularly when Kennedy was running for President in 1960. My father was having none of it, however. He even embarrassed the hell out of me once when he called politicians "liars and crooks" in the presence of Governor Tawes, Robert Kennedy, Hale Boggs, and Louis Goldstein. He wasn't asked to run for dogcatcher after that decidedly non-diplomatic refusal to join the Democratic state political machine.

My father was a man who knew his mind ... and his limitations, to quote Clint Eastwood. Rest in peace, Dad.

Chapter Three
Burl Ives

It was a picture-perfect day on July 13, 1957, with a slight warming breeze caressing the snug harbor at Solomons Island, Maryland, at the southern-most end of Calvert County where the Patuxent River meets the Chesapeake Bay. I had risen early to net from the wharf pilings of my father's marina the succulent blue crabs that my grandmother, Annie DeBoy, would mold into crab cakes. The steamed crustaceans with grandma's magic touch were prized by visitors to the marina who would enjoy a lunch or dinner on the screened porch of the big white house at the entrance to the marina. The popular marina had become a favorite refueling and overnight spot for boatmen on their way from points south to Florida as well as locations from Florida north to Maine.

My grandfather, Frank DeBoy, who partnered with dad on the marina, was an irascible man who didn't like small sailboats tying up at the long 150-foot main wharf facing Mile Lakes Island a half-mile or so out in the harbor because their owner-pilots didn't buy much gas. He was adamant about docking only larger gas, diesel, and other yachts at the main wharf.

At noon that day, I noticed a small sailboat about twenty feet long slowly making its way to the smaller alcove docks. This was near the imposing white house where my grandparents lived and where they could keep an eye on the boats and yachts during the night. As the boat slowly neared the dock where I was standing, I quickly saw that it was America's favorite balladeer and folk singer, Burl Ives, at the helm. I was scheduled to begin studying folk music at the prestigious Peabody Conservatory of Music (second only to the Julliard School of Music in New York at the time) in Baltimore, Maryland, that fall. So, it was the perfect opportunity to attempt to converse with the best performer in the field.

I was a bit surprised by the fact that Burl was slowly guiding his small Pacific Seacraft Flicka named *Sparrow* into the smaller wharf docks. I recognized him right away as his huge bulk of a body sat at the helm in the rear of the boat. His weight then must have exceeded 300 pounds because the bow of the sailboat had risen inches off the surface of the water while the rear of the vessel had sunk. Ives was holding a head of lettuce in one hand while deftly guiding *Sparrow* into one of the small side docks.

I ran onto the dock as Ives threw me the ropes. I quickly looped them around the pilings and tied them tight. Burl had trouble rising from his seat and sitting down. I greeted him. He seemed amusingly surprised by what I said: "It's a pleasure seeing you, Mr. Ives. I see the doctor has put you on a diet."

"Yes, dammit!" he exclaimed, munching on the lettuce. "I wish I could have a mess of crabcakes instead."

"My grandmother at the house here makes great crabcakes," I responded. "If she has any in the refrigerator, I'll ask her to fry some."

"Thanks," Burl replied, "but my doctor will disown me if I don't lose some weight. What's your name, young fellow?"

"Dick Lore," I answered.

"By the way, who was that grumpy old guy who shoved me away from the main dock?" he asked.

"That's my grandfather," I sheepishly replied. "Sorry about that. He doesn't like sailboats because they don't buy much gas, but my father, who owns the marina, is thinking of letting him go."

Ives said nothing more about it and sat back down munching on the lettuce. Then he called down into the small boat cabin to his wife, Helen, asking her to hand him up a glass of iced tea. After he got the tea, he began lighting up a cigar, the mouth-end of which he dipped into the tea.

"My doctor says I have to eat this," he said while holding up the head of lettuce, "and stop smoking these damned stogies."

Down to the Sea in Ships

That was the start of an eight-hour visit with a man I had longed to meet. I had recently purchased his latest record album, *Down to the Sea in Ships* (1956), which featured a dozen or so folksongs of the sea. This was something I loved since I was slated to study piano, the guitar, and voice concentrating on folk songs at the Peabody, about eighty-five miles to the northeast. I mentioned this to Burl and he agreed to autograph the album for me. I quickly ran up the steep hill to our large three-story Victorian-style home overlooking the marina where the cawing of seagulls awakened me every morning from my bedroom with a panoramic view of the harbor.

Grabbing the album and my guitar, I ran back down to be with Ives for, as it turned out, the next eight hours. Burl remained sitting at the helm of the *Sparrow* while I sat perched on the wharf within touching distance of him. As I handed him the album, he said he would invite me aboard, but there wasn't enough room for both of us. Even Helen couldn't join him. I also sensed that he and Helen were having domestic problems. This was highlighted fourteen years later when they were divorced in 1971, leaving Burl to marry his second wife, Dorothy Koster Paul, in London, England, two months later.

All of that was in the future as I sat on the wharf and handed Burl the album while laying the guitar gently down on the wharf. I was in a euphoric state because my favorite folk singer and one of my favorite actors and I were hitting it off as star-and-fan.

"Helen, hand me my pen!" Burl shouted into the cabin. "My young friend here wants an autograph!"

A thin hand with the pen appeared from the cabin and Ives inscribed the back of the album with words I treasure to this day: *"To Dick Lore, a fellow laborer in the vineyards. Burl Ives, July 13, 1957."* Ives also wrote the words *"To Dick Lore, with best wishes, Burl Ives"* on the front cover.

The first number on the album was "Jack Was Every Inch a Sailor," a folksong from Newfoundland and Labrador. I happened to know the words and music to the ballad and Burl did something that touched me deeply. He again shouted down for Helen to pass his guitar up to him.

"Go ahead, Dick, you start with the first verse and I'll follow with the rest," he instructed.

Excusing myself, I ran the few steps to the marina house where I kept my own guitar, returned to the *Sparrow*, then strummed it for tuning and sang (Burl grabbed his guitar and joined me in the second verse):

'Twas twenty-five or thirty years since Jack first saw the light. He came upon this world of woe one dark and stormy night. He was born upon his father's ship as she was lying to 'bout twenty-five or thirty miles southeast of Bachalieu.

When Jack grew up to be a man, he went to Labrador. He fished in Indian Harbour, where his father fished before. On his returning in the fog, he met a heavy gale, and Jack was swept into the sea and swallowed by a whale.

The whale sent straight to Baffin's Bay 'bout ninety knots an hour and every time he blew a spray, he sent it in a shower. On moving on, says

Jack, I went to see what he's about. He grabbed the whale by the tail and turned him inside out...

[Verse]:

Jack was every inch a sailor, five and twenty years a whaler. Jack was every inch a sailor. He was borned upon the bright blue sea.

James Dean

It was quite a thrill. I was doing a duet with the greatest balladeer America had ever known. We finished the song and laid our guitars aside.

I mentioned to Burl that I had really enjoyed his supporting role as the sheriff in the film *East of Eden* (1955) with James Dean, whom I said showed great promise. I immediately saw a scowl on his face and quickly surmised that he and the young actor had not gotten along. Burl hesitated, looked a little perplexed, and didn't answer. Dean, of course, had been killed at the young age of twenty-four in a car crash on September 30, 1955. This abruptly ended the career of a young actor who showed the promise of becoming another Rudolph Valentino. Dean's death came only two weeks after he finished his role as Jett Rink with Elizabeth Taylor and Rock Hudson in George Stevens' memorable classic, *Giant* (1956), based on the novel by Edna Ferber.

"Oh, so you didn't get along with him?" I surmised.

Burl seemed a little embarrassed at first, but I pressed on.

Ives told me the story of the difficulty he and Raymond Massey, who played Adam Trask, the father of Dean's character, had with the young actor in his first film. Both Ives and Massey considered him highly untrained. Dean displayed the quirky mannerisms of method acting and often mumbled and stumbled on his words. Ives and Massey were particularly perplexed at Dean in the scene where he caresses a 100-pound block of ice in his father's icehouse before shoving all the frozen blocks down a chute onto the ground.

"It was like he was making love to the damned thing!" Ives told me.

An Ode to Ice

"Actually, I can relate to that," I remarked, pointing across the roadway leading down to the marina to a long black building that nearly touched the harbor waters. "That's my father's icehouse. I came down with a severe case of German measles when I was only ten years old. My temperature reached a death-threatening 107 degrees Fahrenheit. The nearest hospital or doctor was twenty-one miles away in Prince Frederick, the county seat. Dad called Dr. Page Jett, the only practicing doctor directly associated with the hospital then, in 1946. Dad asked if an ambulance should speed me to the hospital, but Dr. Jett said, 'no,' that the journey may kill me. The doc grabbed his black bag, jumped into his 1940 Hudson and sped to our home in what must have been record time in those days. After deftly running up the curved staircase to my bedroom where my father and mother were frantically holding cold towels over my forehead, the doctor felt my head."

I saw that I had Burl Ives' attention and continued on with the story.

"Your boy could be dead in an hour or even sooner if we don't get his temperature down quickly," Dr. Jett grimly remarked. "Don't you own an icehouse, Dick?"

"Yes," Dad replied. "It's just down the road."

"Get down there and bring back as much ice as you can," the doctor ordered. "That's the best prescription for him right now. Chop up the ice into small pieces and we'll place them in your bathtub. We're going to wrap the boy in a blanket and put him in the tub on top of the ice. I'll stay here and watch his temperature and see he doesn't freeze to death during the night."

Dad didn't need further prompting. As heavy a man as he was, he flew down the stairs, out the front door, and hopped into his new 1946 Buick. With screeching tires, he raced the short distance to the icehouse. We never knew how he did it so quickly by himself, but he was back with a big 100-pound block of ice, which he chipped into small pieces and threw into several small buckets. With one full bucket in each hand, dad raced them upstairs to the bathroom and emptied them into the bathtub. Then he picked up my ten-year-old fever-wracked body and raced me to the bathroom while mom covered me in a light blanket. Dad gently laid me down on the pile of cold ice. My only thought then was that I had planned to go to the small local movie theater to see Errol Flynn and Olivia de Havilland in *The Adventures of Robin Hood* (1946). I was determined not to miss that film, deathly sick or not. Dad managed to calm me down, telling me that Robin Hood, his merry men, and Maid Marion, would wait for me to get well.

I screamed as dad put me on top of the ice in the bathtub, but he quickly calmed me down. Dr. Jett, dad, and mother stayed with me all night, gently lifting me in and out of the tub whenever deadly hypothermia threatened to set in. The doctor kept a constant watch on my pulse and temperature. As the distant rays of early morning began to creep over the waters of the Patuxent River, the doctor said I could be released from my icy prison and put back in bed. My temperature was now close to normal and I felt warmer as heavy blankets were laid over me.

"The doctor told my parents that he had never seen anyone with as high a temperature as I had come out of it alive," I concluded.

I looked straight at Burl Ives while thinking he would probably not believe what sounded like an unlikely tale.

"That's quite a story, young man," Burl remarked. "I'll bet you now recoil at the sight or even mention of ice."

"No sir," I responded. "Those cold ice chunks saved my life. I promised that I would try to never take another drink without filling the glass with ice. Unlike James Dean, I may not be making love to a block of ice, but I will always be grateful to its life-saving gift to me. But, please, tell me more about your acting with Dean."

Marking His Territory

"He would do crazy things," Ives responded, shaking his head. "He often went off the set by himself to get into the method mood. The dumbest, most disrespectful thing I saw him do was when he suddenly walked onto the set, unzipped his pants, and urinated in all four corners of it like a dog marking its territory. Such stupid antics drove Elia Kazan [the director] crazy at first, but he eventually used part of Dean's craziness as a means to enhance the rebellious nature of Cal's character."

What Kazan did must have worked because Dean was nominated for a Best Actor Oscar, but lost to Ernest Borgnine for *Marty* (1955). It also paved the way for the actor's most iconic role in *Rebel Without a Cause* (1955) and his more restrained part in *Giant* (1956), for which he won a second and posthumous Academy Award Best Actor nomination.

Wind Across the Everglades

Being a lifelong movie buff (then and now), I suspected Burl may be going somewhere to star in a movie. I was correct. He said he and his boat were contracted to appear in a film later titled *Wind Across the Everglades* (1958) that was to be filmed on location in Everglades National Park in Florida. He and Helen were headed there via the Inland Waterway.

The movie was the first starring role of later Oscar winner Christopher Plummer. It was also to be the film debut of Peter Falk in a small part and included former superstar stripper Gypsy Rose Lee and renowned circus clown Emmett Kelly.

When I first saw the film, I considered it an inept bomb. It wasn't until more than fifty years later that I saw it again and appreciated it more. Burl had, indeed, personified the role of Cottonmouth as he swaggered and slogged his way in and out of the bogs of the Everglades. It also managed to capture some of the flavor of that national park.

MacKinlay Kantor

Famed Pulitzer Prize-winning author MacKinlay Kantor also had a minor role in *Wind Across the Everglades*. In 1968, shortly after my best-selling book *Mysteries of the Skies: UFOs in Perspective* was published, I was invited by Borden Deal—a columnist for *The Herald-Tribune* in Sarasota, Florida—to the first of two of the regular weekly writers' luncheons hosted by Kantor in Sarasota. Deal had praised my book in his column and recommended it to Kantor and the other writers who were there. They invited me to one of their luncheons where the food was great and the booze flowed freely.

I sat beside Kantor at the head of the long lunch table when he mentioned his long-time relationship with Burl Ives, whom he considered the king of folksong balladeers. I mentioned that I had met Burl, who was on his way to Florida to star in *Wind Across the Everglades*. Kantor asked what I thought of the movie. I replied that I thought it was pretty bad and was disappointed that Ives had starred in it. Looking me straight in the eye, Kantor responded: "I was also in it."

Whoops . . . I thought I had stuck my foot in it again, but Kantor saved me. He said he agreed with my assessment and had told Budd Schulberg, the film's producer, that, after the triumphal release of the classic *On the Waterfront* in 1954, *Wind Across the Everglades* was a real "stinker."

Kantor was a devoted friend to Burl Ives and admired the actor-folk singer as a treasured twentieth century balladeer. He had introduced Ives to the imminent author and intellectual giant Carl Sandburg, who called Ives "the greatest balladeer of any century."

At my first Sarasota Writers' Luncheon in 1968, I also met the prolific crime fiction writer, John McDonald, whose books featured the private eye Travis McGee. McDonald told me that, even though Kantor had won the Pulitzer Prize for his Civil War novel *Andersonville* (1955), his masterpiece was really the longer book *Spirit Lake*, published in 1961. I agreed, adding that it was the only novel in which I actually experienced the sensation of smell while reading it.

Also at the long table was Walter Farley, famed for his novel *The Black Stallion* (1941), which was published when the author was still in high school. Other writers who appeared as visitors like myself at the Friday luncheons included William L. Shirer, Buckminster Fuller and Art Buchwald. The luncheons began in November 1952 and lasted weekly for thirty years. They were a top draw in Sarasota with writers flocking to the area in the hope of being invited to one of Kantor's weekly gatherings. I was one of those lucky writers.

The Itinerant Singer

Back at dad's marina, I asked Burl Ives about his earlier life. He said he began his career as an itinerant singer ("a hobo, really," he told me) strumming the banjo. He managed to launch his own radio show, *The Wayfaring Stranger* (ca. 1940), which brought traditional folk songs to the airwaves.

Before his radio show debut, Ives traveled across the U.S. during the early 1930s earning his way playing the banjo and taking odd menial jobs. In

Mona, Utah, he was jailed for vagrancy and singing "Foggy Dew." For some inexplicable reason, the authorities deemed it "a bawdy song."

In early 1942, following his short jail stint, Burl was drafted into the wartime U.S. Army. He was stationed at Camp Upton and became a hit by joining the cast of Irving Berlin's *This Is the Army* (1943), a role he repeated later on Broadway. He received a medical discharge in September 1943 and was soon sharing an apartment with actor Harry ("Henry") Morgan, who would later co-star in Jack Webb's *Dragnet* (1967) and *M*A*S*H* (1972).

Burl Ives' big year for film was 1958 when four of his best-known movies were released. Sitting beside the *Sparrow* in 1957, I mentioned that I wish I could have seen him in his seminal acting role as Big Daddy on Broadway in Tennessee Williams' Pulitzer Prize-winning play, *Cat on a Hot Tin Roof* (1955). I asked if there were any plans to make the hit play into a movie. He said there had been some talk that it would be, but nothing definite had been set. This was back in the days when movies were made at a fast clip with no ten or more years of gestation periods with long shoots.

At the marina, I asked what his next movie role might be. He said he had just signed a contract to star with Gregory Peck in what was then an unnamed western. That film quickly became *The Big Country* (1968), an epic adventure that co-starred Jean Simmons, Charlton Heston, Carroll Baker, and Charles Bickford. The movie, completed and released a little more than a year after my visit with Burl, won him an Oscar as Best Supporting Actor.

Besides *The Big Country*, 1958 also saw the release of *Wind Across the Everglades*, *Cat on a Hot Tin Roof*, and the film based on Eugene O'Neill's *Desire Under the Elms*, also starring Sophia Loren and Anthony Perkins. Loren later said that Burl was "a kind, gentle man" and was her favorite co-star. Quite an impressive feat and a banner year for the folk singer who previously had mainly only supporting roles in films.

The Lost Dutchman

Burl's interests were hardly limited to folk singing and acting. He was fascinated with the mysteries of life as well. As he sat on the *Sparrow*, he called down for Helen to hand him up his pipe with some tobacco. She did. He packed some tobacco into the pipe and puffed it until the smoked swirled up, out, and over the harbor. Then he turned to me.

"My doctor told me that this pipe and my cigars would kill me someday, so I suggest you stay way from them, young fellow," he remarked, "but I don't think I will go out of this world that way. I plan to go out aboard one of my boats sailing on one of the oceans of the world . . . or maybe the Chesapeake Bay"

"It's interesting you say that, Mr. Ives," I responded. "Did you know that, when Maryland was one of the thirteen original colonies, it became one whose sole purpose was for its farmers to grow, cultivate and sell tobacco? So, you're in the right state to enjoy your smoke."

"No, I didn't know that," he remarked. "Interesting. . . ."

Then Burl told me of someone he knew who was a park ranger with an encyclopedic knowledge of the legendary Lost Dutchman's Gold Mine in the Superstition Mountains. This was a popular spot in the Superstition Wilderness area east of Phoenix, Arizona.

As the smoke from his pipe swirled about his head, Ives said his friend told him the mystery started with Jacob Waltz, a German immigrant who reportedly discovered a glistening mother load of gold in the wilderness. He told Julia Thomas—the boarding house owner who had cared for him for many years—of the location. It was also reported that a number of individuals who were searching for—and a few who even claimed to have found—the mother lode had been mysteriously killed, some in particularly grisly ways. Also, some members of the local Apache Indian tribe were said to "believe that the hole leading down into hell is located in the Superstition Mountains."

Chapter Three: Burl Ives

The Inveterate Sailor

I also asked Burl how be became interested in sailing.

"I've loved the water and sailing as long as I can remember," he responded. "I'm not sure what came first, the singing or sailing. I barely remember it, but my parents told me I actually sang before a meeting of Civil War veterans when I was only four years old. Sailing may have come along shortly after that. I started with a twelve-foot centerboard boat, then graduated to a sixteen-foot sailboat. I'm sitting on the *Sparrow* now and I love her. She has been good to me and I hope I have been good to her. She is now proudly displaying the figurehead of the *Mattie F. Dean*, which itself is worth more than the boat herself."

The *Mattie F. Dean* was a Chesapeake Bay bugeye schooner that may still be lying in its graveyard in Annapolis, Maryland. During its sailing years, it was a real workhorse in the oyster farming industry. Annapolis was also where Burl kept the *Sparrow*. He told me he couldn't wait to fly from wherever he was to the Maryland capitol so he could board her and sail the Chesapeake. He wasn't one to hang around with the Hollywood or Broadway elite for long.

The Fond Goodbye

As dusk with its bright, streaking, red rays covering the sky, I knew that my time with this striking, highly talented artist was coming to an end. It would become the most personal and rewarding time I would spend with a celebrity.

I stretched my hand out over the wharf and shook hands with this extraordinary gentleman.

"It was very nice visiting with you, Dick," he said. "Good luck at the Peabody and keep following your star."

"Thank you very much, Mr. Ives," I responded. "I have never enjoyed a visit with anyone more. Good luck to you with the film."

With regret that I had to leave a man that I considered a giant not only in body but in spirit as well, I climbed the steep hill to our family home with the strains of "Jack Was Every Inch a Sailor" ringing in my ears.

I awoke late the next morning to the usual cawing sounds of seagulls outside my window. As I came downstairs, my parents greeted me smiling.

"Burl Ives was here about eight o'clock this morning," Dad said. "He wanted to thank you for your visit with him."

I was somewhat stunned. For a man as big as Burl to climb that steep hill up to our family home was, to me, amazing. It sent me a message that he also enjoyed and would remember the time he spent with me. At a slim 180 pounds, I had trouble myself daily scaling the hill.

"Why didn't you call me?" I asked.

"He said not to wake you."

"You should have," I remarked in a voice of utter dejection.

"Mr. Ives said you were the perfect fan," Mom interjected. "He said he couldn't remember enjoying a visit with a fan more and considered you as more of a young colleague. He wished you well at the Peabody."

To this day, I have never forgiven my long-deceased parents for not waking me that morning. I have also never forgiven myself for not trying to get a contact address or phone number for this great artist (there was no Internet or e-mail back then). I am sure he would have agreed. Sixty years later, I think of Burl Ives with an ever-renewed sense of affection.

The Final, Silent Farewell

On April 15, 1995, I was sharing a ride to work with a neighbor near where I live in Santa Clarita, California, when I heard on the radio that Burl Ives had passed away. The report said that he was a lifelong cigar and pipe smoker and was diagnosed with oral cancer less than a year before. I remembered back to the day I met him when he said he would not succumb from the effects of smoking. Sadly, he was wrong, but he had led a long, productive life bringing a wealth of folk music, films, concerts, records, and his own people-friendly personality to the world. Burl had quickly gone through several unsuccessful surgeries, then decided against more. He fell into a coma and died on April 14, 1995, at his waterfront home in Anacortes, Washington.

The passing of Burl Ives affected me deeply. As I continued on to work, I could almost see his face in a huge pure-white cloud where I fantasized joining him to reprise our singing together "Jack Was Every Inch a Sailor." Few days have gone by since that I have not thought of him and our visit together in that snug little harbor on the shores of the Chesapeake Bay.

Chapter Four

The UFO Connection

The Mother Ship

It was dark with a nearly foreboding atmosphere on a lonely stretch of road between the Calvert County seat, Prince Frederick, and my home on Solomons Island, Maryland, at 8:15 p.m., April 2, 1958. I was returning home from the Peabody Conservatory of Music in Baltimore, where I was a voice and piano student, when I spotted a single white light hanging stationary over a barn on the left side of the road.

The light remained still for about three minutes. Then it began blinking on and off while moving slowly south toward Solomons, six miles away. After traveling for about mile more, the object again stopped behind some trees and was lost from view.

About a mile north of home, the UFO again stopped and hovered over another barn, also on the left side of the road. The object had obviously been pacing my car. I purposely slowed down, then suddenly sped up several times and the object followed suit.

Suddenly, the UFO began blinking on and off, then started to perform some fantastic maneuvers. In an instant, it appeared at one end of the sky and, only a split second later, reappeared at the other end.

After performing these incredibly fast maneuvers half-a-dozen or so times, the light again stopped. Then, as I strained my neck to watch in a complete state of shock and wonderment, a brilliant large red light descended at an unbelievably fast speed and merged with the much larger white object. It was almost as if it had been swallowed. At this point, my car radio, which had been operating normally, began to emit a loud screeching sound, which continued to the end of the encounter.

The blinking white light continued to follow my car. As I approached the Patuxent River on the right side of the road, the still-blinking light slowed considerably, crossed the river and headed south until it disappeared.

It was a strange, eerie encounter. I have often wondered if the large white light was a mother ship gathering its offspring to its galactic bosom.

The Patuxent River Cigar

Nearly seven months later, on November 20, 1958, I was only days away from reporting for duty as a draftee in the U.S. Army on December 2. I had just finished my shift cleaning freshly shucked oysters at my father's oyster house, J.C. Lore & Sons, on Solomons Island, directly facing the wide expanse of the Patuxent River, a main tributary of the Chesapeake Bay.

It was 5:15 p.m. A red streak of light hung over the river, but the visibility was still sharp and clear. A few of the other oyster shuckers were with me.

"Look!" someone yelled, pointing at the sky. "What the hell is that?"

My sight was quickly drawn to three slender cigar-shaped objects resembling long, narrow, freak cloud formations that hung low over the river directly across from the oyster house. At first, the objects seemed to be reflecting the sunset itself. Then they began moving slowly across the river into St. Mary's County.

Suddenly, a fourth object appeared seemingly out of nowhere. It was so large that it dwarfed the other three UFOs. As we watched, this large object unbelievably began expanding from both ends at once. The objects appeared to be only a few hundred feet away. By this time, about fifteen other shuckers had joined us.

The larger red object with a tinge of yellow, along with the other three UFOs, hovered over the river in clear view for five or ten minutes. Then the larger object began a slow ascent into the sky until it came to a stop at an estimated 20,000 feet altitude. Suddenly, it changed color and shape to a round, silvery disc that quickly disappeared to the northeast at a tremendous speed.

I sent reports on both of these sightings to the headquarters office of the National Investigations Committee on Aerial Phenomena (NICAP) in Washington, D.C.

The Keyhoe Factor

My interest in UFOs (flying saucers) began several years before my 1958 sightings. I had read the first three books by Major Donald E. Keyhoe: *The Flying Saucers Are Real* (1950), *Flying Saucers from Outer Space* (1953) and *The Flying Saucer Conspiracy* (1955). These books, along with volumes by other authors, piqued my interest in the subject. I began collecting sighting reports from newspapers and magazines.

I knew that Keyhoe was often referred to as "Mr. UFO." He was already an established writer in the science fiction and aircraft testing fields. As an investigative journalist for *True* Magazine in the late 1940s and early 1950s, he tested and flew experimental aircraft to evaluate their performance. In 1949, however, his life took a dramatic turn when the *True* editor asked him to investigate the earlier flying saucer reports, beginning with the Kenneth Arnold sighting over Mt. Rainier, Washington, in June 1947.

At first, Keyhoe was skeptical of the reports. He quickly changed his mind, however, after interviewing a number of pilots and military officers with whom had had contacts in the Pentagon. These officials reported seeing unexplained objects in the skies, many of them at close range.

The result was the article, "Flying Saucers Are Real," which appeared in the January 1950 issue of *True*. The well-researched article hit a national nerve and became what still remains one of the most widely read articles in U.S. publishing history. Later that year, Keyhoe expanded the article into a full-length book, *The Flying Saucers Are Real*, which sold an amazing half-a-million paperback copies. Keyhoe had entered the history books as the author of the first article and book on UFOs.

Keyhoe and Lucky Lindy

Several decades before his first UFO book, Keyhoe managed the 1927 U.S. tour of aviation pioneer Charles Lindbergh following Lucky Lindy's historic flight. On May 20 of that year, Lindberg took off from Roosevelt Field on Long Island in his small Ryan monoplane, *The Spirit of St. Louis*, on the 3,610-mile, thirty-four-hour flight to Paris.

After clearing St. John's, Newfoundland, he was lost from sight. At 10:30 p.m., May 21, he landed at Bourget Field in the French capitol, becoming the first person to fly solo across the Atlantic. At times during the perilous flight, he flew only ten or so feet above the churning ocean waves.

It was a truly historic event that captured the imaginations of millions of people around the world. The flight immediately made Lindy the most popular man in America. He quickly conferred with Don Keyhoe on a coast-to-coast tour, which drew millions of people at various venues around the country.

The tour prompted Keyhoe to write his first book, *Flying with Lindbergh*, which was published only a year after the New York-to-Paris flight. It quickly became a best selling account of the historic journey.

Chapter Four: The UFO Connection

The Birth of NICAP

In 1956, Keyhoe co-founded the National Investigations Committee on Aerial Phenomena (NICAP). Another co-founder, Townsend Brown, became the first director. He lasted less than a year, however. His financial ineptitude caused his downfall. He was replaced by Keyhoe, who led it to being the largest and most renown UFO organization in the United States and, possibly, the world. It held that position for the next dozen or so years.

Known as a perpetual gadfly to the U.S. Air Force for its suppression of UFO reports, Keyhoe immediately began pressing hard for Congressional hearings. The NICAP president came down hard on the Air Force's Project Blue Book, which continued to denounce the subject.

Enter Carl Jung

Even the world's most famous psychologist, Dr. Carl G. Jung, the foremost pupil and early devotee of the father of psychology, Dr. Sigmund Freud, got into the UFO act. In 1958, he published his own UFO book, *Flying Saucers: A Modern Myth of Things Seen in the Skies*, in Switzerland.

In his book, Jung wrote: "I would like to call the reader's attention to Keyhoe's books, which are based on official material and studiously avoid the wild speculation, naivety, or prejudice of other publications."

In 1958, Jung briefly corresponded with Major Keyhoe. One of my prized possessions is one of the original letters Jung sent to Keyhoe, who gave it to me during the last week or so of our tenure at NICAP. It is reproduced here as Jung wrote it in his less-than-perfect English from his home in Zurich, Switzerland, on October 13, 1958:

> *Dear Major Keyhoe,*
> *My recent experience with APRO [Aerial Phenomena Research Organization] shows me that I must be careful in getting mixed up with*

UFO-organisations. Although I am vividly interested in these questions, I prefer to detach my name from oganisations of this kind. This does not mean, that I am not perfectly willing to contribute whatever I can, to the research-work, such organisations are concerned with. If I am able at all in help in psychological matters, I am glad to do so, but I prefer it in an in-official way.

I enclose a report in the "Neue Zurcher Zeitung" of Oct. 1st 1958, which is unfortunately inconclusive.

Sincerely yours

[s] C.G. Jung

Joining the NICAP Staff

In early 1965, while working as an assistant editor for a subsidiary of *U.S. News & World Report* in Washington, D.C., I met Richard H. ("Dick") Hall, the Assistant Director of NICAP. Like me, he was a folk song enthusiast. I had been performing these songs at the Unicorn coffee house in the nation's capitol when he approached me and invited me to his apartment. That same evening, he hired me as a staff member at NICAP headquarters. Dick and I quickly became good friends.

About a month into my tenure as a NICAP staffer, I met Donald Keyhoe. He was impressed by my knowledge of UFOs and what NICAP was doing to keep the subject alive in its attempt to persuade Congress to hold hearings on a sientific study of the phenomenon. Like Dick Hall before him, Don Keyhoe also quickly became a friend and mentor.

I learned a lot I didn't know about UFOs from Keyhoe. I also visited with him and his wife, Helen, at their spacious country home near Luray,

Virginia. Both were interested in the fact that I had been a folk singer and pianist and asked me to play and sing for them. I saw that they had the words and music to "Old Man River" from the Broadway musical *Show Boat* (1927) in the bench of their piano. I played and sang that perennial favorite. They appeared to be enthralled by my rather meager peformance.

Science Fiction and Aviation Stories

I also had a couple of brief discussions with Keyhoe about his earlier science fiction and aviation writing. Except for his book *Flying with Lindbergh* in 1928, I wasn't very familiar with his large output of science fiction and aviation articles. He did tell me that these stories were a natural lead-in to his quickly developing interest in UFOs.

This was soon after the first such credited report of the modern era came from Kenneth Arnold, a small plane pilot who, while flying, saw nine discs over Mt. Rainier in Washington State in June 1947. He described them as being "like saucers skipping over water." Thus the term "flying saucers" was born, inaugurating a huge wave of sightings known as the Great UFO Wave of 1947.

Mysteries of the Skies

Soon after I the joined NICAP, another staff member and friend, Harold Deneault, and I began discussing writing our own UFO book. We wanted not just another flying saucer tome. What was there about the subject that hadn't really been explored yet? A quick look at the NICAP files and bookshelves convinced us that none of the books had fully explored the UFO sightings prior to 1947. Our work would focus on the pre-1947 era of reports dating back for about 200 years. I even conducted extensive research on the so-called airship sighting wave of 1896 and 1897.

A proposal for the book, entitled *Mysteries of the Skies: UFOs in Perspective*, was accepted by Prentice-Hall, Inc., in Englewood Cliffs, New Jersey. It was published in 1968 and was well received by critics and the public alike. In 1969, I wrote *Strange Effects From UFOs*, published by NICAP later that year. Although both books have been out of print for many years, they are still being sold on both Amazon and e-Bay. Both tomes are also listed in the Library of Congress card files.

2001: A Space Odyssey

During the early Spring of 1967, I received a call at NICAP headquarters from Dr. Frederick ("Fred") Ordway III. He said he worked with Wernher von Braun at NASA's Marshall Space Flight Center. (Later, he would work with the Apollo spaceflight teams that would send astronauts to the moon.) Now, he said, he was the technical advisor for Stanley Kubrick's *2001: A Space Odyssey* (1968). He also said he was a friend of Arthur C. Clarke, whose writing inspired the film and who was also working with him and Kubrick on the movie.

Ordway quickly asked if I would have lunch with him the following day to discuss his work on the film. I quickly agreed.

The next day, we met at a restaurant near the Dupont Circle headquarters of NICAP. Ordway was impeccably dressed as we ordered lunch and drinks.

Fred Ordway told me that he and his family had moved to near the huge studio in England where Kubrick was filming the movie on a mammoth, elaborate set.

"Every detail of the movie set has to be perfect," Ordway said, sipping his cocktail.

Fred added that both he and Kubrick had been interested in UFOs and the real possibility that they were a result of alien beings surveying earth. He added that they had both read one or more of Keyhoe's books. He also said that Kubrick particularly wanted to garner some thoughts about how astronauts could survive years-long journeys to other planets.

I answered that my own theory had to do with the possibility of cryonic internment. This was in vogue at the time with experiments in Southern California and elsewhere. In theory, astronauts could be frozen in coffin-like containers and later thawed out and revived when they were nearing a distant planet.

While the successful outcome of cryonic internment had never been perfected then or now, some people had been cryonically frozen, including baseball great Ted Williams. The theory was that those who died of a particular disease could later be revived and survive once a cure for that disease was found. I knew that a scientific member of NICAP's Los Angeles Subcommittee, Dr. Leslie Kaeburn, had done some research on the subject and referred Ordway to him.

Following further discussion, Fred Orway thanked me and left. I later learned that he had seen Dr. Kaeburn and the cryonic internment of astronauts was depicted in the early scenes of the film, which was released in April 1968.

The work Ordway, Clarke, and Kubrick did on providing accurate details in the film placed *2001: A Space Odyssey* far above most other sci-fi films of that or any other era and many still consider it to be the best such film of all time.

Joe Franklin and Simon Oakland

Shortly after my book, *Mysteries of the Skies*, was published, I was invited by famed New York talk show host, Joe Franklin, to appear on his program. Appearing with me would be John G. Fuller, a UFO colleague and the author of

The Interrupted Journey: Two Hours "Aboard a Flying Saucer" (1966). Fuller had also been well-known for his "Trade Winds" column for the *Saturday Review*.

In Franklin's New York studio, we also met actor Simon Oakland who was slated for his own segment on the show. I knew Oakland as an excellent supporting actor in such films as *I Want to Live!* (1958), *Psycho* (1960) and *The Sand Pebbles* (1966). Simon told Fuller and I that he had long been fascinated by UFO reports and asked Franklin if he could be on the same segment as Fuller and myself. Joe gave the OK.

Following a discussion of *Mysteries of the Skies*, the talk quickly turned to Fuller's book about the strange abduction case of Betty and Barney Hill. This involved a couple from Portsmouth, New Hampshire, who were abducted aboard a flying saucer on the night of September 19, 1961. NICAP's New Hampshire Subcommittee had thoroughly investigated the case and determined that it was an authentic report by reliable witnesses.

The most controversial aspect of the case was that the Hills experienced two lost hours during their journey home. Those hours were reportedly spent aboard a UFO where the intelligent humanoid occupants submitted them to a physical examination. Following the abduction, a psychiatrist, Dr. Benjamin Simon, spent seven months treating Betty and Barney Hill. He reported that neither of them were psychotic and that "both consciously and under hypnosis, they told what they believed to be the absolute truth" about their abduction from that lonely rural New Hampshire road.

One of the most fantastic bits about the case involved the star map presented to Betty Hill by her kidnappers. The map showed a configuration of stars that would not be discovered by astronomers until years after the abduction!

"That is the most fantastic case I have ever heard about," Oakland remarked. "So, you really believe it is authentic?"

"The evidence definitely seems to be there to label it as a reliable report by equally reliable witnesses," Fuller replied.

"That's scary stuff," Franklin said. "I've never heard of witnesses being kidnapped by aliens from space."

"It *is* unbelievable," Fuller responded, "but it apparently happened."

"Good God!" Simon Oakland exclaimed. "Is this a new trend? Should we all be scared that we may be abducted on board a flying saucer from another planet?"

"Probably not," John replied. "These cases are rare, but they do exist. We'll have to wait and see what happens as more and more UFO sightings and encounters are reported."

"You know, I believe it," Simon remarked. "I've always thought that, of the many millions of plants in our universe, Earth can't be the only one inhabited by intelligent human-like beings."

"'Intelligent' may be the operative word," I said, wryly joining in. "We haven't done such a great job of using our own intelligence in this world of constant warfare."

"Amen to that," Franklin remarked.

UFO Sighting Investigations

Most of my function at NICAP involved heading the organization's twenty-five-to-thirty subcomittees around the world, evaluating UFO reports, and writing and editing the monthly *The UFO Investigator*. I also personally investigated several UFO reports in the field, including:

The Benedictine School Encounter

December 2, 1966. Ridgely, Maryland. Investigators included James Falk, Chairman of the Non-Linear Programming Group, and James Pomeroy, Computer Programmer, both of the Research Analysis Corporation, McLean, Virginia. Witness: Marie Wood, third and fourth grade teacher at the Benedictine School for Exceptional Children.

As she was driving down a lonely stretch of country road at 9:45 p.m., Wood spotted a brilliant flash of light that moved up and down and hovered over a line of trees. She described it like "two dessert dishes put together." It had evenly-spaced portholes around its side and was twice the size of a car.

The object also kept changing color from green to white. After maneuvering over the trees, it suddenly rose straight up and disappeared "in a flash."

At times during the sighting, the witness said, there was an unexplainable "buzz" coming from her car radio. The radio worked fine after the UFO disappeared from sight. This was typical of numerous electro-magnetic (E-M) effects reported by flying saucer witnesses.

The next morning, Wood's car would not start.

"The battery was gone," she remarked.

The witness spent a restless night at home. At 4:30 a.m., she said "a brilliant light filled my entire bedroom."

Following our interview at the school with Marie Wood, we followed up a lead that there may have been other sightings in the area. We traveled to the office of the Sheriff at Easton in a homey type of jail overlooking a body of water. The sheriff's wife was cooking dinner for the prisoners.

Fifteen minutes later, the sheriff returned home. He said he received an anonymous call on the morning following the Wood encounter. The caller said that, at 4:30 that morning, he witnessed a bright red glow east of Easton followed by "an object that kept bobbing up and down."

A Landing at South Hill

April 21, 1967. South Hill, Virginia, a few miles above the North Carolina border.

At nine p.m., Clifford N. Crowder, manager of the Mobile Chemical Warehouse, left his office when his car headlights illuminated an object sitting in the middle of the road about 500 feet away. As he closely approached the object, a blinding flame suddenly spurted from its underside. The UFO rose straight up, leaving the road burning.

Four small holes were discovered in the macadam surface of the road the next morning. After learning of the report the next day from a subcommittee member in Richmond, Virginia, NICAP staff members Don Berliner, Leon Katchen, and I drove to South Hill. We were joined there by William Powers, an assistant to Dr. J. Allen Hynek at Dearborn Observatory at Northwestern University. Hynek was still the Air Force's official spokesman.

Crowder told us that the small UFO was about twelve feet in diameter, fifteen-to-twenty feet high, and "shaped like a water tank standing on end." It sat on legs that were approximately three feet high.

Crowder's neighbor, Norman Martin, a tobacco farmer, also reported seeing at the same time as the Crowder sighting "the biggest burst of light he'd ever seen." The light brilliantly lit up a nearby oak tree.

After Berliner, Katchen, Powers, and I completed our investigation, we heard that J. Allen Hynek stated that Crowder's sighting "simply defies explanation."

There were also other sightings in the area at the same time as the Crowder encounter. These included police officers who saw "strange lights that moved like lightning" as they left the ground and were joined by two more lights in a diamond formation. Police chased the object at speeds up to seventy-five miles per hour. The UFO dipped up and down, then sped toward South Hill. One orange-yellow light split into two separate objects, then "came back together" and disappeared behind some trees.

Congressional Hearings

One project the NICAP staff eagerly participated in was the hearings before the Commitee on Science and Astronautics, U.S. House of Representatives, on July 29, 1968. I closely worked with Keyhoe, Dick Hall and rest of the NICAP staff, and Dr. James E. McDonald in preparing for the one-day symposium.

Besides McDonald, the other five speakers included Dr. J. Allen Hynek and well-known astronomer Dr. Carl Sagan. Congressman J. Edward Roush (D-IN) was chairman of the symposium. Roush also strongly believed that some UFO reports could represent visits from other planets. He joined the NICAP Board of Governors later that year.

In his lengthy statement, Hynek showed signs that he was breaking away from the usual negative Air Force stance on the subject. He said: "The Air Force position is that there is no evidence that UFOs represent a threat to national security. Consequently . . . it is not their mission to be scientifically curious about the hundreds of unidentifies in their own files." At the same time, he warned that we cannot afford "to overlook something that might be of great potential value to the nation . . . Can we afford not to look toward the UFO skies? Can we afford to overlook a potential breakthrough of great significance?"

McDonald followed with startling statements of his own: "The hypothesis that these are extraterrestrial surveillance [objects] I regard as most likely . . . They appear to be craft-like, machine-like devices . . . [There is] just too much other consistent evidence that suggests we are dealing with machine-like devices from somewhere else."

Chapter Four: The UFO Connection

The Colorado Project

A few months following the South Hill case, I worked with the rest of the NICAP staff providing sighting reports and other information to the newly-formed University of Colorado UFO Project, sponsored by the U.S. Air Force. The eagerly-anticipated project, headed by Dr. Edward U. Condon, promised an unbiased, objective investigation.

We transmitted to the project a number of top reports from the NICAP files. We soon discovered, however, that the main objective of Condon and his cohorts was simply to tow the Air Force line. They would do so by denying any possibility that some of the reliable reports could bolster the idea that at least some UFO encounters were real and not hoaxes, misinterpretations, or figments of the imagination.

By May 1968, Don Keyhoe was hopping mad and decided to cut off any further reports to the project. Like the rest of the staff, he initially had high hopes that the project would provide impartial, objective proof that the subject cried out for continued scientific investigation. Still, Keyhoe wasn't entirely sure.

"Despite our misgivings, we pledged our assistance," Keyhoe wrote. "After working with most of the project staff, we began to hope for a majority-controlled impartial study—a hope shared by many of the Congress, the press, and the public. Unfortunately, this hope steadily dwindled."

On January 8, 1969, the Air Force was so anxious to release what it called the *Final Report on the Scientific Study of Unidentified Flying Objects* that it was able to get Bantam Books to release its mammoth 965-page paperback book in an incredibly short time—twenty-four hours!

As expected, the report described itself as "the definitive scientific answer to one of the world's most fascinating riddles." Even famed *New York Times* columnist Walter Sullivan got into the debunking act with his pithy introduction. He wrote that the report highlighted "the fallibility of even such sober observers as policemen, airline pilots and radar operators." He even suggested that "techniques of conditioning" may have been applied to credible witnesses.

"One cannot help but view our points of view on a great many things with new skepticism," Sullivan concluded. "Anyone who reads this study will, I believe, lay it down with a new perspective on human values and limitations."

My Day With Hynek and Vallée

In early 1969, following the Congressional hearings, I had the opporunity of meeting with Dr. J. Allen Hynek and his colleague, Dr. Jacques Vallée. It was Vallée who later wrote the Foreword to Ann Druffel's excellent book *Firestorm: Dr. James E. McDonald's Fight for UFO Science* (2003). I met Hynek and Vallée at Hynek's office at the Dearborn Observatory at Northwestern University in Chicago.

Our conversation quickly turned to McDonald, who was a good friend as well as a UFO colleague. As the Senior Physicist at the Institute of Atmospheric Physics at the University of Arizona, he was in a good position to persuade his fellow scientists to take a serious look at the subject.

Vallée and Hynek told me how McDonald had stormed into Hynek's office, pounded his fist on the astronomer's desk, and exclaimed: "You've betrayed your responsibilty to science, Allen! You should have spoken out years ago!"

While quickly puffing streams of smoke from his pipe, Hynek responded: "You just don't understand the situation, do you, Jim? Where were you when I tried to get support from the academic community?"

As Hynek continued his work, Vallée took a long lunch hour with me. He knew of my fondness for old books and the writings of Jules Verne. He walked with me to the university library and showed me the original editions of several Verne books, including *A Tour of the World in Eighty Days* (1873), republished many years later as *Around the World in Eighty Days*, and *20,000 Leagues Under the Sea* (1870).

During our long lunch break away from Hynek, Vallée confessed to me a certain fondness for McDonald. He expressed some thoughts about the physicist that he would include, several decades later, in his Foreword to Druffel's book.

Vallée wrote that McDonald "was the man who burst on the scene . . . demanding action, digging into the cases with great energy, exposing the false explanations. He [had] a formidable reputation as an independent thinker." He added that McDonald's life was "highly relevant to our time."

Vallée also hoped that McDonald and Hynek could eventually join forces to provide at least "the germ of a unique scientific breakthrough" in the study and investigation of UFOs. He ended his discourse by lamenting that "a world where people like Allen Hynek are ignored [and] where someone of the caliber of James McDonald is left to die alone and misunderstood is a world crying out for drastic reform . . . What is at stake here is our own spirit and the uncertain future of human intelligence."

Dr. James E. McDonald

No question about it. Dr. James E. McDonald was a human dynamo, a man with unexcelled energy, particularly when he zeroed in on subjects that particularly interested him.

McDonald had already begun looking into the well-documented UFO reports from highly qualified witnesses when my future wife, Martha ("Marty") DeGroat, and I first met him at NICAP headquarters in 1966. He spent several hours looking over the NICAP files and came back literally wiping the sweat from his brow on that hot late spring day.

"Whew!" he remarked. "You have some really interesting reports from highly reliable witnesses."

That started a close relationship with McDonald as both a senior scientist and UFO investigator. Marty, then Assistant Director Dick Hall, and I became good friends with McDonald. He even stayed at our home in Bethesda, Maryland when he was in the Washington, D.C., area. Dick was a particularly close friend which began when he supplied McDonald with some of NICAP's most well-researched reports.

During his visits to our home, McDonald often kept us up for most of the night discussing the latest UFO reports and investigations. His energy was boundless and his detailed knowledge of the subject surpassed ours.

Jim McDonald was also a threat to the U.S. government, which was determined to undermine good sighting reports. He became concerned that he might have become a target for harm because he knew too much about UFOs and the government's continued attempts to deny all sighting reports.

During one of our nights together, Jim said that one of his small luggage bags—with UFO information inside—during an airplane flight was stolen and replaced by an identical bag. There were also later reports that he may have been followed by cars of the type he felt were typically used for surveillance or undercover work. He also said that the cars had no front or rear license plates.

Unfortunately, Jim McDonald had some personal issues in his life that propelled him into a state of depression. On June 13, 1971, his body was found under a bridge on a desert drywash outside Tucson, Arizona. A pistol and a suicide note were reportedly found beside his body.

McDonald's remarkable story and his untimely death at the young age of fifty-one is superbly recounted in Ann Druffel's *Firestorm*.

The CIA Connection

Sometime after I became Assistant Director (and, later, Vice President and Secretary-Treasurer) at NICAP during the early summer of 1967, a young man with a cocky, superior attitude came to NICAP as a new staff member. On his first day at work, Stuart Nixon approached my desk overlooking Dupont Circle in Washington and announced: "Gordon, I am here to coordinate some changes that will need to be made here." Suddenly, Nixon drew back, as if he had said too much.

"What changes are you talking about, Stuart?" I asked. "Who sent you here?"

"Oh, never mind," Stuart replied. "Sorry . . . I shouldn't have said anything. I'm just here to help you guys through the rough times."

A red flag had been sent up. That was obvious. Nixon wasn't very subtle about it. Only a few days later, he told me that the official NICAP photographer, William ("Bill") MacIntyre, had been shot down in his helicopter in Vietnam in 1965, about the same time I joined the NICAP staff. He was on a secret mission with the Central Intelligence Agency (C.I.A.), Stuart openly remarked.

What the hell was this guy trying to do? I wondered. Recruit me for the C.I.A? Was this an open move by the agency to take over NICAP? Ironically, Don Keyhoe himself may have opened the door for that to eventually happen since he became the director and appointed Admiral Roscoe Hillenkoetter, the first Director of the C.I.A., Chairman of the NICAP Board of Governors. Other board members, including Colonel Joseph Bryan and Dewey Fournet, had also been known C.I.A. operatives. They were among the many contacts Keyhoe had established in the military, the Pentagon, and the intelligence agencies.

That evening, I called Don Keyhoe at his home in Luray, Virginia, and told him what Nixon had related to me. Silence.

"What do you think, Major?" I asked. "Could Stuart Nixon be a C.I.A. operative with a nod to infiltrate the NICAP files?"

"No, he's too stupid for that, Gordon," Keyhoe told me. "He hasn't got the brains."

"Maybe that's how the agency operates," I retorted. "They wouldn't just come out and announce they were set to take us over and move us out the door."

"Naw, I don't think so," Keyhoe responded. "Roscoe wouldn't do that."

"Maybe the Admiral doesn't even know about it," I remarked. "If you don't mind me asking, how did you come to hire Nixon?"

"I can't really go into that, Gordon," Don said with a rather uncomfortable tone to his voice. "Let's just say it was a favor to a friend."

"Well, we can only hope that favor doesn't eventually translate to the end for NICAP," I said. "We've all worked too hard and put too much of our own lives into this effort to see that happen."

"Oh, I know, Gordon . . . ," Don remarked. "Hell . . . I trust these guys. I don't think Roscoe or Joe Bryan would hoodwink me. They know how hard and long I've worked to keep this going."

I pointed out to Keyhoe that this was the way the CIA often worked . . . Pitting friend against friend. Entrenching someone in the NICAP staff who appeared to be less than highly intelligent.

The Final Days

Following the release of the Condon Report findings in January, 1969, the prospects for NICAP to continue as a viable organization began to quickly go downhill. Adding to that downward slide was Keyhoe himself. Being an organizational and money manager was not his cup of tea and that was pounced upon.

During the last quarter of the year, I was told by Dewey Fournet, one of Keyhoe's old friends and then still a government hotshot, that changes were eventually going to have to be made. He didn't say it would mean firing Keyhoe, but it didn't take a genius to figure out that would have to be done if the organziation were to regain any kind of financial footing.

I spent many sleepless nights on the phone with Fournet at his home in Baton Rouge, Louisiana. Dewey told me that, if NICAP was to be saved, he would have to know how the finances were handled. I told him that I could provide that information while being wracked with guilt over what may be happening to Don Keyhoe.

The main aim now was to save NICAP as a still viable UFO organization. My friend and former Assistant Director Dick Hall became my listening board and offered many helpful suggestions. I naievly believed that Fournet and a few other board members really wanted and intended to save NICAP as a UFO-study organization. I was also assured that my job would be safe.

Not so. As the days and weeks wore on, the ghosts of past C.I.A. actions (including the tapping of the phones at NICAP headquarters and my home in Bethesda) bore down on me. I contacted Dick Hall and expressed my fear that a C.I.A. takeover may be in the works. I suggested that he and I and a few other NICAP staff members should begin to xerox copies of the most important sighting cases and other documents for safekeeping in our personal files.

Dick still didn't believe that a C.I.A. takever was in the works, but he agreed to my suggestion. At the time, our financial officer and I were the only staff members still left. With Hall, we set about contacting former staff members Ted Bloecher and Isabel Davis. For several weeks, there was a frantic flurry of activity as we wore out the xerox machine copying UFO reports and other significant documents for safekeeping.

I soon learned, however, that Keyhoe's and my time at NICAP were to be short-lived.

On December 1, 1969, J.B. Hartranft, Jr., a NICAP Board of Governors member, had lunch with me at an upscale restaurant near his office in Bethesda, Maryland. Hartranft, the Founder and President of the Aircraft Owners & Pilots Assocation, had written the introduction to my book, *Mysteries of the Skies*.

I suspected that the time had come for changes to be made at NICAP. Without going into details, Hartranft confirmed this to me. He said that changes were necessary because of top management's inability to get the organization out of the deadly financial bind it was in. Again, I was assured that my job would be safe.

As I left Hartranft's office, I had an uneasy feeling. *How was the Board going to justify firing Keyhoe without getting rid of me as well?* I wondered. Keyhoe as President and myself as Vice President and Secretary Treasurer were the only two NICAP operating officers.

I didn't have long to wait. In a secret meeting two days later, on December 3, the NICAP Board with Colonel Joseph Bryan III presiding, fired both Keyhoe and myself. Apparently, the Board members felt they had to terminate me in order to "smooth over" their getting rid of Keyhoe. A few days later, Dick Hall said it was obvious to him that I had been the "scapegoat" in the firing. Hall repeated this in a detailed, blistering letter to the Board of Governors. He particularly decried the "shoddy" way it was done.

Adding insult to injury, in a letter to the NICAP subcomittees and others, the Board called both Keyhoe and I inept businessmen responsible for the financial downfall of the organization. The fact that I had made it clear to Dewey Fournet that I had nothing to do with handling the finances—that had always been Keyhoe's bailiwick—obviously fell on deaf ears.

Chapter Four: The UFO Connection

The CAUS Report

It wasn't until a couple of years later that I learned through Citizens Against UFO Secrecy (CAUS) that Colonel Bryan was an active CIA agent even as he led the charge to fire Keyhoe and I. Following is a summary of the CAUS findings I wrote in the June-July 1979 of my own *UFO Research Newsletter*:

NICAP and the CIA Connection

Has the National Investigations Committee on Aerial Pheneoma (NICAP), once the leading and most respected UFO organization in the world, been secretly controlled by the all-powerful Central Intelligence Agency since the group's founding in 1956? Following months of intensive investigation by Citizens Against UFO Secrecy (CAUS), Inc., the answer is a tentative "yes."

It was done quietly. Neither fortmer NICAP Director Major Donald E. Keyhoe nor the former assistant directors (Richard Hall and Gordon Lore, now UFOR President and Editor) made the direct connection until it was too late. They were aware, however, that some sort of surveillance was being undertaken during the 1960s. It was obvious, on more than one occasion, that the NICAP headquarters office telephones had been tapped, particularly during discussions with Keyhoe of important UFO cases, and that Lore's phone in Bethesda, Maryland, was similarly "bugged."

According to CAUS, in the January 1979 edition of its newsletter, Just Cause:

"At least two CIA covert agents worked themselves into key positions" with NICAP about the time of its founding in 1956. The first was

"Count" Nicolas de Rochefort, of the CIA's Psychological Warfare Staff, who became the UFO group's vice chairman. The other was Bernard J.O. Carvalho, who became Chairman of the membership subcommittee.

When Keyhoe assumed the reins of leadership in January, 1957, he persuaded Vice Admiral Roscoe Hillenkoetter, first Director of the CIA, to join the NICAP board of governors. The Admiral had been Keyhoe's classmate at the U.S. Naval Academy and admitted that the CIA had been interested in UFOs since reports had attained nationwide attention in June 1947.

By early 1962, Keyhoe was on the brink of forcing Congress to hold open hearings on UFOs and the Air Force's (AF) handling of the matter. He was relying on Hillenkoetter to criticize AF policy, but the former CIA Director suddenly resigned from the NICAP board, leaving Keyhoe in the lurch. The congressional effort collapsed.

The NICAP infiltration continued. In late 1959, Colonel Joseph Bryan III (USAF-Ret.) asked Keyhoe if he could see some "really hot cases." Skeptical at first, Keyhoe was placated when Bryan publicly stated that UFOs are extraterrestrial and that the policy of officially withholding UFO information was "dangerous."

Bryan was the founder and first head of the CIA's Psychological Warfare Staff, but Keyhoe was apparently unaware of this. Bryan, who denied communicating with the CIA about NICAP, became the group's chairman and, as such, shared responsibility for the firing of Keyhoe and Lore as NICAP's operating officers in late 1969.

A similar denial came from Karl Pflock, Chairman of NICAP's Washington, D.C. subcommittee in the late 1960s and early 1970s. Pflock was a former briefing officer for the intelligence agency.

Chapter Four: The UFO Connection

Enter G. Stuart Nixon, who joined the NICAP staff around 1966 and was instrumental in the ousting of Keyhoe and Lore. He met with "several past and present CIA employees on a frequent basis" and claimed to have had many converstions with Bryan.

Early on, Nixon told Lore that he hoped "nobody would be too upset by what I intend to accomplish at NICAP." Lore pressed him, but he clammed up. Later, he began downgrading certain potentially excellent UFO reports, especially the photographic cases for which he was responsible. He labeled as "hoax" numerous reports that looked good to the rest of the staff.

In 1969, Nixon was against publication of a special UFO report in book form that Lore authorized and wrote entitled Strange Effects From UFOs, *which included as one if its main sections an analysis of occupant cases. The report was well-documented and the occupant cases were given high marks by a special NICAP scientific panel, but Nixon disagreed, saying NICAP had no business getting into such a way-out fringe area.*

Lore also knew that Nixon had been seeing one or more members of the board . . .

Following the ouster of Keyhoe and Lore, Nixon was named Executive Director [of NICAP] and Jack Acuff President. Acuff had been head of the Society of Photographic Scientists and Engineers, a group that had been on the KGB's (Russian secret police) spy list, obstensibly because the society had many members who were photo analysts with the Department of Defense's intelligence units and with the CIA. Acuff began working with the Federal Bureau of Investigation and met with KGB agents, according to CAUS.

"Since taking over NICAP," the CAUS newsletter stated: *"Acuff has converted the organization from being a vocal and persistent critic of the government's UFO policies to being a rather 'passive recipient' of civilian UFO reports. The group's investigative network, the subcommittees, were disbanded shortly after Acuff took the job."*

In the early 1970s, NICAP was operating on a budget of about $50,000 annually. Acuff Associates, however, took around $35,000 of this for "contracting services," and Acuff later indicated that NICAP owed him approximately $20,000. Paltry sums—$76 one year, $20 the next—went into "general research." NICAP and its once-respected newsletter had become mere shells of their former selves.

Last year, Acuff pulled a stunt that outraged many NICAP members and former members. He sold the organization's outdated mailing list to Samisdat, a fanatical neo-Nazi group in Canada.

Meanwhile, William F. McIntyre, former photographic consultant to NICAP and a friend of Nixon's, began telling ufologists that Acuff wanted to merge with Samisdat or sell the UFO group to them. This action caused some former NICAP employees and members to start the Ad Hoc Committee to Preserve NICAP.

(Around 1968, Nixon almost jokingly told Lore that McIntyre had been on a "secret" mission to Vietnam. He had been shot down and spent several days on a raft. Lore asked Nixon if McIntyre was with the CIA, but he just shrugged his shoulders and indicated his friend was involved in all sorts of unusual pursuits).

During this battle, McIntyre admitted "he was a former covert agent of the CIA." He also said Acuff had worked for the agency.

By September, 1978, Acuff wanted out of NICAP, "claiming the organization owed him a rather large sum of money." An ad-hoc committee member, Richard Hall, proposed a coalition with the Center for UFO Studies, the Mutual UFO Network, and the International Fortean Organization, but nothing came of it.

After Acuff's resignation last October, [Richard] Hall made a move to be appointed his successor, but this, too, was unsuccessful.

Then several retired CIA officials were offered Acuff's job. One of them—Alan N. Hall—accepted. One of the leaders in this move was Charles Lombard, "a former CIA covert employee" and aid to Senator Barry Goldwater (R-Ariz.), a NICAP board member.

(UFOR is indebted to David Branch, Pasadena, California, for supplying us with this information, as well as to CAUS.)

The NICAP Fall

In a 1973 telecon with Keyhoe during a launch at the National Press Club of his final UFO book, *Aliens From Space: The Real Story of Unidentified Flying Objects*, I again asked him if Stuart Nixon could have been a CIA agent. He repeated that Nixon was "not smart enough." He did acknowledge that Stuart had been a disrupting influence on the NICAP staff and added: "The biggest mistake I ever made was not firing him!"

To this day, nearly half-a-century later, I still feel guilty that my effort to save NICAP had to be done by essentially confirming Keyhoe's financial ineptitude. However, he was still someone I greatly admired and respected. I thought that, perhaps, some of that guilt could be somewhat assuaged by the fact that the organization was taken over by those who intentionally aimed to destroy it.

This was what infuriated me. During the fourteen or so years of its existence under Keyhoe's direction, NICAP had done more than any other such entity in bringing scientific credibility to reliable UFO sightings. It also had persuaded many scientists such as Jim McDonald to continue their own efforts to keep the reliable reports in the public and scientific eye.

Thanks is due to a special friend, the late Dick Hall, for his unflinching support on my behalf during a most difficult period.

UFO Research Associates

In early 1971, I began my own organization, UFO Research Associates (UFOR), and continued to investigate sighting reports from around the country and other parts of the world. My wife, Marty, and I also published the monthly *UFO Research Newsletter* from our home base.

One of the sightings that impressed me most during the fourteen or so years that UFOR remained in existence occurred in California in 1976. The sighting was investigated by Paul Cerny, a former NICAP subcommittee leader who worked with me on this and several other reports. Following is an account of this amazing sighting as published in our newsletter:

> Bill Pecha, 39, is "a rather fearless, healthy, husky individual [with] a keen mind and photographic memory." The heavy machine mechanic has perfect eyesight. But his highly stable physical and mental attributes were severely tested at 12:45 a.m., September 19, 1976, outside his home in Colusa, California.
>
> While Pecha was watching television alone, the set and air conditioner "suddenly went dead." A circuit breaker had probably "kicked out from a short." The witness went outside to check. Approaching the corner of his mobile home, "he became increasingly aware of a static electricity

effect on his body." The hair on his head, arms, and chest stood up. His head hair also crackled and snapped.

Pecha looked up into the clear, full-moon sky and was startled to see a tremendous circular UFO hovering at about 50 feet over his barn and the corner of his home. He watched for four-to-five minutes as his heart beat rapidly.

The estimated diameter of the object was a whopping 140 feet. Its "dome had vertical ribbed sections." The surface between each of these sections was concave. . . .

There was "a slight peak or point" on the gray dome . . . The craft's edges and rotating perimeter had the appearance of stainless steel. A smaller section—around "a large diameter light source"—at the bottom of the saucer rotated counterclockwise and slower than the rim. Six narrow appendages three-to-four inches in diameter hung six-to-eight feet from the bottom of the UFO and "gave the appearance of a loosely dangling heavy flexible conduit with frayed ends."

The craft headed over the field behind Pecha's home. The "appendages were immediately retracted into the bottom." Two "hook" arms on the bottom were also retracted. Simultaneously, "a small door opened on each side just above the arms and a light mounted on a curved piece of tubing protruded out and slightly downward. The lens area . . . looked like many glass cubes clustered together." The two side lights emitted "a bluish-white beam of light."

A large red light came on in front of the strange craft as it backed toward Slim Davis' home and crop dusting airfield a half mile away. The large light on the bottom-center "intensified to a bright white cone-shaped beam downward which reached only halfway to the ground and stopped in mid-air!" The UFO maneuvered over Davis' home and airplane hanger, "lighting up everything like daylight."

At about this time, Pecha observed two more similar objects approximately 70 feet in diameter hovering over the 500,000-volt power lines "a couple hundred yards beyond the Davis airfield." The craft "appeared to be almost resting on the lines, each one between two power poles, but separated by one span section between [the] poles."

A brilliant white light, which illuminated the power poles, was emitted from each object. The power lines "were glowing red for some distance out on each side of the poles." Then a power blackout of the surrounding area occurred.

Pecha made a beeline for his home, yelling for his wife, Lenda. He ran into the mobile home and peered out of the back window. The UFO, its large bottom light illuminating the area, was hovering over Davis' home.

Lenda Pecha joined her husband, and the couple watched as the mysterious object "suddenly shot off at an incredible speed towards the foothills" 18-20 miles away. According to Pecha, the large UFO covered this distance in 2-3 seconds and illuminated "the tops of the hills for a second or two." Then it sped back to hover again over the Davis home and light up the area.

"Everywhere around the immediate countryside, all the lights were off; ranch yard lights and the whole town was in darkness except for the moonlight and the UFO," stated Mutual UFO Network Western States Director Paul C. Cerny, who investigated the incident and sent his report to UFOR.

Chapter Four: The UFO Connection

By now, Pecha began experiencing real concern for his family's safety. His two children, eight and ten years old, were still asleep. He began turning from the window when he saw the UFOs over the power lines "suddenly break away at the same time, shooting up and out of sight."

Pecha rounded up his family and headed for the door as the TV set and air conditioner resumed functioning. The family jumped into their pickup truck, and Pecha "raced backwards out the driveway with the lights deliberately turned off." The backup lights were on, however, which "may have attracted the UFO."

Pecha floored the accelerator, attaining speeds up to 90 m.p.h. The object paced the truck. The UFO would "appear on one side, then cross over to the other side of the truck within a few hundred feet."

The mechanic slammed on the brakes in front of a friend's house. Les and Gayle Arant joined the Pechas and saw the UFO, now "over the edge of town again, somewhat higher in the sky." Then it rapidly climbed at an angle and disappeared toward Sacramento.

Elaine McGowen, a Sheriff's Department employee, and her son, Fred, also saw the object. Pacific Gas and Electric officials said the nine-minute blackout was "of undetermined nature. All of Colusa County and some adjoining areas were affected."

Some leaves on the tops of the trees in the area of the Davis home and airfield "were turning brown ... as if heated or scorched...."

As the UFO manuevered over the Davis home, "their dogs reacted, howling and barking in an unusual manner."

A remarkable sighting and up-close encounter with an unidentified flying object....

As of this writing during the summer of 2016, UFO sightings from around the world continue to be reported. The spirits of Major Donald E. Keyhoe, Dr. James E. McDonald, Dr. J. Allen Hynek, Dr. Jacques Vallée, Richard H. Hall, Ann Druffel, and many others devoted to a scientific investigation of flying saucer reports from credible sources live on. Someday somehow the truth will be known in the lingering hope that Mankind will be enlightened by the knowledge of our friends from outer space.

Chapter Five
Chaco Canyon High: Ecstasy in New Mexico

From 1980 to 1984, I spent a lot of time living in Taos, New Mexico, with my late wife, Marty, and stepson, Jim Triche. We were on a spiritual quest at an apartment on one of the the mesas that had been populated by the native Anasazi Indians. We also lived in a house beside the sacred Taos Mountain, which became my own spiritual center.

The mountain, also known locally as Pueblo Peak, is 12,305 feet high. An imposing part of the Sangre de Cristo Mountains, it is an outcropping of the Rocky mountains. It is also considered by many to be one of the seven sacred mountains in the world.

The house Marty and I shared during the spring and summer of 1984 provided an up-close view of the mountain. I often laid in the tall grass and gazed up at the faraway peak. During one of these soliliquies, I had my eyes closed as a caressing breeze blew over me when I felt a wet tongue on my face. I opened my eyes and saw it was a wandering cow which also managed to serenade me awake the next morning or two as it poked its head through my open and screenless bedroom window.

Taos History

Taos is now renowned as an artist's colony. Its human history is believed to date back at least 6,000 years when nomadic hunter-gatherers swept through the area leaving behind potshards, arrowheads, pictographs, and other evidence of their existence. About 950 years ago, the Native Americans of Taos Pueblo—which is still occupied today—began to populate their villages.

Following skirmishes with Spanish conquistadors over a 150-year-long period or so, Taos became the headquarters for famed mountain men such as Kit Carson and Jim Bridger. During the last two years of the nineteenth century, artists began their migration to the area, drawn by the power and beauty of Taos Mountain and the valley surrounding it.

In 1955, Taos Ski Valley opened and has drawn skiers from all over the world. It was near the valley on a road onto the mountain that I found a welcomed stream trickling down while the sunlight hit the tree leaves following a light rain. This invoked an almost eerie spiritual aura. I often spent a lot of solitary time sitting on a rock meditating at this spot.

Introducing MDMA

Soon after Marty and I settled into our Taos home, we met a small group of people who were part of an outcropping of individuals from the western states acknowledging the virtues of the proper use of the psycho-active drug MDMA (3, 4-*methylenedioxymethamphetamine*). It is better known today by its street name Ecstacy. It was being lauded as a "love" or "hug" drug because of its apparent ability to bring out the best instincts, emotions, and actions in those who use it.

As early as 1914, MDMA was synthesized by chemists who incorrectly believed it could be used as an appetite suppressant. Several hundred scientists, psychiatrists, psychologists, chemists and others began experimenting with it and quickly documented its effects on those who used it. They found that the advantages far outweighed the disadvantages when it was properly dispensed, used, and supervised.

MDMA Advocates

As news about MDMA spread across the country, more and more advocates began coming forth calling for medical/scientific studies of the drug. These included Dr. John H. Halpern. He led a team at Harvard University's McLean Hospital in Belmont, Massachusetts to study the therapeutic use of the drug in helping end-stage cancer patients obtain relief from depression.

"There is anecdotal evidence that MDMA can help them resolve the anxieties they experience without doping them up on tranquillizers," he reported.

Enter "the Godfather"

The man most responsible for spreading the word about the beneficial aspects of MDMA and who is also known as "the godfather of Ecstasy" is Alexander ("Sasha") Shulgin. He was described by various pundits as a medical chemist, biochemist, pharmacologist, psychopharmacologist, author, and teacher. He was also a kind, gentle man with a white beard springing from his face.

Sasha came into the lives of my wife and I along with a small group of friends from Taos and other areas who were anxious to discover how the drug could benefit our lives. As an unofficial outcropping of possible clinical trials of MDMA at the University of Washington in Seattle, Sasha wanted to include us in a six-month non-government-sanctioned study of the drug which he hoped would be of significant benefit to any trials that may be forthcoming.

Shulgin was credited with introducing MDMA to interested psychologists, psychiatrists, and pharmacists in the late 1970s for psychopharmaceutical use. He started his rise up the scientific ladder in 1941. At the age of sixteen, this brilliant young researcher began studying organic chemistry as a Harvard University scholarship student. In 1943, during World War II, he dropped out of school and joined the U.S. Navy where he began his intensive study of psychopharmacology.

In 1954, Sasha received his PhD degree in biochemistry from the University of California at Berkeley. Following post-doctoral work and a brief stint as a research director, he began working as a senior research scientist at Dow Chemical Company. It was during this period that his future goals and research were shaped by a series of psychedelic experiences.

"I understood that our entire universe is contained in the mind and the spirit," he enthused. "It is indeed there inside us and there are chemicals that can catalyze its availabilty."

Meeting MDMA

Shulgin set up a home-based laboratory on his property in Lafayette, California, that he dubbed "The Farm." He held pharmacology seminars for DEA agents. Then he was introduced to MDMA by someone in the medicinal chemistry group for which he was an advisor at San Francisco State University.

Sasha soon learned that MDMA had been synthesized. Then it was patented as early as 1912 by Merck scientists "as an intermediate of another synthesis in order to block competitors, but was never explored in its own right." This allowed Shulgin to develop a totally new method of synthesizing the drug.

Sasha introduced his substance to hundreds of psychologists, psychiatrists, and lay therapists around the country. These included his wife Ann, a lovely woman whom he met in 1979 and married two years later. My own wife, Marty, and I also fell in love with Ann when we met her in Taos.

"Chaco Canyon High"

The entire time our group participated in this unofficial trial, we ingested MDMA in pure liquid form indistinguishable from water. In early June 1984, Sasha and Ann led our small group of about ten people on a weekend outdoor journey I later termed "Chaco Canyon High." We loaded our campers and headed out over the bumpy road from Taos on a clear, warm, picture-perfect day for the two-hour journey in northwestern New Mexico to the Chaco Culture National Historic Park.

We parked our vehicles, gathered around together and began hatching out a plan for the two days we would be there. We first noted that the area was very dry and barren with crumbling stone houses that were many centuries old.

One member of our group had done his research and filled us in on some brief history of this remarkable location. Nearly a thousand years ago, what he termed as perhaps the most sophisticated society north of Mexico settled in the expansive canyon. Historians said the estimated 1,100 or so inhabitants comprised the heart of "the largest and most important religious, economic, cultural and political center" in what is now the continental United States. He added that a fairly recent discovery indicated it was probably also a meeting place for people from hundreds of miles around.

Historians now consider the masonry techniques that the Anasazi Indians employed to be very advanced for the time. The most famous "town" in the canyon is Pueblo Bonito, which was constructed with jacal masonry with workers depositing huge mounds of mud to hold the stones in place. This kind of advanced masonry was used throughout the canyon.

Somehow, it seemed the perfect place for our "spiritual high."

After completing our brief tour of the canyon, we met at a central location where Sasha began dispensing the MDMA. There were very few other visitors around and we weren't very worried since the drug had not yet been placed on the FDA's Schedule 1 list.

Marty and I took our usual drink of the clear liquid. Normally, for most users, it takes about forty-five minutes for the effects to kick in. Most of the time, however, I was able to begin feeling those effects in little more than a minute or two. As I drank, I saw a collared lizard scurrying about around my feet while a small group of swallows flew quickly by us. Later, a lone eagle with outspread wings leisurely flew overhead. During our Chaco Canyon high, the regal bird returned several times. We took it as a positive sign that we were making progress in our spiritual quest.

The following is taken from my letter to Sasha Shulgin about my experience with MDMA that Saturday:

June 9, 1984

"Chaco Canyon . . . My total intake of MDMA included the initial dosage plus two supplements. Within a minute of the first dosage, I began feeling a stirring, an elation, and the spinal arthritis pain was alleviated. . . .

"About an hour and a half later, I took a supplement. Quickly, I felt light. Free. The pain had greatly lessened. I felt a need to be near, to touch, and hug the other people around me. Then everything became incredibly quiet and still. It was as if the concept of time-space had been caught in a stop-frame. A sense of oneness with everyone and everything around me permeated my being. A small rabbit darting around on the ground, a tiny lizard on a rock, a bird circling the canyon . . . All was One. Even the thought of death brought no fear.

"My thoughts—and Love—turned to Marty. We took a second supplement. I was on an even higher plane. Marty began to open up. The blocks started to crumble. Her face glowed. She became a different, more loving person. With a sense of deep gratitude, I began to see her in a different light. A photograph I took of her at this time showed a smiling, open, caring, loving person who was very much a reflection of her True Self.

"That night, the closeness increased and soon turned into a beautiful expression of togetherness that neither of us had ever felt before ... The feelings between us were deeply loving, sensual, sexual. There was a great caring and sharing of one for the other. All past bitterness, anger, resentment, and marital game-playing had faded. We were in *the moment*, a part of the Cosmos together. It was the single most beautiful moment of being together either of us had ever experienced. ...

"In the six days since the MDMA experience, I have felt a new sense of purpose, Love and understanding. I realize that my own limited perception of other people and things around me has been untrue. Unreal. The only reality is the experience of the Oneness. ..."

My second letter to Sasha related two other memorable MDMA experiences at home in Taos.

June 23, 1984

"12:13 p.m.: Initial dose.

"12:20: Pain in back begins to dissipate. Heart expands. I dance around the room.

"12:50: Time stands still as I look at Taos Mountain with a sense of Oneness. Stillness. Quiet.

"1:45: I get flashes of Marty and me deep in space and feel much love for her. It's as if we had made a pact of Love and support before the dawn of history. Back to earth. Felt the presence of space creatures enter my being with Love. Flashes of what I can only describe as visual "spots" from Egypt to Atlantis. I feel that Marty and I were together in Atlantis.

"2:05: First supplement. Feel a strong connection with Space and the planets. My origins lie there. Playing Gustav Holst's *The Planets* [1916]. The music of Mars courses through me. I am in Space again, the void. I am Home. Free. Mars, the bringer of war. I see conflagration, the history of the world in battle. It really is a cleansing. From the conflagration comes a period of understanding, wisdom, and Love. Pockets of deep understanding admist the fire and destruction. Space surrounds me. Both Marty and I are there . . . I feel us billions of years in the past *and* the future. We are a part of the Universe. A great Love permeates me. . . .

"4:05: Second supplement. Dancing to the music of Johann Strauss. Free-flowing body movements. Frenzy of movement, then quietness.

"5:35: Hard stiffness in my lower back is loosening up. Energy is running up my spine . . . Am literally bouncing to the music of Strauss.

"5:45: Feel the presence of Space Beings all around me. They are trying to impart some message. I feel we all have a benevolent tide of extraterrestial beings surrounding and protecting us. They want us to grow and expand.

"6:14: Flowing in *perfect* harmony and rhythm to Strauss' *Emperor Waltz* [1889]. Have not felt such total freedom of movement in several years. . . .

"6:30: Laid on the mesa in the tall grass. Wind blowing. Looked up slightly to the northeast. Lovely white rays bombard that area of the sky. Then I saw a rainbow colors. Felt a close affinity to that spot in the sky. That is where my thoughts and heart will be tonight. I experience a real closeness to the *aliveness* of space. . . .

June 28, 1984

"Morning. A strong presence of Space surrounds me. It is full. Vibrant. Alive. Space Beings appear to be calling. I go into the mountains. Beside my favorite snow run-off mountain stream, the Space Beings appear to be trying to transmit a message. I am feeling high . . . Detached. I feel that I want to leave my pain-wracked body and "get on with it." The feeling of being drawn to Space persists throughout the day.

June 29, 1984

"10:15 a.m. I take my daily walk along the mesa. A calmness. A Oneness with the land infuses me. I reach the barbed wire fence, beyond which cows graze. Around several earth mounds are about a dozen prairie dogs scampering about. Suddenly, my heart expands and, for a moment, I become One with these creatures. As I return home, I feel a Oneness with the land and everything else around me. I let my bare back touch a spot on the ground and experience the healing power.

June 30, 1984

"12:05 p.m. Initial dose of MDMA. Begin to feel light. Flow with Debussy's *Clair de Lune* [circa 1890]. Considerable lessening of back pain. . . .

"1:30: Much pressure in the body. Feel as if it is ready to explode in all directions. Heavy. Into a 'the-body-is-not-me' mode. Feel powerful eruptions from inside like I need to go through the death experience . . . Then comfort. A joyous *knowing* that there is no real death. Body is much more free. . . .

"2:12: Ferocious, unknown anger setting in. Hands trembling again. Frantically beating legs, particularly knees where arthritic pain is centered.

Very hot. [*Note: This is not an uncommon feeling in MDMA users and close supervision is needed to prevent a serious overeheating of the body that can result in death*]. Feeling of death surrounds me ... Still, I somehow know there is *nothing* to fear.

"2:34: First supplement. Feel the eternalness of unseen things. The *real* things.

"2:50: A silent and numbing 'roar' is bearing down on me like a freight train. Double, blurred vision for a few moments. Feel a definite connection with energy caught in the heart chakra connected by the breastplate to the back ... Could it be the key to completely loosening the arthritic 'crystals?' Energy has loosened considerably. Feel 100 percent better. ...

"4:00: Exhausted. I am 'coming down.' Much improvement in the body.

"4:50: Quiet. Begin to feel a love *of* myself. *For* myself. It is very freeing. ...

"6:45: The clouds are still. Quiet. I experience a powerful Oneness with Space. Want to leave my body and join that Oneness. Death feels closer and closer. I feel resigned to it, but I draw back. What is this death I feel inside me? Perhaps Life and Death are both the same. I feel a connection, a kinship between them. I think I *must* try to experience death symbolically, but am afraid it may turn into the *real* thing. I call a friend for advice.

"7:15: My friend tells me to draw an encircled pentagram around my bed. I do so to the strains of Tchaikovsy's mournful *Pathetique Symphony* (1893). Marty is nearby. I try to feel the death experience to the sounds of the 'Hopelessness' and 'Death' movements. Great sadness at first. Then body movement. Surprisingly, the fear leaves and, briefly, I pass beyond the portals of life. An encompassing, beautiful white light radiating Love surrounds me and, for the first time, I *feel* and *know* that physical death is not to be feared. It is a wonderful new beginning, a rebirthing. Feel a renewed sense of life and purpose. Oh, God, the glory of *feeling*! The Love! I experience the pain as an ally, not an enemy. I can use it for insight and understanding, not for self-destruction. I no longer feel the pall, the aura of death around me.

"8:30: I am trying to integrate a new 'me.' There is a renewed sense of purpose, hope, and knowledge that I am far vaster than my pain-wracked body. The pain doesn't seem to matter as much now. To hell with it! It's telling me it will completely disappear only after I have pushed that invisible 'integration' button. . . . [*As I type this several days later, I feel my heart expand at the thought of my pain. Why? The answer comes as tears flow and the heart seems to know. Using the pain with Love and Understanding instead of constantly fighting it with deep animosity will enable me to end it. A 'bolt' from my heart area caresses my pain and, strangely, I feel a deep Love for it. It is my teacher.*]

"9:45: Realization and clarity are pouring in on me. I see things in a much more objective, different and fulfilling light."

"Two Extraordinary Letters"

Sasha and Ann Shulgin were obviously impressed by my musings. They wrote Marty and I a follow-up letter dated July 10, 1984, from their home at The Farm in California:

> *Two extraordinary letters from you. We are deeply grateful to you for . . . writing the kind of account which we need most. . . .*
>
> *Gordon, your arthritis problem and your efforts to find out why it's there and what to do about it are potentially of immense value to many other people whom we know . . . You are a pioneer, as is anyone who tackles problems in this particular way. . . .*
>
> *I would suggest one thing . . . Be patient. Try not to push yourself too much too fast. You've spent a long time with this load of pain and imbalance and the best rule I know is: treat yourself with the same*

patience and compassion with which you would treat a close and dear friend. You are, after all, the closest and dearest friend you have. . . .

Anger at the arthritis is acceptable, but anger at yourself is counter-productive. It takes up a great deal of energy and thinking space and tends to muddy the spiritual waters . . . You need all your energy to discover what you can about the causes and cures of your arthritis and you need all possible love for yourself to aid in your healing. . . .

When you are discovering and working on deeply buried origins of problems, it is well to have a bit of space and time between sessions with any psychoactive material. The unconsious does a lot of work between experiments and a lot of work goes on during sleep . . . It's important to give the sub- and unconscious room to do their quiet work too.

Also, don't fall into the trap [of] letting yourself believe that only through MDMA sessions will wisdom and intuition be released. Insight goes on all the time and MDMA contains only a key to your self-healing ability, not the healing ability itself. Don't confuse the chemical key with the world it unlocks, which is, after all, inside you and nowhere else.

Marty, thank you for your honesty and openness . . . It's a deeply satisfying thing for both of us to know that two people who have chosen to share their lives can rediscover their commitment and love for each other. It is this loving which makes both of you part of the important network that stretches worldwide now when it is most desperately needed . . . We thank you both for being so very courageous and so very willing to increase the God-consciousness in yourselves.

The Aftermath

Three months after our small group began experimenting with MDMA, our involvement in what was to be a six-month commitment came to an abrupt end. We received the news from Sasha Shulgin that the Drug Enforcement Administration (DEA) was slated to declare MDMA a dangerous drug and would place it on Schedule One of its forbidden drugs. This included heroin, LSD, and marijuana. The drug, now popularly known as Ecstacy, was making its way across the country. It was quickly becoming a street drug and unsupervised use was causing adverse effects, even a few deaths.

Later in 1984, the DEA announced it was taking what it termed "emergency measures . . . to make trafficking in MDMA punishable by 15 years in prison and a $125,000 fine."

Protests began pouring in. Dr. Philip Wolfson, a psychiatrist from San Francisco, said that outlawing any use of the drug was "a bloody shame. Now, all scientific exploration will be halted. We're not going to get the chance to see the real potential of the drug."

During the ensuing quarter of a century, Sasha and other pharmacologists continued to extol the possible benefits of MDMA while also warning against unsupervised use. Ever so slowly, progress was being made for a series of government-sanctioned clinical trials. Early in 2016, the Multidisciplinary Association for Psychedelic Studies (MAPS) said the Federal Drug Administration (FDA) could approve MDMA for limited use as soon as 2021 "if the clinical trials perform according to plan." A safer medical version of the drug would be used.

MAPS had already studied twenty patients with post-traumatic stress disorder (PTSD) and found that the great majority (eighty-three percent) no longer showed signs of the disorder after two months of treatment. Even the follow-ups conducted four years later showed that "the benefits stuck."

Phase Two of the required three phases included 136 individuals who were given MDMA combined with psychotherapy for their PTSD symptoms. As of this writing in April 2016, MAPS is planning to meet with the FDA to urge approval of Phase Three trials. This final phase would involve hundreds of subjects.

"Phase 3 starts around 2017 and it will take four-to-five years to finish," stated Brad Burge, MAPS Director of Communications. "That will put it at early 2021 for [possible] FDA approval."

Dedicated scientists and pharmacologists continue to push for more safe use of MDMA to treat anxiety and depression in autistic, cancer, and other patients with life-threatening diseases. Little by little, progress continues to be made. In 2015, a careful and systematic review of neuro-imaging in those that used MDMA found that there was "no convincing evidence that moderate MDMA use is associated with structural or functional brain alterations."

A Sad Farewell

Unfortunately, my late wife Marty and I lost contact with Sasha and Ann Shulgin following our move back to Los Angeles later in 1984. I subsequently learned that Sasha stayed close to his home at The Farm in Lafayette, California, during the latter part of his life. In April 2008, he had surgery for replacement of a defective aortic valve, but his health began a slow deterioration. In April 2014, Ann announced on her Facebook page that Sasha had been diagnosed with liver cancer and was on a rapid downward spiral. On the last day of May, she reported that her frail husband was "experiencing his last moments in peace and without pain."

On June 2, 2014, Alexander ("Sasha") Shulgin, a brilliant scientist who was also a participating member of Mensa International, quietly passed away at home surrounded by his wife and family. He was just fifteen days short of his eighty-ninth birthday.

I had the pleasure of knowing Sasha Shulgin as he was still formulating his operating theory. He was a controversial figure, but my late wife and my dealings with him were positive and uplifting. The field he represented and the issues he raised are still being debated today.

Boggs family near the U.S. Capitol building in 1950. From left to right: Cokie, Congressman Hale, Tommy, Lindy and Barbara Boggs.
(*Photo scan by Jay Triche from the Author's Collection.*)

G.I. Rupert Lore & Sons Marina, Solomons Island, Maryland.
(*Photo scan by Jay Triche from the Author's Collection.*)

A U.S. Coast Guard vessel with President Harry S. Truman aboard docks at the Lore Marina in 1950.

James Cagney. (*Photo scan by Jay Triche from the Author's Collection.*)

Rita Hayworth, star of *Miss Sadie Thompson* (1955). (*Photo scan by Jay Triche from the Author's Collection.*)

Burl Ives. (*Photo scan by Jay Triche from the Author's Collection.*)

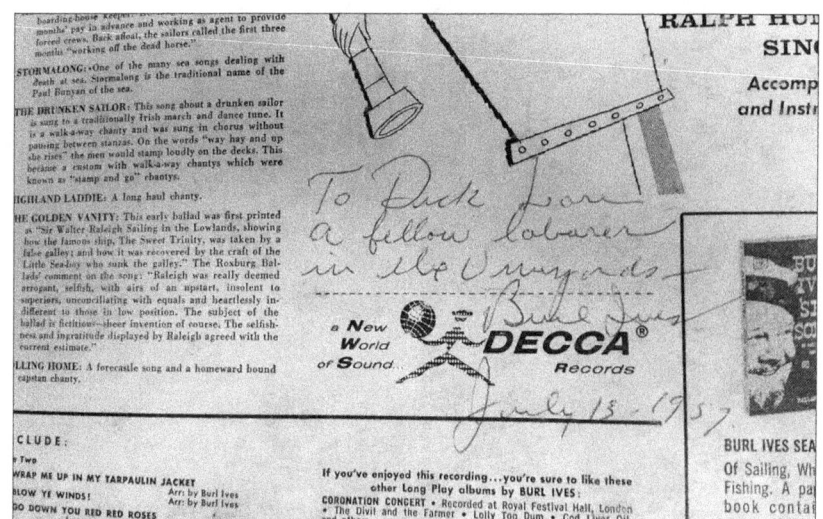

Burl Ives' autograph on the back of the author's copy of the singer's Down to the Sea in Ships record album. (*Photo scan by Jay Triche from the Author's Collection.*)

Robert Mitchum, star of *The Night of the Hunter* (1955). (*Photo scan by Jay Triche from the Author's Collection.*)

Robert Mitchum is a menacing presence in *The Night of the Hunter* (1955). (*Photo scan by Jay Triche from the Author's Collection.*)

Major Donald E. Keyhoe (USMC-Ret.) at the NICAP door in Washington, D.C. (*Photo scan by Jay Triche from the Author's Collection.*)

I Aim at the Stars. (Photo scan by Jay Triche from the Author's Collection.)

Major Donald Keyhoe's first book was *Flying with Lindberg* (1928).
(Photo scan by Jay Triche from the author's collection.)

The author, left, and Harold Deneault, work on their book *Mysteries of the Skies* (1968). (*Photo scan by Jay Triche from the Author's Collection.*)

(*Photo scan by Jay Triche from the Author's Collection.*)

NICAP staff members Gordon Lore, left, and Leon Katchen
investigate UFO landing site in South Hill, Virginia, on April 21, 1967.
(*Photo scan by Jay Triche from the Author's Collection.*)

Dr. J. Allen Hynek, left, walks with Dr. Jacques Vallée.
(*Courtesy of Dr. Jacques Vallee.*)

Dr. Antonia Rodriguez clearing negative entities from the author's home in Canoga Park, California on September 15, 1985.
(*Photo by Jay Triche from the Author's Collection.*)

Asmodeus. (*Courtesy of Wikipedia. The Free Encyclopedia.*)

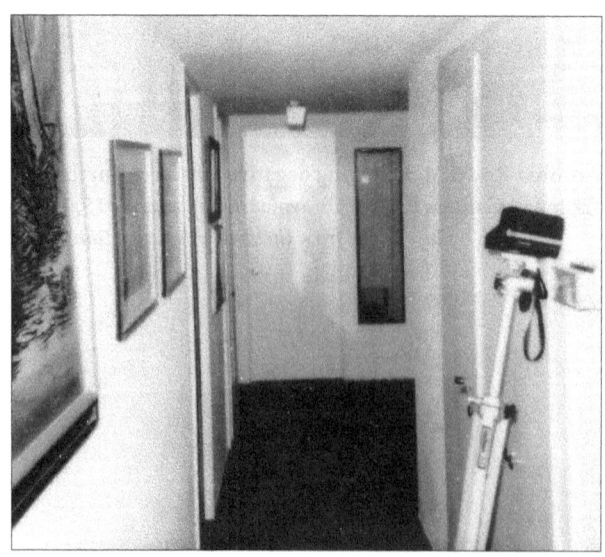

Image on door during exorcism of author's home.
(*Photo by Jay Triche from the Author's Collection.*)

Tina Louise. (*Photo scan by Jay Triche from the Author's Collection.*)

Jodie Foster. *(Photo scan by Jay Triche from the Author's Collection.)*

Lesley Ann Warren in a scene from *Victor/Victoria* (1983).
(Photo scan by Jay Triche from the Author's Collection.)

Tom Hanks. (*Photo scan by Jay Triche from the Author's Collection.*)

Walt Disney Concert Hall today.
(*Photo scan by Jay Triche from the Author's Collection.*)

Joseph Cotten. (*Photo scan by Jay Triche from the Author's Collection.*)

Ken Howard. (*Courtesy of United Press International.*)

Chapter Six

The Psychic Connection

It began with a thunderous bang. Like a gigantic sledgehammer had hit the wall of the three-bedroom house where my wife Marty and I were living on Hamlin Street in Canoga Park, California. *BOOM! BOOM! BOOM!* The sounds nearly knocked me out of my kitchen chair. Somehow, however, I knew it wasn't an earthquake. It was something even more sinister.

Marty had retired for the night on this dark evening in early 1985 and did not hear the banging. I quickly ran outside to the pool-patio area. After turning the patio lights on, I immediately noticed that the concrete wall extending from the house to the end of the lengthy patio was covered with many thousands of black beetles.

Marty and I had been studying for our B.S. degrees in Metaphysics at the American National Institute for Psychical Research and Development (ANI) in Calabasas, California. However, nothing had prepared us for what was happening . . . or what would continue to occur for the next several months. The thunderous bangs were only a prelude to an incredible series of events that would result in an exorcism of our home.

"An Evil Presence"

I reentered the house and felt I was being drawn to the small back bedroom. There was something there . . . something evil. It was calling me.

I closed the door and left the light off. It would be easier for me to tune into whatever was occurring in that limited space where a small cot-like bed sat. The bed was surrounded by several shelves containing part of my extensive book collection of many volumes on the psychic and occult.

Suddenly, I got it!

My God! I thought. *I've drawn an evil presence into our home!*

That was only the beginning. Much more was to come. I had already learned that, if I opened my inner self to the spiritual aspects of life, the negative influences could hitch a ride on that positive band of energy. In spades!

That first night in the back, unlit room not only caught me by surprise. It grabbed me by the throat and didn't let go.

My attention was immediately drawn to the bed. Lying there in a pool of ghoulish blood was the image of a young girl who had been brutally murdered. I knew it was only a psychic image, but it shocked the hell out of me. Her murderer had also grabbed me by the throat and was squeezing tightly.

Choking, I lunged for the door, but was knocked down. A dark mist filled the room as I slowly found my footing. The closet door flew open and I felt that was where the demon had been lurking for its prey. The prey happened to be me!

I grabbed the door handle and tried to open it, but I was dragged back by the invisible demon and thrown on top of the bed. I was having none of it. I only knew I had to leave that room saturated with pure evil as quickly as I could.

My next attempt to open the door succeeded. I closed the door and locked it shut.

The doors in the rest of the house, however, remained unlocked for the next several months. This may have given the evil entity a portal through which he could wreak his havoc.

Astounding Daily Events

Daily and nightly events came quickly and dramatically. These included:

- The bright white curtains throughout the house turned a filthy- looking black color.

- Small black rat-like droppings lined the edges of the floors.

- Several pictures hanging on the walls showed the forming of ectoplasm.

- As I walked through the living room one day, all three of our cats were thrown over the couch to the other side by an invisible force.

- One afternoon, as I walked past them, all the pictures and photographs lining the living room wall fell to the floor.

- Early one morning, I found that the securely closed cabinet door containing several hundred of my record albums had mysteriously opened. The albums were piled on the floor.

- On several occasions late at night, when I was alone in the bathroom, a dark slime descended down the wall onto the sink.

- Several times during the day, Marty and I clearly saw two men wearing hats and what looked like 1950s-style clothing appear at our front door and loudly knock. When we opened the door, however, no one was there.

- The periodic loud banging sound against the side of the house and the appearance of swarms of black beetles on the outside wall continued.

Psychics Over the White House

It was time to consult with Dr. Antonia ("Toni") Rodriguez, the President of ANI. She was a well-known psychic and spiritual advisor whom President Ronald Reagan and First Lady Nancy Reagan called upon when they felt she was needed.

Most of the general public didn't know it (then or now), but it was no secret in the political corridors of Washington, D.C., that the Reagans called upon several psychics and astrological advisors during their White House years. These included astrologers Jeane Dixon and Joan Quigley. Nancy Reagan was fiercely protective of her husband and was particularly concerned about the impact astrological predictions could have on his safety.

The Reagans also gave the go-ahead to special psychic projects aimed at keeping up with or surpassing similar projects in the U.S.S.R. In the early 1970s, this was confirmed to me by Dr. Melvin Gravitz, a psychologist in Bethesda, Maryland, who said he had been a part of a White House-CIA psychic project in the 1960s and early 1970s. This was when both America and Russia put psychic developments on a fast track. Unfortunately, most of these projects were aimed at weapons development and improving the spy networks.

Chapter Six: The Psychic Connection

I was involved with Toni Rodriguez and ANI in one of these projects straight from the White House. (See below.)

The Exorcism

The exorcism at our home in Canoga Park occurred during the late afternoon and early evening of September 15, 1985. Toni Rodriguez, dressed in a turquoise blue dress and outfitted with what she termed "cleansing candles," and her small entourage, quickly went to work. Also included were my stepson, Jay Triche, and his wife, Carol.

Toni took her time, slowly moving through the house. She zeroed in on areas she felt had been contaminated by evil entities. In the back bedroom, she reported feeling sick when she cleared the closet where she believed the demon was lurking. She said the demon may have been Asmodeus (described by some as "the king of demons" and by others as the Devil himself) or one of his demonic henchmen.

As Toni left the back bedroom, an image of an evil-looking face with a long beard-like projection dangling from its jaw appeared on the door. It remained there for the rest of the evening. The face was eerily also similar to the image of Asmodeus (see photo section).

Toni Rodriguez was methodical and thorough. In only a few hours, the house was cleared and remained so for the rest of our residency there. No more ectoplasmic-like outcroppings on the pictures. No more black beetles on the patio wall or pounding against the walls of the house. No more rat-like droppings. The black curtains had quickly turned a pure white. The poltergeist activity also ceased. The photos and pictures remained on the walls. The cats were left alone. The record albums remained in their cabinet. Finally, there were no more strange men who suddenly disappeared at the front door.

American National Institute

In 1975, Toni Rodriguez opened ANI in a bucolic setting near The Commons in Calabasas, California. It was small as colleges go with a short string of low black, gleaming buildings and a small student body. A tall, green hill that was often alive with goats provided a welcome rural setting.

I later discovered from the California Board of Education that, at the time, ANI may have been only one of two colleges in the United States that offered bachelors, masters and doctoral degrees in Metaphysics. The other was JFK University in Berkeley, California.

Top Secret: The Aura Project

Only a few weeks after the evil influences were flushed from our home, I found myself working on a project with Toni in her office when the phone rang. To my surprise, it was Edwin ("Ed") Meese, President Reagan's official Policy Counselor, calling from the White House. Toni quickly switched to speakerphone mode.

"Hello, Ed," Rodriguez greeted. "Haven't heard from you in quite a while. How are Ronnie and Nancy doing?"

"They're doing fine," Meese replied. "They are contemplating a proposed project they are interested in that may also interest you."

"Really?" Toni responded. "Tell me about it."

"As you know, there has been a lot of terrorist activity during this trying decade," Ed related. "The Reagans were wondering if you could come up with a proposal for a project that could reliably identify possible terrorists and their intentions at such venues as airports, train stations, and bus terminals. It would have to be something that potential terrorists would know nothing about."

I immediately sat up at stiff attention. I could hardly believe it. I was listening to a strange request from one of the two or three top officials in the White House.

Toni was quick to respond.

"It would probably have to be under the cloak of aura reading," she said. "I'm teaching that to a group of students now at the institute. A few are becoming quite adept at it. Everyone has an aura that can be read. The colors of the aura can reliably determine what kind of individual a person might be."

Rodriguez went on to explain that it would be difficult if not impossible to absolutely determine if someone might be or become a terrorist. Expertly reading someone's aura, however, might identify that person as a *potential* terrorist... or not.

Toni explained that the colors of an aura could tell a lot about the kind of individual someone might be. On the negative side of the coin, a quivering black aura usually denotes such feelings as evil, hatred, and malice. Dark indigo: malice. Dark red: anger. Scarlet: hidden anger. Lime yellow: deceit, dishonesty, etc.

"Can you get out an initial six-month proposal complete with how much money you will need?" Meese asked. "We will probably put a Top Secret label on it, so only a few of your most trusted colleagues should know about it."

Toni responded that she could have a proposal ready in a few weeks. Following the call, she turned to me.

"Well, Mr. Author, how are you on writing proposals?" she inquired.

"I've had a little experience," I replied. "Maybe you would want someone more experienced."

"No," Toni said. "We can't trust any outsiders and I'm not sure I'd pick any of my other students to do this."

"Thanks, Toni," I acknowledged. "I'll give it my best shot."

There was a lot to be done in a couple of weeks to have the proposal ready. If we got the go-ahead, individuals sworn to secrecy would have to be expertly trained in aura readings. These readings would be in transportation venues throughout the United States as well as through individual photographs and films.

I knew it would be a hell of a difficult, even potentially unreliable, project. Several questions raced around my mind. How would we know if someone emitting a black or dark red aura was a potential terrorist or had recently had a knock-down-drag-out fight with his/her spouse? We would also have to contend with other similar questions.

Extensive training would also have to be considered. Also, how could we reliably keep the project at a Top Secret level?

About three weeks later, shortly before Thanksgiving, I came up with an initial six-month project proposal. It would have a $150,000 price tag on it, possibly more if required.

It was only a few days after we sent the proposal to the White House that we heard it had been approved for further investigation. The next step? Meese would send a White House investigator to ANI to spend several days with us to determine if we had all our ducks in order enough to do the job.

That was our downfall. I was worried from the start that Toni would not create the proper confidence that we could covertly do the kind of job the White House required.

The official first visited the ANI office and briefly perused the large file and student rooms. He offered suggestions on how our layout could be improved in order to better provide more security, but he seemed to be impressed.

It was when the official joined us for a Thanksgiving dinner at Toni's home that our hoped-for project quickly unraveled. I had urged Rodriguez to have the meal at another location, even at a nearby restaurant. She, however, insisted it be in her home.

The problem was that Toni was not a good organizer, with papers spread out on a couch and table. Even a copy of the proposal was there in plain sight. An even bigger problem was that she had kept her ailing, nearly unresponsive father in a large elevated bed in the front hallway. The room was dark with a brightly lit cross hanging over the bed. When the envoy saw that, he was visibly stunned.

"We aren't going to get the go-ahead, are we?" I asked, gently guiding him to the side.

"No, Gordon, I'm afraid not," he quickly responded with what appeared to be an embarrassed smile.

It was as if a negative aura had quickly descended over ANI. Toni pretended to ignore it, but I could see she was deeply disappointed.

"On to bigger and better things," she told me.

Bigger and better things than to work with the White House on an important worldwide problem? They don't come any bigger that that.

Paula Ellis and Rod Steiger

The most interesting student I met and conversed with during my time at the Institute was the lovely and talented Paula Ellis. During lunch and class breaks, Paula and I would often sit outside at one of the picnic tables and talk.

Paula was a singer and occasional actress. She was also the current lover of Academy Award-winning actor Rod Steiger. The actor won the Oscar for his performance as a bigoted Southern sheriff opposite Sidney Poitier in *In the Heat of the Night* (1967). Two years earlier, he had been nominated for his shattering portrayal of a Holocaust survivor in *The Pawnbroker* (1965) and many expected him to take home the gold for that role. Lee Marvin, however, beat him out for *Cat Ballou*.

"Rod really should have gotten his Oscar for *The Pawnbroker*," Paula told me. "Everyone I have talked to thinks that."

"I agree," I responded. "His silent scream in the movie is still one of the great film images. He conveyed a depth of despair that no words could adequately convey. I also thought he was great in *In the Heat of the Night*.

Paula admitted that Steiger could be very difficult and trying. Maintaining steady intimate relationships was not his cup-of-tea. Being a fine actor was. Paula and I agreed that his performances in such films as *The Pawnbroker, In the Heat of the Night, The Sergeant* (1968), *No Way to Treat a Lady* (1968) and even *On the Waterfront* (1954) were crown achievements in acting.

I thought Paula was a truly lovely person inside and out. She was also the third wife of Steiger and had a son, Michael, by him. I had also met the beautiful Claire Bloom, Steiger's first wife, about thirty years before (Chapter Ten). It is Paula, however, that I still miss most. Such enlightened friends don't come along very often.

I left the school late in 1986 following a downward spiral from which ANI never recovered. In 1988, I became the General Manager of Beverly Hot Springs in Los Angeles. It would be my best venue yet for meeting celebrities.

Chapter Seven

Beverly Hot Springs

One of the two main venues I had of meeting and interacting with those in the celebrity world came when I was the General Manager at Beverly Hot Springs for nearly five years, from 1988 to 1992. These celebrities included many film stars.

The waters constitute the only natural mineral hot springs spa in Los Angeles, located about ten miles from the downtown area. It is near the elite Beverly Hills section of the city. The Paramount movie studio is also nearby.

A constant strong flow of pure mineral water with temperatures from ninety-six-to-105 degrees rise up from an artesian well that Richard Grant, a real estate speculator, found when he purchased the springs with the enticing label, "Nature's Own Formula."

Development of the mineral water spa began in 1984. Then the well was used as the underground foundation for the development of Beverly Hot Springs. When I came on board as a staff member in 1988, I quickly became a regular, nearly daily user of the healing waters. This helped to alleviate my arthritis, relax the muscles, and improve skin problems.

The Korean owners opened the spa in the Asian tradition of nude bathing (swim suits optional) with separate facilities for men and women in the same building. Soon after its opening, many prominent celebrities began pouring into the spa to relax and enjoy the benefits of the water and the Korean-style massages.

My job at the spa was to make daily rounds and check for any problems that needed to be resolved. I also acted as the public relations officer and the English language editor of the owners' bi-weekly newspaper *The Corea Times*.

Catherine and Daniel Mann

One of the first people I met as General Manager at Beverly Hot Springs was Catherine ("Cathy") Mann, who quickly became a good friend. She was a friend of one of the spa's co-owners, Dr. Huh. She was also the former wife of famed movie director Daniel Mann.

In the 1950s and 1960s, Cathy was right into the middle of Hollywood filmmaking. She was beside her husband when he led three of the top female stars to Best Actress Academy Awards during the 1950s and in 1960. The first Oscar went to Shirley Booth for *Come Back, Little Sheba* (1952). This was followed with an explosive performance by the bombastic Anna Magnani in Tennessee Williams' *The Rose Tattoo* (1955). Last and least (according to the star herself and just about everyone else) was Elizabeth Taylor in *BUtterfield 8* (1960). There were at least two other Oscar-nominated performances with Susan Hayward in *I'll Cry Tomorrow* (1955) and the great Paul Muni in *The Last Angry Man* (1959), thanks to Daniel Mann.

Being the movie fan I am, I immediately got into a conversation about the films Cathy's ex-husband directed. We both decried the fact that Mann had never won the Oscar for Best Director, but that may have been because none of the films he helmed won the Best Picture prize.

"It was a shame," Cathy piped in. "Danny led three of the top Hollywood stars to Best Actress Oscars, but he never won one himself."

Chapter Seven: Beverly Hot Springs

"What did Danny himself and you think of their performances?" I asked Cathy as we sipped some green tea on the second floor of the spa.

"He loved Shirley Booth," Cathy responded. "She was the easiest to direct. No trouble at all. Sweet and gentle. Then came Magnani, who upheld her reputation of being difficult to work with. Danny nearly pulled out what little hair he still had on the top of his head directing her. Nonetheless, he also thought it was the best acting job of the three film divas."

"What about my favorite actress, Elizabeth Taylor?" I asked.

"Liz was a different kettle of fish," Cathy responded. "She hates to be called 'Liz,' by the way. It's always Elizabeth or Mrs. Whoever She Was Married to at the Time."

"I read that Liz [pardon me, Elizabeth!] hated her role in *BUtterfield 8* and felt she should have won the Academy Award for any one of the three previous back-to-back films for which she was nominated [*Raintree County* (1957), *Cat on a Hot Tin Roof* (1958) and *Suddenly, Last Summer* (1959)]," I remarked. "I guess you could say she made up for it by winning her second Oscar for *Who's Afraid of Virginia Woolf?* [1966]. That time, she gave a performance truly worthy of the Best Actress Academy Award

"Absolutely correct," Cathy responded. "During the making of *BUtterfield 8*, she got seriously ill and the doctors had to give her a tracheotomy to save her life. After she received her Oscar, Elizabeth said it was the first time in Academy history that anyone got the golden statuette for having a tracheotomy!"

The films of Daniel Mann was not the only topic Cathy and I discussed. We were both working our way through the early stages of spiritual fulfillment. (I am now eighty and still nowhere near the "fulfillment" part. On to the next lifetime. . . .) Our favorite meditation retreat was at the superbly beautiful and eerily quiet (it was only a few minutes away from a heavy traffic area in Pacific Palisades, California) Self-Realization Fellowship Lake

Shrine, founded in 1952 by Swami Paramahansa Yogananda. Cathy loved the quiet beauty of the snow-white swans in the lake while my favorite spot was standing before the urn containing a portion of the ashes of Mahatma Gandhi. Yogananda and Gandhi were friends and Gandhi dictated in his will that a portion of his ashes would go to Yogananda while the bulk of his remains were to be scattered on the surface of the Holy Ganges.

For the last thirty-five or so years of her life, Cathy continued her spiritual quest and became a resident of several Buddhist meditation centers in Los Angeles and the Carmel Valley. I lost contact with Cathy shortly after I left as General Manager at the spa. I have always fondly thought of her as an avid reader and a lifelong student of spiritual consciousness, being and enlightenment. She was also a brilliant, charming and beautiful human being. I can only hope she found no little measure of enlightenment when she died in May 2006 at the age of eighty-three.

Star Trek: The Next Generation

My main on-going relationship with well-known patrons of Beverly Hot Springs was with the main cast of *Star Trek: The Next Generation* (1987-1994). Patrick Stewart, Jonathan Frakes, LeVar Burton, and Brent Spiner had been filming the series at nearby Paramount Studios and used the spa (sometimes daily) to relax.

I became pretty good friends with LeVar Burton, who shared many of my interests. These included UFOs (see Chapter Four) and the spiritual and paranormal. (A few years prior to our meeting, I had gotten my B.S. degree in Metaphysics [Chapter Six]).

LeVar was raised Catholic and attended the St. Pius X Seminary in Galt, California, with the intention of becoming a priest. He felt, however, that there was something more to a spiritual life than being a priest and following a strict dogma. He began reading other spiritual literature, including some on Hinduism and Buddhism. Then he left the seminary to study and graduate from the University of Southern California's School of Theatre.

One day, as we were sitting naked in the eucalyptus-strewn sweat room at the spa, I told LeVar that I suddenly had a psychic vision of him as a high priest who used healing crystals on the ancient continent of Atlantis. He responded that I was the second person who had told him that in recent months.

Only three years after graduating from high school, LeVar hit it big with his acting debut as Kunta Kinte in the 1977 television mini-series, *Roots*, based on the novel by Alex Haley. It was a huge success. He reprised the role in the follow-up 1988 TV film *Roots: The Gift*.

I still remember Burton's classy response when he was asked about the social impact of *Roots*.

"It expanded the consciousness of people," he remarked. "Blacks and whites began to see each other as human beings, not as stereotypes."

As of this writing on Memorial Day of 2016, LeVar Burton has been named as the co-executive producer of a highly anticipated reboot of *Roots* on the History channel.

LeVar went on to become the host and executive producer of the *Reading Rainbow* series for PBS. It ran for an incredible twenty-three seasons, winning over 200 broadcast awards, including twenty-six Emmys. Burton himself took home twelve Emmy Awards as the show's host and producer.

The single day I remember most with the *Star Trek* crew occurred on a sunny October 25, 1991. I was in my General Manager's office when I received a call from someone at Paramount. The caller insisted that I tell the crew to immediately return to the studio. I already knew that at least one of the actors, Brent Spiner, who portrayed Data in the series, was angry at the studio for insisting that he always be on call, even when he was off the set.

"The studio doesn't own me, dammit!" he told me.

I asked the Paramount staffer the reason I could tell the actors they had to quickly get dressed and return to the studio. She said that Gene Roddenberry, the creator of the *Star Trek* franchise, had died. I saw Patrick Stewart standing by his locker and delivered the sad news to him. He immediately summoned Burton, Frakes, and Spiner, who quickly dried themselves, dressed, and ran toward their van in the spa parking lot.

I continued my visits with LeVar Burton until I left Beverly Hot Springs in 1992 to accept a position as an editor with a publishing firm in Southern California. I have, however, always remembered my visits with Burton, who was often joined by Nick Mancuso, another actor who has obtained respected supporting actor status in Hollywood films.

Tina Louise

Soon after taking my new job at Beverly Hot Springs, I met Tina Louise. I was in my office when I was called into the first floor lounge area. Tina was sitting alone in one of the comfortable, soft lounge chairs. I immediately recognized her. Nonetheless, I was somewhat shocked by her unkempt appearance. She even wore a worried look.

In order to break the ice, I began telling her how much I enjoyed her performances in such films as *Day of the Outlaw* and *The Trap* (both released in 1959). It was her Hollywood film debut, however, in *God's Little Acre* (1958), based on the novel by Erskine Caldwell, that most impressed me. Acting opposite Robert Ryan and Aldo Ray, she shone as the bright star she is. It also opened the door for her to act as a leading lady for such big male stars as Ryan, Robert Taylor, and Richard Widmark. Tina further honed her craft by studying with Lee Strasberg at the Actors Studio.

The role that firmly catapulted Tina to the top came in 1964 as Ginger Grant in the television comedy *Gilligan's Island*. I asked her how she felt about playing Ginger.

"I didn't like it at all at first," she admitted.

"Why is that?" I asked, although I suspected I had already correctly guessed her answer.

"I thought it would typecast me as being sexy and dumb," she answered, "but it did help to spread my name wide and far. So, I am grateful for that."

"Good," I responded. "So, what can I do for you?"

Tina shuffled uncomfortably in her chair. Then she said she wanted to receive free passes to the spa for as long as she wanted. The idea was that she could generate more patrons to the spa merely by her presence. I said I didn't have the authority to grant her request, but would ask Dr. Huh, one of the spa's co-owners. Again, I already knew the answer.

Dr. Huh turned her request down. He said that, if the word got out, a number of the other celebrities would also want free passes. When I told Tina, she appeared to be genuinely distressed. I suspected she may have been having financial problems and she did not look her best. I apologized, wished her well, and never saw her again.

Years later, I remembered reading that Tina Louise said: "The best movie you'll ever be in is your own life because that's what matters in the end."

Tina is now in her eighties and is still getting acting parts. I recently read a report that, as of late 2014, she was due to act in a spiritual drama, *Tapestry* (2014), and a horror flick, *Late Phases* (slated for post-production in 2017).

Daryl Hannah

Soon after giving Tina Louise the news she didn't want to hear, I met the beautiful Daryl Hannah. I was manning the check-in counter at the spa when she leisurely strolled in wearing a magnificent designer dress that highlighted her stunning beauty. I don't easily swoon like a lovesick teenager when meeting a lovely woman, but I nearly lost it with Daryl. She smiled at me as she plopped her purse on the counter and began searching for her checkbook. It took me a couple of seconds before I was able to speak.

"Good afternoon, D . . . D . . . Daryl!" I stuttered like a lovesick schoolboy.

Jesus, I thought, *she must think I'm a real idiot!*

Daryl gently smiled, however, as I stumbled around under the counter for a spa ticket.

"It's all right," she said. "I'm in no hurry. Compose yourself. I won't bite."

"Bite me, Daryl!" I silently screamed. *"I'm here to be consumed!"*

"I'm sorry, Daryl," I said.

"That's all right," she smiled with a patient look that said it all: *This happens to me all the time!* "What's your name?"

"Gordon Lore," I stuttered while summoning the courage to talk like a grown man. "I'm the General Manager here. Please *pardon-mois*, but seeing the real Ayla in person bowls me over."

"Ayla was just a film role, so I won't knock you unconscious with my club and drag you into my cave," she gently said.

I resisted the temptation to respond: *Hit me with whatever you like and drag me into your lair! I'm yours!*

Ayla is the strikingly lovely cave dweller in the 1986 film version of Jean M. Aurel's best-selling *The Clan of the Cave Bear* (1980). The movie was described by at least one film critic as being "a richly detailed, beautifully filmed screen version" of the popular novel. It tells the story of cave dwellers nearly 40,000 years ago on a prehistoric journey described as "humankind's long march toward civilization."

I would have marched with Daryl anywhere and made the long march a never-ending one. At the time I met her, I believe she was still dating John F. Kennedy, Jr. The fact that she would even acknowledge my existence after being in such exalted company impressed me.

Even before I met Daryl, I had been following her career. She made her film debut in *The Fury* (1978), starring Kirk Douglas and John Cassavetes. This was quickly followed by her performance as a knockout blonde mermaid in Ron Howard's fantasy *Splash* (1984) starring Tom Hanks, followed by *Wall Street* (1987) with Michael Douglas in his Academy Award-winning role. Then she played the title role of *Roxanne* (1987), a modern take on the classic Edmond Rostand play, *Cyrano de Bergerac* (1897). The late great film critic Roger Ebert said her performance in that celluloid effort was both "gentle" and "sweet."

The sweet and gentle actress went on to star with the late great Peter O'Toole in *High Spirits* (1988) and she appeared in *Crimes and Misdemeanors*, directed by Woody Allen, and *Steel Magnolias*, both released 1989. She also snagged the lead role in a remake of the cult classic *Attack of the 50 Foot Woman* (1993). It was her role as the one-eyed killer in Quentin Tarantino's *Kill Bill* (2003), however, that is one of her more memorable film ventures.

Hannah went on to give Marilyn Monroe a run for her money when she reprised that film legend's role in *The Seven Year Itch* (1955) in a 2000 theatrical production at London's West End Theatre. She was praised for her apparently little-known talents as a comedienne.

Sandwiched somewhere between her affair with JFK, Jr. and her film career, was (and still is) her involvement as a true environmental crusader.

She is a strong advocate of solar power and used her celebrity status as a promotional tool when she joined with more than 350 farmers and their families and a cadre of supporters in an effort to end an attempt to bulldoze the nation's largest urban farm in the City of Angels. The farm had been established following the bloody Los Angeles riots in 1992. It enabled city dwellers to grow food for themselves. Hannah proved she meant business when she chained herself to a walnut tree in the farm for a numbing three weeks! She even spent some time in jail for her noble effort.

Daryl hardly stopped there. She also used her celebrity status in an attempt to end what was described as "sexual slavery" around the world. She even traveled the globe to film a documentary on behalf of that effort.

On August 30, 2011, the actress was arrested in front of the White House in Washington, D.C. She was part of a sit-in against the proposed Keystone oil pipeline that would stretch from Canada down through the U.S. to the Gulf Coast. Less than a year and a half later, on February 13, 2013, while again protesting the pipeline, she was arrested at 1600 Pennsylvania Avenue with Kennedy during a climate change protest against the ongoing Keystone effort. She was convinced that the pipeline would be devastating to the health of the North American environment.

I saw Daryl several more times during my stint at Beverly Hot Springs and even dared to flirt with her. To my surprise and delight, she played the part, even blushing when I told her how beautiful she looked.

I never told my late wife, Marty, about this. Years before my meeting Daryl, I had made a fool of myself over the lovely Susan Strasberg, the daughter of famed Actor's Studio head Lee Strasberg in New York (see Chapter Ten).

Jodie Foster and William McNamara

Actress Jodie Foster was at the top of her game when I first saw her as a patron of Beverly Hot Springs in 1989. Earlier that year, she had won both an Oscar and a Golden Globe for Best Actress playing a rape survivor in *The Accused* (1988). It was an incredible performance based on the true story of a woman who was brutally gang-raped by a group of drunken men in a bar in the historic whaling port of New Bedford, Massachusetts.

When Jodie walked up to the ticket desk with a female friend who kept clinging to her, she flashed a big smile. She also tried to persuade her friend to "lighten up" on her obvious expressions of affection.

I had recently seen Foster again in director Martin Scorsese's controversial film, *Taxi Driver* (1976) in which she played a twelve-year-old prostitute opposite Robert De Niro. She was nominated for a Best Supporting Actress Academy Award for that part. She also won a National Society of Film Critics award for her role in the movie.

Would-be presidential assassin John W. Hinckley, Jr., was a highly mentally disturbed young man who had seen Jodie in *Taxi Driver* and was obsessed by her. On March 30, 1981, he tried to kill President Ronald Reagan in the hope that the act would impress Foster. The incident subjected Jodie to intense media attention and garnered Hinckley thirty-five years of incarceration. In 2016, he was permitted to live with his mother in Richmond, Virginia, under ultra-strict monitoring conditions.

I had also just seen *Stealing Home*, which had only been released a few months earlier in August 1988. Foster played opposite Mark Harmon and William McNamara (see below).

"Good afternoon, Jodie," I remarked as she approached the check-in desk. "I'm Gordon Lore, the General Manager. Welcome to Beverly Hot Springs."

"Thank you, Gordon," she responded.

"I saw *The Accused*," I remarked. "You gave a superb performance. Frightening, but great. As you know, the crime occurred in an historic whaling port. Too bad they had to bring such violence into the confines of one of the great whaling towns . . . By the way, didn't you start your career as the Coppertone girl on TV?"

"I did," Jodie said, flashing a smile.

"You must have been very young . . . maybe two or three years old."

Jodie held up three fingers.

"You and your friend enjoy the waters, Jodie," I remarked.

I saw Jodie only one more time. It was in 1991, at about the time *The Silence of the Lambs* was released. Her role as FBI agent Clarice Starling with Anthony Hopkins as Hannibal Lecter was rewarded with a second Best Actress Oscar.

The movie itself won lasting fame as one of only three films to win Academy Awards in all of the main categories, including Best Picture, Actor, Actress, Director, and Screenplay. The other two films were *It Happened One Night* (1934) with Clark Gable and Claudette Colbert, and *One Flew Over the Cuckoo's Nest* (1975) with Jack Nicholson and Louise Fletcher. *The Silence of the Lamb*s is also preserved in the National Film Registry.

Not long after seeing Jodie for the first time, I also met the promising young actor with whom she co-starred in *Stealing Home* (1988), with Mark Harmon as the lead actor. I was relaxing in the hot waters when a young man sat down beside me. I introduced myself and offered my assistance if he needed anything.

"I'm Billy," he said, holding out his hand.

"Yes," I responded. "William McNamara. I just saw you with Jodie Foster and Mark Harmon in *Stealing Home*. Jodie is a patron here as well."

"I know she is," Billy remarked. "She recommended this place to me. It's great for relaxing following a long day in front of the cameras."

"Thank you, Billy," I said. "Let me know if I can do anything for you."

I never saw Billy at the spa after that, but did follow his career. I discovered that he is an internationally well-known animal rights advocate who also studied with Lee Strasberg in New York.

Later, I was particularly impressed with McNamara's acting chops as a perverted killer opposite Sigourney Weaver in *Copycat* (1995) and in a more family-oriented role in the TV movie *Doing Time on Maple Drive* (1992). He also channeled the roles of Montgomery Clift in *Liz: The Elizabeth Taylor Story* (1995) and Ricky Nelson in Stephen King's *Nightmares and Dreamscapes* (2006).

Lesley Ann Warren

A regular spa visitor I became friendly with was the charming, effervescent actress Lesley Ann Warren. I was manning the reception desk at the springs when she came in several times dressed in what I called her Apple Annie outfit. She sat on a chair opposite the desk waiting her turn to purchase a ticket.

Despite her down-and-out street outfit, I recognized Lesley immediately. I had read that she was filming with Mel Brooks in a nearby Los Angeles neighborhood a little known film by the comedian called *Life Stinks!* (1991). Lesley approached the desk wearing what appeared to be a shy smile.

"Good afternoon, Lesley," I greeted. "How are you today?"

"I'm OK," she replied. "A little tired and feeling grimy. I'm looking forward to a wonderful soak in the mineral waters. What's your name?"

I introduced myself. Lesley looked a bit taken aback, but she had a sparkling twinkle in her eye.

"How did you recognize me, Gordon?" she somewhat shyly asked.

"I'd recognize you anywhere, Lesley," I responded, "ever since seeing you in *Victor/Victoria* when it was first released in 1982. What a great, effervescent performance that was. You were the real blonde spitfire. You deserved all the plaudits."

Lesley had garnered a Best Supporting Actress Oscar nomination as well as a Golden Globe nod for *Victor/Victoria*. She also won People's Choice and New York Film Critics awards for the part.

Lesley actually blushed at one point in our short conversation. She kept coming back and, each time, tried to fool me in her street costume. I kept recognizing her, however.

Being a lifelong movie buff, I consulted my extensive library to find out more about this lovely lady. I discovered that she was the daughter of Margot Warren, a nightclub singer in New York. Lesley followed her own star, however, and studied under the famed teacher of the stars Lee Strasberg at his New York-based Actors Studio. At only seventeen years of age, she was then the youngest student to be accepted at the Studio.

Warren went on to shine on Broadway in *110 in the Shade* (1963). This quickly led to her getting the title role in *Cinderella* (1965), the Rodgers and Hammerstein television musical. From there on, there was no looking back. Lesley had become a true bona fide star.

I had a couple of informative and very enjoyable conversations with Lesley as she lounged around the reception area of the spa. I asked her what she thought about her *Victor/Victoria* performance. Her answer surprised me.

"I hated it at first," she said.

"Why?" I probed.

"I thought my performance as the crazy peroxide blonde was way over the top," she elaborated. "I believed the audience would boo me off the screen."

"Guess what, Lesley?" I interjected. "You were wrong. The audience loved you. *I* loved you in the part. You played it to ditzy blonde perfection. No one could have done it better. But, tell me . . . What is your formula for

Chapter Seven: Beverly Hot Springs

success as an actress?"

"Pretty much the same as it is in life itself," she replied. "I learned so much from Lee Strasberg. My own philosophy is to follow your own heart. Follow what it is telling you. Fight for what you believe in. In the heart lies the truth to whatever you want to do either professionally or in life itself. Follow your heart and your own instincts and you will succeed."

The last time I saw Lesley, she was wearing a regular light yellow dress and looked absolutely charming and beautiful. That was how I have always remembered Lesley Ann Warren.

Oliver Stone

No doubt about it. Famed Hollywood Director Oliver Stone is a unique individual. At times, he is quiet, then explosive, opinionated one minute and willing to objectively listen the next. I first saw him standing alone and stoic beside the small marble alcove wall on the second floor of the spa.

After introducing myself, I invited him to sit down. I had heard he could be a terror. It just depended on what mood he was in.

I already knew that Stone had won his first Academy Award in 1979 for adapting the true prison story, *Midnight Express* (1978), into a gripping film. He also penned the screenplay for Brian De Palma's violent, over-the-top *Scarface* (1984), starring Al Pacino. I had read that Stone may have based his *Scarface* script on his own cocaine addiction. He also credited his work on the film as the impetus for him to kick the habit.

When I met Stone, his three-hour film *JFK* (1991), starring Kevin Costner, was the rage. I had read that Oliver was virtually certain that Lee Harvey Oswald did not act alone. He may even not have been the one to pull the trigger that ended the life of President John F. Kennedy in Dallas, Texas, on November 22, 1963.

"If you study the Zapruder film along with the sequence of the shooting, the timing, and consider the wounds and the autopsy finding, it makes no sense," Stone supposedly remarked.

The director also reportedly said that was an indication that the CIA files on Oswald were virtually ignored by the Warren Commission. *JFK* tells the story of the investigation into the assassination by New Orleans District Attorney Jim Garrison, superbly performed by Kevin Costner. It was a riveting film, but many critics, historians and politicians took issue with Stone for his "depiction of an assassination plot hatched in the highest echelons of the American government."

Stone also pointed out that CIA Chief Alan Dulles, along with his top aides, had been fired by Kennedy two years before the assassination. Dulles, however, was still charged with heading the investigation. Stone had been convinced that Dulles was responsible for keeping certain important information from the Warren Commission.

In 1992, a year or so after I met him, Stone screened *JFK* for certain members of Congress on Capitol Hill. The screening reportedly was a major factor in the passage of the Assassination Materials Disclosure Act of 1992.

The director also related that Jim Garrison had a chance to see *JFK* shortly before he died in 1992 and "he was a very happy man" with it. Stone also gave a small part in *JFK* to Garrison as Chief Justice Earl Warren.

Oliver won his first directing Oscar for *Platoon* (1986) followed by a second gold statuette three years later for *Born on the Fourth of July* (1989) The screenplay for *Platoon* was partially based on Stone's combat experience in Vietnam.

Meanwhile, Oliver Stone continues his effort to strip away the cover-ups of important information from the U.S. government and its intelligence agencies. He believes that "our government has been snooping in our lives ever since we became an empire after World War I."

Frank Langella

One of the more interesting, laid-back celebrities I met at Beverly Hot Springs was Frank Langella. He is a well-regarded film and stage actor who has coughed up an impressive list of character roles. I knew he had risen to motion picture prominence in two 1970 films: *The Twelve Chairs* directed by Mel Brooks and Frank Perry's *Diary of a Mad Housewife*.

In 1977, Langella performed the title role of *Dracula* on Broadway. Following that run, he starred with the great Laurence Olivier in the 1979 film version directed by John Badham. I had recently seen Frank in the film version when I noticed him relaxing in one of the second floor spa chairs at the springs. I approached him and introduced myself as the General Manager. Then I mentioned that I had seen him in *Dracula*.

"What did you think of it?" he asked.

"Excellent," I responded. "You, the rest of the cast and the production designers, in particular, did a hell of an impressive job."

"That's what we were aiming for," Frank related in his smooth, elegant voice. "The producers and director were looking for a much more sophisticated, even darkly elegant version that suggested the true origins of the Dracula legend. They also gave the production team, the costume designers, and set decorators *carte blanche* to come up with a way to make the picture shine in a muted color sort of way."

"I remember film critic Roger Ebert saying it was an elegant, welcome take on the Bram Stoker novel that had previously been overdone in a somber, black-and-white caped Dracula rising from the coffin style," I remarked.

The late great film critic was effusive in his praise: "What an elegantly seen *Dracula* this is, all shadows and blood and vapors and Frank Langella stalking through with the grace of a cat. The film is a triumph of performance, art direction, and mood over materials that can lend themselves so easily to self-satire. There have been so many Draculas (Bela Lugosi played him three times, Christopher Lee five) that the tragic origins of the character have been lost among the gravestones, the fangs and all those black cloaks. This *Dracula* restores the character to the purity of its first film appliances in F.W. Murnau's 1922 *Nosferatu* and Bela Lugosi's 1931 version."

High praise indeed. I also thought so at the time. At a recent viewing of the film while preparing for this book, however, I did not have as high an opinion of the cinematic effort as I did then. I wasn't convinced that the darker version effectively strode the line between its color and black-and-white photography.

I thought the 1992 version directed by Francis Ford Coppola and starring Gary Oldman, Winona Ryder, Anthony Hopkins and Keanu Reeves was better with its visually striking set designs, excellent direction and nearly impeccable acting.

I also asked Frank what he thought of the performance of whom I called the original "bat-man", Bela Lugosi. He said that he was grateful for the continued appreciation of Lugosi's original *Dracula* (1931) and other related films.

I only spent about fifteen minutes with Langella, but I did continue to follow his career. I was particularly impressed by his all-out role as Clare Quilty in the second film version of Vladimir Nabakov's *Lolita* (1997), directed by Adrian Lyne. It was a chilling performance, better even than that of Peter Sellers in the 1962 version by Stanley Kubrick.

Langella also gave what I considered an excellent, Oscar-worthy performance in George Clooney's *Good Night, and Good Luck* (2005) playing William S. Paley, the former CBS chief executive. This was followed by the *Frost/Nixon* film directed by Ron Howard in 2008, for which he was nominated for a Best Actor Oscar.

Chapter Seven: Beverly Hot Springs

Tom Hanks and Rita Wilson

It was in 1990 or 1991 that I met Tom Hanks and his wife, Rita Wilson. As I was making my rounds of the spa, I saw them sitting at a table in the small second-story cafe. They were sipping green tea. After introducing myself, both Tom and Rita commented on what "a great place" the spa was. Great for letting the hot soothing mineral water relax the muscles and clear the skin.

At the time I met him, Tom was still relatively early in his film career, but he already had a number of impressive credits on his resume, most of which I had seen. These included *Splash* (1984), *Volunteers* (1985), *The Money Pit* (1986), *Big* (1988) (who could forget a miniature Tom dancing on the piano keys?), and *Joe Versus the Volcano* (1990).

During our short visit, I asked Tom what his philosophy was on good film acting. (Rita merely continued sipping her tea as Tom was conversing with yet another admiring fan.)

Tom responded something like this: "If you're going to act in a film, do your best to do it right. Otherwise, it will live on forever. Try to make the acting as real as you can in relation to the character you are playing. And you've got to have some pretty good idea who and what you are in life. Then bring that into your acting. When you act on film, what you do and say remains forever."

I thought there must be something more to great acting than that, but it sounded pretty good, so I didn't press the issue. A few minutes later, Tom and Rita stood up and excused themselves.

The year after I left the spa, Tom's star in Hollywood began to take on a shining glow. He would shortly win back-to-back Best Actor Academy Awards for *Philadelphia* (1993) and *Forrest Gump* (1994). Then came *Apollo 13* (1995), *Saving Private Ryan* (1998), *The Green Mile* (1999), *Cast Away* (2000) (virtually a one-man acting *tour de force*), *The Da Vinci Code* (2006), *Captain Phillips* (2013), *Bridge of Spies* (2015), and *Sully* (2016).

Not bad for a guy sipping green tea with his wife in a mineral water spa in the middle of Los Angeles or someone whose net worth as of 2016 was estimated to be as high as $390 million!

Sam Neill

One afternoon, while making my rounds at the Spa, I saw the Irish-born New Zealand actor Sam Neill by himself in a chair on the second floor. I approached him, introduced myself and sat down next to him.

"Is there anything I can do for you, Sam?" I asked.

"I'm fine, Gordon, thank you," he responded. "Great place you have here."

"It's not mine, I responded. "I wish it was. It's great for fighting back at my arthritis . . . By the way, I just saw you and Meryl Streep in *A Cry in the Dark* [1988]."

The Australian film was originally released under the title *Evil Angels*. It is the story of a woman who claimed her baby was taken away and killed by a dingo. The authorities thought differently, however. The incident quickly turned into one of the most infamous murder cases in Down Under history.

"Incredible, wasn't it?" Sam remarked. "The case, I mean."

"So was the film," I interjected. "One of those real 'did-she-or-didn't-she' mysteries. Superbly acted by both Meryl and yourself."

I had also seen Sam in *Dead Calm* (1989) with another Australian actor, Academy Award winner Nicole Kidman. That movie was also a real thriller.

Sam told me a little about his early life in New Zealand and his role opposite Judy Davis in *My Brilliant Career* (1979). He said his father's family owned the largest liquor retailing business in New Zealand.

After I left the spa, Sam went on to win international acclaim in several films, including the original *Jurassic Park* (1993) and *Jurassic Park III* (2001). Since then, he continues to build up his acting resume in a number of distinguished, notable film and TV appearances.

Conclusion

Other celebrities I briefly met but did not have significant interaction with included baseball great Joe DiMaggio (he decried the fact that his highest annual salary as a baseball player was only $100,000 compared to the then $2 million a typical rookie player earned; and no, I didn't ask him about Marilyn Monroe), Matthew Modine (the star of the critically acclaimed *Birdy* [1984] and *Memphis Belle* [1990]), and Jean-Claude Van Damme (he had just come on the Hollywood scene as an up-and-coming action star).

With few exceptions, my contact with famous celebrities came to an end when I left Beverly Hot Springs in 1992. As I rapidly enter the twilight of my years on this planet, however, I fondly remember the many beautiful people from around the world (including the Canadian Province of Newfoundland and Labrador) I have met.

Chapter Eight

Frank Gehry and the Walt Disney Concert Hall

The Walt Disney Concert Hall in downtown Los Angeles, California, is a masterpiece of modern architecture. Home of the Los Angeles Philharmonic, the structure was built to accommodate a near-perfect tonality that rings the rafters of the entire hall with a booming stereophonic sound.

Plans for the building and its actual construction were a long time coming. In 1987, Lillian Disney started the project with a gift of $50 million to begin constructing the hall as both a tribute to her late husband, Walt, and as a gift to the people of Los Angeles.

World-famous architect Frank Gehry and his cadre of project architects designed the building's architecture, acoustics and massive organ. The completed designs were delivered in 1991. Construction on the massive underground parking garage began in 1992 and was completed in 1996 at an equally massive cost: $110 million. This project put a big dent in plans to keep the cost of the entire project to no more than $200 million.

Space Age Technology

In 1993, as the Associate Editor of *Dimensional Stone* magazine, I became one of the first journalists to write and publish an article on this project entitled "Disney Concert Hall: Space Age Alliance of Computer Technology and Stone." An introductory prelude said: "In a bold move that could revolutionize the dimensional stone industry, aerospace-derived three-dimensional computer technology is being used to design the $200 million Walt Disney Concert Hall—including its dazzling array of limestones from three countries."

In preparation for the article, I visited with Frank Gehry and several of his project architects in Gehry's cavernous two-story working office in Santa Monica, California. There, I saw four working models of the concert hall. These included the overall hall itself, the hall with the Dorothy Chandler Pavilion, a projected new building, and the hall's interior.

Catia 3-D

As other architects and designers labored at their desks armed with slide rules, charts and computers in the long, spacious office complex, I shook hands with Frank Gehry. He acknowledged that I was one of the first writers of a stone publication to approach him about writing an article on what was then a project he hoped would help keep him on the very top rung of the architectural world.

Gehry also explained to me that, in 1990, he began searching for new computer technology that could improve upon the usual two-dimensional architectural drawings that were then standard in the industry. He said he felt there were what he called too many "layers" that had to be penetrated between the architect's rough drawings and the final building. This put at risk the loss of "the original feeling" of the design and forced artistic compromise due to budget constraints.

"The main problem," Gehry continued, "was that of documenting three-dimensional shapes in two-dimensional drawings."

The architect and his associates searched for a software program that would solve documentation problems as well as construction uncertainties. Gehry and his principal associate, James Glyph, rediscovered Catia. This is a 3-D software program from Dassault Systems, a French firm that had been producing the program for the computer and automobile industries. Gehry had previously used the program for a large fish sculpture in the 1992 Olympic Village in Barcelona, Spain, and a bus stop in Hanover, Germany. As far as he knew, however, this would be the first time Catia would be used on a stone construction project.

Designing "In the Model Format"

Then Gehry turned me over to George R. Metzger, one of the ten project architects at Frank O. Gehry & Associates. Metzger lost no time getting down to brass tacks:

> We design in the model format. We don't do drawings first and then make a model from the drawings. We have a rough scheme of the project and get right into the model building. Therefore, the record of the design is the model.
>
> As we refine the design, we then move up from $1/16''$ to $1/8''$ to $1/4''$. As our designs got more complex, we were presented with the problem of how to document and record the sculptural shapes of the models themselves.
>
> Catia allows you to build true three-dimensional surfaces that are very complex and will give you any point on the surface. A conventional system would only build a flat two-dimensional plane and some curves divided by edges.

Once we discovered a method to record these shapes in the computer, the next step was to figure out how to pull the information off the model and feed it into the computer. We've experimented with several different systems for extracting information from the model. First, we used hand-measuring devices that picked points on the various curves. Then we recorded the measurements on paper and input them into the computer.

Reading the Data

It is at this point, Metzger explained to me, that the ceiling-mounted infrared cameras "read" the data from a digitizing wand with light sensors while someone uses the wand to touch key points on a model. This enables the architects to digitize in points around the surface.

The architect continued:

The most recent thing we have been experimenting with is a piece of equipment from the dental industry. It's a mechanical arm for measuring. The arm has a pointer, which you can place on the tip of the object you want to measure. Then you can push a button to physically measure and insert the information into the computer. It's similar to a dental drill without the drill bit on the end. Once we digitize in three points, we can build the surfaces into the computer.

The X-Y-Z Coordinates

Craig Webb, another project architect, continued with the Metzger explanation.

"Those devices put in the X, Y, Z 3-D coordinates down to four or five decimal points," he explained. "This is much more accurate than what you typically deal with in architecture—plus or minus a millimeter."

Chapter Eight: Frank Gehry and the Walt Disney Concert Hall

George Metzger jumped into the explanation again as I listened attentively. He said that the Catia system allows for close and accurate examination of all the stone shapes.

"On the stone surfaces, we try to figure out ways to make the stone pieces repeat so we can be more economical in the fabrication process," Metzger explained. "We attempt to cut the large number of stone pieces the architect must typically deal with down to a reasonable number . . . like a thousand different types. We work with each of the unusual shapes with the idea of imposing a rational geometry on the surface."

Limestone Mock-Up

Metzger directed my attention to a mock-up limestone wall—close to the concert hall models—that was fifteen feet high and thirty feet long. Its imposing but precise curved cut was the major attraction in the American Pavilion at the Venice Biennial in Italy in 1991.

The wall was constructed with St. Pierre Angle Roche Dure Evielle, a rough-honed finish limestone from the Carrieres de St. Pierre Aigle Quarry in Sigma, France. It was one of four limestones from six quarries in three countries that were being considered to sheath the exterior of the concert hall. It was chosen after Gehry and his team looked at and studied around 150 limestones in the same color range.

The other limestones under consideration were Giallo Dorato from the Fratelli Grassi, Morseletto, and Vittorio Grassi quarries in Vicenza, Italy; St. Maximin Roche Franche Fine Limestone from Rocamat St. Maximin Quarry in France; and Subtle Saffron from the American Limestone Company, Dallas, Texas. I saw samples of each of these stones on display on the second floor balcony of Gehry's office.

"Hanging the Stone"

"There are so many possibilities for hanging stone on the building," Metzger joined in as I continued listening intently. "I believe there will be a stick system with a horizontal support member that picks up the stone. With that as a general system, there are a lot of other options such as the spacing verticals, which is how the edge of the stone will be held. It was impractical for us to dictate a specific system to the various people we have been talking with. In the near future, we are going to try to bring someone on board who can customize the system to fit the desired means of construction."

3-D Computer Technology

Metzer told me that he believed 3-D computer technology would be an important, even indispensable, adjunct to future stone construction. He elaborated:

> We've demonstrated things that stone fabricators might do if they're interested. They might add stone joint widths. Architects could get more accurate dimensional information on the stone pieces themselves. They could experiment with curved back surfaces versus flat back surfaces and how those will vary. As is evident in the wall mock-up, that offset can be quite considerable. They'll need to understand that before they fabricate. They could also add trimmed edges to the sides of the stone elements.

Enter Richard S. Smith, the owner of Certified CIM Consulting (C- Cubed), of Mission Viejo, California. He was hired to train the architects on the Catia system. As a test, the limestone wall mockup was constructed. My interest didn't lag as Smith gave a detailed explanation:

> We modeled three-dimensionally. Then we extracted the data, created shop tickets, and faxed those to France, where the stone was cut. We're

patterning the entire concert hall. From there, the patterns will go out to subcontractors to either do shop tickets or come up with some kind of direction-controlled machine to cut the stone.

We're hoping the fabricators and installers will pick up our computer information and add to it. For instance, the installers may choose to develop their support structure behind the stone in the computer system because it would be quite advantageous for them to figure out shapes and quantities of the pieces they need.

Installers will probably use computer information to survey the building. We've looked at several surveying devices that can both pull up dimensional information directly from the computer, then work in the field to locate the corners of each piece of stone. It can be determined where a stone is supposed to go within an accuracy of one millimeter. We've tested it on the mock-up and it looks like it's going to work. Everything is maintained digitally in a three-dimensional database.

A Number of Stone Applications

Smith meticulously described how the Catia program could create any number of stone patterns. It could locate the square footage of a wall and count the number of stones and determine their radii. The system could also read out information on whether or not the stones in a particular area are the same or unique.

Smith added that Catia can work with precise cut lines for each stone until it meets all seismic and esthetic requirements. To reduce fabrication costs, the number of unique stones is minimized. Through Catia, the size, shape, thickness, weight, density and other characteristics of each stone can be quickly and accurately determined. This, he thought, could well be a boon to prospective contractors in submitting accurate cost bids. Smith added that every one of the many project consultants would have access to the system.

Limestone "Wrappers"

Everyone involved with Frank Gehry and his architectural team contributed to creating the bold, striking, contemporary design for the Walt Disney Concert Hall. This design was in a style reminiscent of the best of Frank Lloyd Wright, the premier architect of the twentieth century.

Ayn Rand (see Chapter Ten) and Howard Roark would be proud.

Gehry told me he called the limestone walls "wrappers." The tall walls would curve around the front of the complex and between the lobbies, walkways and other spaces, he elaborated. They would also penetrate the inside of the hall as a lead into the rest rooms, stairways and fire exits.

The architects related to me how important it was to Mrs. Disney that there would be a garden adjoining the hall. The entire city block not occupied by the wall itself would be turned into an outdoor garden with stairways, fountains, planted terraces and plazas. There the public could enjoy a natural setting without having to pay an admission price to the hall.

Search For the Perfect Sound

Gehry and his team were acutely conscious of how important it would be for the hall to accommodate as near-perfect an acoustical sound as possible. With his primary architect, Michael Maltzen, he visited many concert halls throughout the world searching for the ideal acoustical configuration. They were lucky to find it in Tokyo's Suntory Hall. Gehry even hired Minoru Nagata, Suntory's acoustician, as his own principal acoustic consultant.

The hall was originally slated for completion by the end of 1996 for regular concerts by the Los Angeles Philharmonic starting with its 1997-1998 season. Its final completion, however, didn't come until several years later, mainly due to high cost overruns.

During the interim from projected completion to the actual time the hall opened for concerts, there were divergent opinions among many observers about the project. Some called it "about as attractive as a used shoebox" while others lauded it as a beautiful creation destined to be the envy of orchestras and concertgoers everywhere. In a *Los Angeles Times Magazine* interview, Ernest Fleischmann, Executive Vice President and Managing Director of the Philharmonic, likened it to "an incredibly beautiful organic kind of flower with its petals unfolding."

The Completed Hall

It took more than ten years after I wrote and published my article that the Walt Disney Concert Hall was finally completed and open for business. Upon its completion in 2003, the project cost about $274 million. The highest single entity cost was the parking garage at a whopping $110 million.

When the Los Angeles Philharmonic began to practice in the hall, it rehearsed Maurice Ravel's elegantly orchestrated *Daphnis and Chloe* ballet (1912). The playing by the orchestra members made the hall superbly come alive with what has been called "a new sonic dimension [that] caused every square inch of air" in the hall to merrily vibrate. Esa-Pekka Salonen, then the Music Director of the Philharmonic, couldn't have been more pleased.

"The sound ... was my greatest concern, but now I am totally happy and so is the orchestra ... ," he enthused. "Everyone can now hear what the Los Angeles Philharmonic is supposed to sound like."

Salonen and the others involved in the massive project were convinced that the Walt Disney Concert Hall "remains one of the most successful grand openings of a concert hall in North American history."

The Frank Gehry Story

Gehry has been tagged with the envious label of "the most important architect of our age" by *Vanity Fair*. Many of his buildings, including his own residence in Los Angeles, have become renowned around the world. His best-known works include not only the Walt Disney Concert Hall, but also the Guggenheim Museum in Bilbao, Spain; the New World Center in Miami Beach, Florida; the Weisman Art Museum in Minneapolis, Minnesota; and the Cinemathique Francaise in Paris, France.

The eighty-seven-year-old architect was born in Toronto, Ontario, Canada, of Polish-Jewish parents. As a child, he showed signs that he would become an architect. He would build what his grandmother described as "little cities" out of wood scraps.

In 1947, Gehry and his family migrated to Southern California, where Frank graduated from the University of Southern California's School of Architecture. In 1958, at the age of twenty-eight, he designed and built his first private residence. In 1961, he moved to Paris to work for a time with the architectural firm of Pereira and Lickman. By 1967, he was back in California with his own firm, Frank Gehry and Associates.

After lending his architectural expertise to a number of buildings, including the California Aerospace Museum at the California Museum of Science and Industry in 1984, he was awarded the coveted Pritzker Architectural Prize in 1997. Since then, he has continued to win major commissions and has been dubbed "the apostle of chain-link fencing and corrugated metal siding,"

Gehry is also known as a sophisticated classical artist who is familiar with the history of European art as well as contemporary painting and sculpture. He has frequently used concepts of this classical knowledge in his buildings.

Conclusion

Born on February 28, 1929, Frank Gehry is a Piscean who was naturally inspired by fish. In 2015, he designed his first yacht. He also had a yacht of his own.

Gehry is also a great fan of ice hockey. He began an amateur hockey "league" in his office he called FOG (standing for Frank Owen Gehry). In 2004, he designed the trophy for the World Cup of Hockey.

As of this writing in May 2016, even at his advanced age, Frank Gehry continues his work as whom many consider the greatest architect since Frank Lloyd Wright.

Frank Gehry and his band of architects constituted one of the most productive and interesting interviews I have conducted in my more than fifty years as a writer-editor. I learned a lot about the finer points of great architecture and developed a deep appreciation for the work of such innovative artists as Frank Gehry.

Now, in his late eighties, Gehry is still going strong. On Tuesday, November 22, 2016, he joined with twenty others in receiving the nation's highest honor, the Presidential Medal of Freedom, from President Barack Obama. He was in rare company alongside such luminaries as Tom Hanks, Robert De Niro, Robert Redford, Cicely Tyson, Bruce Springsteen, Ellen DeGeneres, Bill and Melinda Gates, and Michael Jordan.

Following is the official White House tribute to Gehry:

Never limited by conventional materials, styles, or processes, Frank Gehry's bold and thoughtful structures demonstrate his architectural power to induce wonder and revitalize communities. A creative mind from an early age, he began his career by building imaginary homes and cities with scrap materials from his grandfather's hardware store. Since then, his work continues to strike a balance between innovation and functionality, resulting in some of the twentieth century's most iconic buildings. Frank Gehry has proven himself as an extraordinary scholar of American innovation."

Chapter Nine

Kidney Kill

During the summer of 1995, I was the editor of *Contemporary Dialysis & Nephrology*, then the top magazine in the renal care field. It was at this time that I came across shocking, disturbing reports that authorities in China were routinely using the organs, mostly kidneys, of executed prisoners for transplantation in top-ranking Communist Party officials and wealthy foreigners who could pay cash for them. In some cases, the reports indicated, the organs may have been extracted even before the prisoners were executed and still alive.

I had originally learned of this practice in the fall of 1994, when I interviewed Robin Munro, Hong Kong Director of Human Rights Watch, Asia. He told me: "While China doesn't have a voluntary organ donation program, it does have a very vigorous and rapidly growing organ transplantation industry." Munro added that the majority of the 2,000-3,000 organs that are annually transplanted in China come from condemned prisoners.

More shocking details came to light during the summer of 1995 at a U.S. Senate Committee on Foreign Relations hearing helmed by Senator Jesse Helms (R-NC). One of the witnesses he welcomed was Harry Wu, Executive Director of the Laogai Research Foundation in Milipitas, California. Other witnesses included officials from Amnesty International (AI)

USA and Anti-Slavery International along with a Research Fellow from the Hoover Institute at Stanford University.

Senator Helms said that he fully trusted Wu, whom he called "one of the bravest souls I know." He still had trouble believing the charges, however, until he saw a BBC documentary on the flourishing trade of human organs in China. He expressed a sense of almost unbelievable shock at what he was learning.

"From what I understand, any person in need of an organ transplant can travel to China, present $30,000 in cash and receive a new organ within hours," the Senator remarked. "The Chinese Public Security Bureau measures the blood type and attributes of all the prisoners on death row... and the best fit is marked for quick execution."

A "Dismal" Record

William F. ("Bill") Schulz, the Executive Director of AI-USA, called China's human rights record "dismal." He confirmed that "executed prisoners are reported to be the main source of organs in China." He added that the prisoners are rarely, if ever, asked for their consent to donate.

Schulz also testified:

> *In the experience of one medical source, the Head of the Intermediate People's Court gave notice of impending executions to the Deputy Head of the court's executive office, who in turn notified the relevant government Health Department. The Health Department official with responsibility for such cases then contacted the appropriate hospitals, giving the number and date of the executions and medical details of the condemned. Use of organs following executions, according to this source, was routine.*

Schultz indicated that, once the prisoner's organs are removed, the corpse is cremated. This made it impossible to verify that the organs had been taken.

"If the family requests the return of the intact corpse," Schultz continued, "it is usually met with a bill for the expenses of the prisoner's upkeep during detention, which is often too large for the family to pay."

Violating International Standards

Schultz had even more to say about how China continued to violate international standards:

The system of organ procurement from executed prisoners in China is part and parcel of a judicial system which fails to ensure due process and violates international standards at almost every stage from arrest to execution. The lack of legal safeguards in China raises the concern that the use of the corpses of executed prisoners as a source of organs may play a role in encouraging the imposition of the death penalty. . . . There is a real risk that the decision to impose the death penalty, already a common punishment in China, and the timing of the execution, will be dictated at least partially by the existence of a lucrative market for organs.

Schultz indicated that executions are rampant in the People's Republic and the death penalty is routinely given for "non-violent offenses, including theft and economic crimes such as bribery, embezzlement, and speculation."

The Harry Wu Story

In a two-hour interview, Harry Wu told me his incredible story. He said he came from a prosperous family. His father was a bank official. He drew a word picture of a peaceful and pleasurable youth, which quickly and dramatically changed with the Communist revolution in 1949. Like other wealthy landowners, Harry's father lost all his holdings.

In 1956, shortly after his graduation from the Geology Institute, Wu responded to a call from China's Communist Party through its Hundred Flowers Campaign. It mandated that citizens (especially students and the *intelligensia*) give their honest opinions on how the party was governing the country. Harry Wu did exactly that: he gave his honest opinion. This ran counter to just about everyone else who told officials what they wanted to hear. In his letter, Wu was critical of some of the party's actions, the most crucial being its supporting Soviet troops invading Hungary that same year.

In the fall of 1956, Mao Zedong, China's leader, said that "the true enemies" of his party had been exposed, presumably through responses to the Hundred Flowers Campaign. One of these "enemies" was nineteen year-old Harry Wu, then a student at the university.

"A Political Troublemaker"

"This was the first time I was singled out as a political troublemaker," Wu later remarked. "Most of my classmates were more pragmatic. They just repeated what the Communists wanted to hear."

Wu continued his fight for freedom for the next few years. He was closely monitored by party officials until, at the age of twenty-three, he was arrested. Harry was charged with being "a counterrevolutionary rightist" and sent to the laogai, China's system of forced labor prison camps similar to the Russian Gulag.

Chapter Nine: Kidney Kill

Surviving the Laogai

Harry Wu told me he was a political prisoner for nineteen long years in twelve different laogai camps. It was rough work mining coal, building roadways, and clearing the land for the planting and harvesting of crops. Like his fellow prisoners, he was beaten, tortured and starved nearly to death. Harry also said he was a witness to the deaths of many of his fellow prisoners from the effects of starvation, brutality, and suicide.

Harry did say that, when he was twenty-three, he met another prisoner who became not only his best friend, but "the most influential teacher in my life." The lean, muscular teacher was called Big Mouth Xing because his mouth was so stretched out and around his face that it seemed to touch both his ears. Xing taught Harry how to survive in the laogai. Wu became genuinely fond of this peasant from a poor village. He was an uneducated thief, but he took Wu under his wing and taught him how to survive the prison camp.

The Immigrant

In 1979, at forty-two years of age, Wu was released from the laogai following political changes in China due to the death of Mao Zedong. As a geologist, he secured a teaching position at the Geoscience University in Beijing. Then, in 1985, he received an invitation from officials at the University of California at Berkeley to become a visiting geologist scholar.

Harry said he may have been premature in coming to America so soon, but he felt the need to live in a free country.

"I came to California with only forty dollars in my pocket and a small suitcase full of clothes," Wu told me. "I knew there would be no money coming to me during my first year as a visiting scholar. So, I had to find what shelter I could. I lived on the street and in the parks when the weather permitted it, but had to go underground into the subway when it rained. I also had to take very low-paying jobs until I could eventually afford a cheap apartment."

By 1988, Harry was beginning to work his way up the employment ladder. He managed to secure a job working for an electronic chip manufacturer where he quickly became an assistant manager.

The China Prison Camp Fight Continues

About a year after arriving in the U.S., Harry was invited to discuss his camp experiences before a class at the University of California, Santa Cruz. As he stood before the students, he quickly realized he was about to become a voice speaking for the many thousands of forgotten prisoners who had perished in the Chinese gulag. While speaking, he began to shed tears, which rolled down his cheeks, but the students were transfixed by what Harry had to say.

Two years after the UC-Santa Cruz speech, Harry met with the curator of the East Asian Studies Department at the Hoover Institute at Stanford University. The curator wanted to discuss his great interest in discovering all he could about China's forced labor prison system and its numerous camps.

Wu told the department curator about his own time in the camps. Intrigued, the curator invited Wu to become a visiting scholar at the institution. That gave Harry a further incentive to begin compiling a catalogue of China's prison camp system, the laogai, translated as "reform through labor."

In 1992, Harry published his book *Laogai: The Chinese Gulag* after he had made several trips to China documenting the existence of the labor camps. He even risked his own imprisonment or worse by secretly recording dialogue and images with camera and video.

Return to China

In June 1995, only days after I interviewed him, Harry Wu embarked on his fourth fact-finding trip to China. He attempted to determine whether or not there may be a link between China's loans from the World Bank and the prison camps. As he reached the Kazakhstan border, however, he was captured and imprisoned as "one of China's most wanted criminals."

For two frightening, harrowing months, Harry was held under constant guard. His arrest sparked an international incident. Chinese officials convicted him of stealing state secrets, but, bowing to outside pressure, instead of keeping him in prison, they expelled him for life from China.

"I Was Not a Hero"

In his book *Troublemaker*, Wu wrote:

> *I came back from the land of the skeletons. I was not a hero. I would have to turn myself into a beast many times, fighting and bullying and lying and confessing, but I would survive ... I want to expose the system [laogai]. I am the needle in the heart, the bone in the throat. Truth is on my side. I went back to China and came out with evidence of evil. This is just the beginning.*

Gathering the Honors

Well before his final trip to China, Harry Wu was already gathering a number of awards. These include the following:

- The Freedom Award from the Hungarian Freedom Fighters' Association (1991);

- The first Martin Ennals Award for Human Rights Defenders (1994);

- The Courage of Conscience Award by the Peace Abbey in Sheraton, Massachusetts (1995);

- The Dutch World War II Resistance Foundation's Medal of Freedom (1996);

- Honorary degrees from St. Louis University and the American University of Paris (1996);

- The Columbia Human Rights Law Review's Award for Leadership in Human Rights (1996);

- Honorary doctorate from the Institute of World Politics, Washington, D.C. (2012); and

- Member of both the International Advisory Council of the Victims of Communism Memorial Foundation and the International Council of the Human Rights Foundation.

Harry Wu also had the honor of showing the Dalai Lama an exhibit at the Laogai Museum on October 7, 2009.

Illegal Transplants Continue

China began its organ transplantation policy in the 1960s. Today, it is one of the largest such programs in the world. In 2004 alone, more than 13,000 transplants were performed in China. This increase can be partly credited to the ongoing practice of prematurely executing prisoners for their organs.

China still claims that it does not support or conduct involuntary organ harvesting. A regulation enacted in the country in 1984, however, made it legal for surgeons to remove organs from executed prisoners irrespective of prior consent from the criminal or obtaining permission from relatives. By the beginning of the 1990s, numerous medical groups and associations along with human rights organizations began condemning the practice. Concerns about the practice again came to light in 2001 when a Chinese doctor seeking asylum said he had performed illegal organ extraction operations.

In 2006, the word started getting out that many prisoners in the Falun Gong system had been executed with the sole purpose of supplying China's lucrative organ transplant industry. Results of an investigation said that there continues to be large-scale organ extractions from unwilling Falun Gong prisoners.

In December 2005, China's Health Ministry finally admitted that the practice of removing organs from executed prisoners for transplants was widespread. In 2007, the Chinese government issued regulations banning the commercial trading of organs. This move was backed by the Chinese Medical Association. Despite these actions, however, in August 2009, *China Daily* reported that around sixty-five percent of transplanted organs were still being derived from prisoners in the country's death row system.

In 2014, Ethan Gutmann, a journalist-investigator, interviewed former inmates in Chinese prisons and labor camps. He also talked with former medical professionals and security officers with extensive knowledge of the country's transplant practices. He reported that, between 2000 and 2008, approximately 64,000 Falun Gong prisoners may have been executed in order to obtain their organs for transplantation.

Conclusion

Up until this writing in 2016, reports kept circulating that China was still providing organs extracted from executed prisoners even though its official departments continue to condemn that practice. This is borne out in part by the fact that China has what is considered "by far the shortest wait time for organ transplants in the world." Also, it is believed that prisoner executions are "timed for the convenience of the waiting recipient."

Foreigners needing organs who have the money (usually in the $30,000-to-$60,000 range) to pay for them can often get them within days of arriving in China. One credible report said: "It may take only one week to find the suitable [kidney] donor, the maximum time being one month." This is compared to up to six years in Canada, four years in Australia, three years in the United Kingdom, and 3.6 years in the United States.

Meanwhile, Harry Wu continued his fight against not only China's dismal human rights practices but of those in other parts of the world as well. However, while taking a well-deserved vacation in Honduras, Wu suddenly died on April 26, 2016. He will long be remembered as a human rights advocate *par excellence*.

Chapter Ten
Quick Takes: From Baltimore to Stockholm

Felix Robert Mendelssohn

In the late 1940s, I began taking piano lessons from a lady in my hometown, Solomons Island, Maryland, at the urging of my father. Dad wanted all three of his sons to become accomplished on musical instruments. My brother, Jon Shaw, also began his guitar lessons.

It was my youngest brother, Joe, however, who rebelled against wanting to become a musical genius. Dad was hoping that his sons would eventually form an assembly that could not only entertain him and our mother and house guests but also perform at outside functions.

This little story, however, has Joe and his violin teacher as the main protagonists. My piano teacher later became Leroy Evans, an accomplished pianist and Baltimore Symphony Orchestra choral director at the Peabody Conservatory of Music in Baltimore, which I later attended for a year (1957-1958). Joe's teacher had a classical composer's name: Felix Robert Mendelssohn. He was the great grand nephew of the renowned German composer of the same name.

Uncle Felix had been a towering name in nineteenth century classical music with such compositions as the *Overture to a Midsummer Night's Dream* (1826), the *Scottish Symphony No. Three in A Minor* (1842) and the *Concerto in E Minor for Violin and Orchestra* (1844).

Nephew Felix never knew his famous great grand uncle, who died long before he was born on September 27, 1896, in Berlin, Germany. In 1937, four years after Adolph Hitler and the Nazi Party came to power, Felix escaped to the United States. In 1942, during the height of World War II, he found a place as a cellist with the Baltimore Symphony Orchestra. He was also a *kapellmeister*.

Dad had somehow learned that Felix was giving private violin and cello lessons above a seventy-eight r.p.m. record store in mid-town Baltimore. This, he thought, would be the perfect teacher for brother Joe. After all, his ancestor was one of the classic composers from the nineteenth century.

Dad had given Joe an old violin that had belonged to his father, Joseph Cobb Lore. He called Felix and arranged for Joe's first lesson.

I was only thirteen or fourteen at the time (the year was 1949 or 1950) and was already a fan of Uncle Felix's great music. I even had a few of his compositions on seventy-eight r.p.m. records. I wanted to meet his ancestor with the same name.

Our mother, Dora Lore, bundled Joe and I into dad's new Buick along with the violin. Mom and I were enthusiastic about meeting Mendelssohn, but Joe could have cared less. He was only nine or ten and had no desire to become a concert violinist.

After arriving in Baltimore, we entered the record store, the old-fashioned kind where you could go into glass-enclosed booths to listen to records prior to buying them. Then we climbed a series of winding steps to Mendelssohn's studio. I immediately discussed his famous uncle's music

Chapter Ten: Quick Takes: From Baltimore to Stockholm

with him. He was particularly impressed by the fact that I was a fan of the *Double Concerto for Violin, Piano, and String Orchestra in D Minor* (1823), which his uncle had composed at the young age of fourteen. It was nephew Felix's favorite composition by his uncle.

Then it was down to business. Felix asked Joe to play something. Joe lifted the violin from its case and began a simple melody he had been practicing. Felix quickly began fingering a tuft of hair that was standing erect on his head. Then his head began to violently shake.

"No! No! No!" he exclaimed. "Where did you learn that, *Meester* Joe?"

Felix grabbed the violin and played the composition the way it should be played. Joe and mother were embarrassed. At the end of that first lesson, it was already clear that Felix thought Joe would never make a decent violinist let alone find a place as a soloist or in a symphony orchestra.

The second lesson a few weeks later was even worse. As we were ready to leave, Mom asked Felix if he thought Joe had any potential as a performing violinist. His answer left no doubt about what he thought.

"No! No! No! *Nein! Nein! Nein!*" he exclaimed. "He will never make a good violinist! He doesn't even like it! Can't you *zeee* that?"

Mom and Joe were clearly convinced, but Dad wasn't. When we got back home, he insisted that Joe have one more lesson. He called Mendelssohn, begging the teacher to let Joe have another lesson with him. Reluctantly, Felix agreed. Dad possessed the power of persuasion, a factor that made him respected and rich in his business ventures. Dad also later told me that he gave Mendelssohn $50, which was considerably more than the maestro charged for his lessons.

The third lesson was an unmitigated disaster. Joe had been practicing a simple composition at home and managed to completely slaughter it when he vainly attempted to perform it for Felix. Grabbing tufts of his hair in both hands, Mendelssohn went to the open window of his second-story studio, put his foot on the ledge and cried: "*Meeezes* Lore, if you don't get him out of here, I will jump out *zee* window and kill myself!"

Mom quickly got the hint. She hastily put the violin back in its case, grabbed Joe and me and practically pushed us down the stairs. Halfway down the steps, mother looked back. She was afraid that the maniacal music teacher might be right behind us. That was the last we saw of Felix Robert Mendelssohn, the great grand nephew of the renowned nineteenth century composer.

Many years later, I learned that Mendelssohn was also a celebrated concert cellist. His career was short-lived, however. I read that, while giving a solo cello concert at Cadoa Hall in Baltimore, he suddenly keeled over and died of an apparent heart attack at the age of only fifty-three.

Claire Bloom and John Neville

One of the most enjoyable short encounters I had with an actor or actress occurred when I met Claire Bloom and John Neville. I had read in *The Washington Post* that these two popular stage and screen actors were slated to appear in their road tour production of William Shakespeare's *Romeo and Juliet* (1597) at the National Theater in Washington, D.C., in 1957. I was ecstatic. I was in love with Claire and fantasized about us being together. She was also only five years older than me!

I put in extra hours on my father's oyster boat to earn the money to pay for the ticket. On the evening of the performance, after parking dad's 1957 Buick, I decided to take a short walk prior to entering the theater. A block or so later, I saw a couple heading toward me. It was Bloom and Neville leisurely strolling toward the theater. I quickly walked up to them, a bit flustered, my heart beating fast.

"Hello, Miss Bloom, Mr. Neville," I greeted. "I'm here to see you both in *Romeo and Juliet.*"

"Well, thank you." Claire responded. "I hope you enjoy it."

"I'm sure I will," I said. "I've seen several of your films and I just wanted you to know how much I enjoyed your performances."

"Thank you again," she remarked. "I haven't made very many yet. Which ones did you see?"

"There was your movie debut with the great Charlie Chaplin in *Limelight* in 1952 followed by *The Man Between* [1953] with James Mason," I replied. "Then you played Queen Anne with Laurence Olivier in *Richard III* in 1955, seen here in the United States last year. I'm sure there will be many more to come."

"That's right," Claire remarked. "You know your movies."

"What's your name?" John Neville asked.

"Gordon Lore," I answered. "I live about seventy miles south of here on the Chesapeake Bay."

"We both hope you enjoy the play," Claire interjected. "You'll have to excuse us. We still have things to do before the curtain goes up."

"It was a pleasure meeting you both," I remarked, "and I'm sure I'll love your performances as the two most famous characters to emerge from the pen of the Bard-of-Stratford-on-Avon."

Claire and John both smiled at that.

"Will we have time to invite him backstage for a short visit after the curtain falls?" Claire asked her co-star.

"I wish we could, Claire, but I'm afraid we don't have the time," Neville answered.

"I'm sorry, Gordon," Claire remarked. "We hope you enjoy the play."

"I'm sure I will," I replied. "'Knock 'em dead,' as they say."

I did enjoy the play and couldn't take my eyes off Claire. At the age of twenty-six, she was a bit too old to play a fourteen year-old girl, but that was standard in the theater. I still loved her as Juliet. Famed film critic Kenneth Tynan agreed with me, saying Bloom's performance was "the best Juliet I've ever seen."

The plaudits for Claire Bloom continued. Following her stage performance as Blanche Dubois in Tennessee Williams' Pulitzer Prize-winning play, *A Streetcar Named Desire* (1947), the playwright himself exulted: "I declare myself absolutely wild about Claire Bloom!"

During her long career, Claire acted alongside such major stars as Richard Burton (with whom she had a torrid love affair), Yul Brynner, Sir John Gielgud, Paul Newman, Sir Ralph Richardson, Paul Scofield, George C. Scott, and the man who would later become her husband, Rod Steiger (see Chapter Six).

John Neville was also well on his way to an illustrious career. He played a number of classic leading roles at London's Old Vic Company and gained fame in the title role of Shakespeare's *Richard II*. I'll always remember him, however, with the beautiful Claire Bloom in *Romeo and Juliet*.

At the Peabody

As a lover of classical and folk music, I had the opportunity of becoming a student at the prestigious Peabody Conservatory of Music in Baltimore. (At the time, the Peabody was considered to be in second place as a music conservatory, just behind the Julliard School of Music in New York City). I majored in voice and piano. My teacher, Professor Frank Leon Bibb, said I had a promising baritone voice. He led me through numerous piano and voice lessons and was my accompanist during my solo concert of folk songs.

Professor Bibb became one of the three main mentors in my life. His three-story town-home near the Peabody was filled with music. He owned what was then considered as one of the largest private collections of opera libretto and music manuscripts in the world. He had previously used many of these during solo concert performances with such opera soprano divas as Lily Pons.

On nearly every Saturday from 1957 to 1965, the year he passed away, a group of devoted students gathered in Bibb's home to listen to the Metropolitan Opera broadcasts. I was in charge of following the music and libretto of these compositions from Bibb's extensive collection. There was not a single opera produced by the Metropolitan during those broadcasts to which he did not have the manuscript.

During the last quarter of 1965, Professor Bibb passed away. I still miss him and honor his memory.

I consider my time at the Peabody as the best single year of my overall schooling. The building itself was constructed in classical Victorian style and boasted one of the largest library collections of Victorian literature in the world. I remember seeing there a First Folio display of William Shakespeare's works from the last year or two of the sixteenth and the first few years of the seventeenth centuries on loan from the Folger Library in Washington, D.C.

Jesse Levine

My best friend during my year at the Peabody was Jesse Levine, a promising violist. He lived next door to me in the student boarding house about a block from the Peabody.

Jesse was only seventeen when I first met him. But, even then, he could make his musical instrument sing. We spent many evenings together discussing classical music.

Our friendship continued for several months after I left the Peabody and shortly before I was drafted into the U.S. Army on December 2, 1958. Even at his young age, Jesse had become a violist with the National Symphony Orchestra in Washington, D.C. I happened to unknowingly sit beside his girlfriend at one of the concerts. She was surprised to learn that Jesse and I were friends. We had a brief meeting in the concert hall and hoped we would meet again soon. We never did, however.

Jesse went on to become the principal violist with the Buffalo Philharmonic Orchestra (BPO). During his distinguished career, he was a soloist, professor, chamber musician, conductor, and music director. He performed in Australia, Europe, Israel, Mexico, South America, and throughout the United States.

Along the way, Jesse became the solo violist on a number of motion pictures. To this day, I still look at the final credits of some of the older films to see if his name shows up. Sadly, Jesse Levine passed away from pancreatic cancer on November 11, 2008.

"Jess was a wonderful guy," said his friend, Charles Haupt, the BPO's concertmaster for thirty-seven years. "He was one of the best violists of his generation and an extremely gifted conductor."

A similar sentiment was expressed by famed cellist and Yale professor Aldo Parisot: "He had the most beautiful vibrato, the most beautiful sound I have ever heard. The sound of Jesse Levine was something unique . . . He used to say that I gave him the vibrato, and he taught me how to conduct. . . ."

I Aim at the Stars

I have always been a life-long movie buff and practically lived in movie theaters while I was growing up. My most interesting film experience came in 1960 when I was in the U.S. Army stationed at DeWitt Army Hospital, Fort Belvoir, Virginia, where I was the Medical Librarian.

Chapter Ten: Quick Takes: From Baltimore to Stockholm

My First Sergeant knew of my great interest in films and picked me and four other non-commissioned officers to attend the American premiere of *I Aim at the Stars*, the story of German rocket scientist Wernher von Braun. My Army companions and I were to be among the many others attending the celebrity-laden function on September 28, 1960. The film would be shown at Loew's Palace Theater in Washington, D.C.

Our First Sergeant had no further information on the event or who would be there. When we arrived at the theater in an Army bus, we were ushered into the theater on a red carpet by the U.S. Herald Trumpeters, the U.S. Army Band and, as icing on the cake, the U.S. Army Chorus.

What had I gotten myself into? I wondered. I made sure my tie was straight, brushed some lint from my uniform, and ran a comb quickly through my hair while everyone watched. We were seated in the front row of the theater with strong overhead lights beaming down on us. I was a little uneasy. We were on display, but I took comfort in knowing we were the honored guests.

The theater was filled with not just any celebrities. They were the *crème-de-la-crème* of society. Leading the way was First Lady Mamie Eisenhower. (I was told that President Dwight D. Eisenhower was slated to attend, but had to cancel at the last minute.) Others who were in the theater—most of whom I got to briefly meet in the reception line after the showing of the film—included both the current Second Lady and future First Lady Pat Nixon.

The Welcoming Remarks were by Lieutenant General Leslie R. Groves, USA (Ret.), who had led the Manhattan Project to develop the atomic bomb during World War II. He was also the current President of the Army Distaff Foundation, Inc.

The main attraction on the stage before the showing of the film was the man everyone came to honor: famed rocket scientist Dr. Wernher von

Braun, who gave the Introduction. He praised the film and star Curt Jurgens' performance while acknowledging that, true to Hollywood form in such biopics, he was never in love with sexy co-star Gia Scala.

Following Von Braun was Curt Jurgens, who played Von Braun. He briefly described the making of the film and the rocket scientist's career.

After the film, my fellow soldiers and I were honored to briefly meet these celebrities in the reception line. Von Braun's handshake was firm and Mamie Eisenhower thanked us for our service to the country. General Groves had a pleasant handshake. He wished me "good luck." We were then escorted back over the red carpet to our bus.

It was all a true film buff's dream.

* * *

I knew a little about Von Braun and his career before I saw *I Aim at the Stars*, but was anxious to know more. I visited several libraries, including the one at Fort Belvoir and the Library of Congress in Washington. I discovered that he was born in 1912 and, by 1960, was one of the most important rocket developers and champions of space exploration. This lasted until his death in 1977.

Before I met Von Braun and for a time after that, I had mixed feelings about the scientist. He had been a Nazi who was involved with *Verein fur Raumschiffarht*, the German rocket society, as early as 1929. In 1932, at the young age of twenty, he began working for the German Army developing ballistic missiles.

Soon, Von Braun gathered together what became known as his "rocket team" to develop the V-2 ballistic missile during World War II. The V-2s were built at a forced labor factory at Peenemunde on the Baltic coast. The rocket later became the forerunner of those used in space exploration programs in both the U.S. and the Soviet Union. The rockets were used against civilians in several countries, the most prominent being England during the infamous Blitz in 1940-1941.

When it became clear that Germany was losing the war in Europe, Von Braun led the surrender of himself and 500 of his top scientists, along with the rocket plans and test vehicles, to the American Army. After relocating to the U.S., he worked with the Army to develop ballistic missiles, which were tested at White Sands Proving Grounds, New Mexico.

By 1950, Von Braun and his team relocated to the Redstone Arsenal near Huntsville, Alabama. There they built the Jupiter ballistic missile. Later, they constructed the Saturn rockets. Von Braun had become the director of NASA's Marshall Space Flight Center and was the architect of the Saturn V launch vehicle. This was the booster rocket later used to propel American astronauts to the moon.

In 1972, Von Braun retired from NASA. His retirement was short-lived, however. He died in Alexandria, Virginia, on June 16, 1977.

The Duke of Windsor

In February 1961, I was on the last leg of my three-month journey through Europe and the Near East as I stepped aboard the luxury liner, S.S. *United States*, in Southampton, England. The weather was relatively calm during the first leg of the trip to Cobh, Ireland. As we left Ireland, however, a fierce storm with near-hurricane-force winds descended on the ship. Having been born and raised on the shores of the Chesapeake Bay, I was used to strong storms. Many of my fellow passengers, however, were not so lucky. For two days, the high winds and waves battered the liner. Passengers in all three classes were sick.

Normally, lifeboat and lifejacket drills were held shortly after leaving Ireland, but they had to be delayed until the storm had passed. On a clear, sunny day, passengers from throughout the ship assembled on the top deck. We began putting our lifejackets on while waiting for crewmembers to show up to provide whatever assistance was necessary.

I sat down on one of the lounge chairs. Suddenly, I felt a hand on my shoulder.

"Young man, would you be kind and help me with my lifejacket?" the voice asked.

"Certainly," I responded.

I stood up and saw that I was facing an elderly gentleman who had his head lowered while struggling with his lifejacket. I grabbed the strings of his jacket and led them around to his back, where I tied them securely.

Then I faced the gentleman and saw that it was the Duke of Windsor, the former King Edward VIII of England. I knew that he and the Duchess were scheduled to be on board, but never thought I would even catch a glimpse of them during the voyage. The Duchess was still ill from the storm and had not recovered enough to join the drill.

"Thank you very much," the Duke said. "Where are you from?"

"A little town on the shores of the Chesapeake Bay in Maryland," I remarked.

"Oh, yes," the Duke responded. "Near Washington, D.C."

"Yes sir," I answered.

"A lovely area," Windsor responded. "I have visited there, but I would like to know more about you and where you are from. Would you join me in first class for a drink?"

"I would be honored," I replied.

As we began our walk toward the First Class lounge, we were approached by a member of the crew, who said the Duchess had requested the Duke's immediate attention.

Chapter Ten: Quick Takes: From Baltimore to Stockholm

"Sorry, young man," the Duke apologized. "Maybe we can have that drink before we arrive in New York."

That drink with the Duke never materialized, but I was anxious to know more about him. After all, I never expected to meet the only *former* king in the thousand-year history of the British monarchy. All the other monarchs had died while still ruling the country.

I already knew a little about the Duke. It was common knowledge that he had abdicated the throne in December 1936 for the woman he loved... Wallis Simpson from Baltimore, Maryland, which happened to be my second home until well into my thirties. Wallis was a divorcee, which threw an additional curve into the abdication procedure, causing what many believed to be the greatest constitutional crisis in British monarchial history.

After returning home, I made a quick trip to the Library of Congress, where I learned more about the Duke's abdication. At his Accession Council on December 12, 1936, King George VI created the title His Royal Highness the Duke of Windsor for his brother. It was a one-time creation that would expire when Windsor died and would never be used again.

The dukedom derives its name from the town where Windsor Castle is located. The castle has been the home of British monarchs since the time of Henry I following the Norman Conquest.

I also knew that the Duke had been the Governor of the Bahamas. I believe it was while he was in that post that I heard he may have been a Nazi sympathizer but still supported his country with the outbreak of World War II.

The Duke of Windsor died in 1972, eleven years after I met him. The duchess followed him in 1986.

I still remember the Duke of Windsor as a kind gentleman who invited me into the First Class lounge of the S.S. *United States* for a drink that we never had. I toast his memory with a hearty shot of King's Bay rum.

King Gustaf VI Adolf

During one of my two trips to Europe in the early 1960s, I boarded the S.S. *America* in New York for the five-day Atlantic crossing to Southampton, England. From there, I journeyed by train to Bergen, Norway, where I unexpectedly ran into my first cousin, Sarah Jane Zahniser, and two of her friends, who were on their own personal tour. Together, we traveled down through Scandinavia. In Copenhagen, we danced and swayed to the music of Louis ("Satchmo") Armstrong and his orchestra in Tivoli Gardens. The Danes were crazy about Satchmo and so were we.

Then we found ourselves in Stockholm, Sweden. During our first day there, the three girls had their own early morning plans, and I was left on my own.

I began to walk through the Swedish capital, stopping at one of the travel agencies to pick up a brochure. There was a lot in the brochure about Stockholm Palace, a sprawling, impressive building that, I thought, must be centuries old. I was right. It had been the home of Swedish royalty since about 1700, when construction began on it about the same time as the beginning of what was known as the Great Northern War.

With my thirty-five millimeter slide camera at the ready, I walked past two of the Royal Guards whose compatriots had guarded the palace and the Royal family since 1523 and entered through the huge front doors. I quickly came upon the massive Hall of State.

The hall was truly impressive with its high ceiling chandeliers and huge rectangular windows. At first, I thought I was alone. This was still before the advent of the tourist season. In the back of the hall, I saw an elderly gentleman sitting alone. He wore thin-framed rather unimpressive glasses and was dressed in a light gray suit. I decided to approach him.

"*God morgon*," I greeted in my very limited Swedish. "Do you speak English?"

"I do, young man," he answered. "Are you from America?"

Chapter Ten: Quick Takes: From Baltimore to Stockholm

"Yes, sir," I replied. "I'm from the state of Maryland on the Chesapeake Bay."

"I know of that area," the gentleman remarked. "Near Washington, D.C, your national capitol."

"That's correct, sir," I continued. "Are you also a visitor?"

"You could say that," he answered with a wry smile. "I live here in another part of the palace."

Suddenly, what he said sunk in. I quickly consulted my guidebook and gulped: "May I ask you name?"

"I believe you may already know it by now," he replied with a knowing smile. "It's Gustaf."

I couldn't help it. I blurted it out: "You're Gustaf Adolf, the King of this lovely country!"

"*Bingo*, I think you Americans might say. What is your name?"

"Gordon Lore," I answered. "I'm from a family that has been in the seafood business for about a hundred years or more."

"What do you do?" Gustaf pressed on.

"I work with my father in the seafood business now, but I aspire to be a professional writer and editor." I replied.

"I believe the Chesapeake Bay has some of the finest seafood in the world," the King stated.

"It does have that reputation," I responded. "Oysters, crabs, and the prized rockfish, in particular."

This opened the door for the King to elaborate on his own interests. He told me he had amassed a library of many thousands of books. (At the time of his death in 1973, he had a personal library of around 80,000 volumes on a wide variety of subjects.) His main interests included archaeology (he even participated in digs in China, Greece, Italy, and Korea), art, architecture, history, botany, fly-fishing, and sports.

I quickly surmised that, even though Adolf was the King, he eschewed most of the pomp-and-circumstances trappings. A modest monarch. Someone willing to talk to a wandering American visitor. I decided I had taken too much of his time. He wished me a pleasant visit and firmly shook my hand.

As I left the palace, I felt honored to have briefly met the very personable King of Sweden.

Anne Revere

I have been a lifelong fan of both film and stage. In 1962, I saw Anne Revere in a small theater production of Tennessee Williams' first Broadway-bound play *The Glass Menagerie* (1945). Anne played Amanda Wingfield, a mother in conflict with her crippled daughter and confused son. The sparse production was staged in a small 100-seat theater-in-the-round in Washington, D.C.

I was in the first row of seats only inches from the same-level action on stage. There was no curtain, just the open stage closely surrounded by the theatergoers.

As I waited for the play to begin, I reflected on Anne Revere and her films. She was born in Manhattan, New York, in 1903. She was also a direct descendant of famed Revolutionary War patriot Paul Revere.

As a talented actress, Revere found a place for herself in Hollywood playing the stoic, wise, loving mother to a number of top stars from Hollywood's Golden Age. She was nominated for a Best Supporting Actress Oscar three times for playing the mother of Jennifer Jones in *The Song of Bernadette* (1943), Elizabeth Taylor in *National Velvet* (1944), and Gregory Peck in *Gentleman's Agreement* (1947). She took home the gold statuette for *National Velvet*. In 2009, Heritage Auctions sold her Oscar for $89,625!

In 1951, Anne's Hollywood career quickly ended for nearly twenty years. She had been a member of the American Communist Party and her name was included on the infamous Hollywood Blacklist. Returning to New

York, she again found work on the stage and received a Tony Award for her performance in Lillian Hellman's *Toys in the Attic* (1960-1961). By 1970, she was occasionally acting in a few movies and daytime soap operas.

During Anne's appearance in Washington in *The Glass Menagerie*, I became so drawn in to her performance that she noticed my enthusiasm. I was the first to yell "Bravo, Anne!" when the play ended.

I wasn't sure that Revere had noticed me, but she had. As the lights dimmed, she leaned over to me.

"You really liked the play, didn't you, young man?" she remarked.

"I did indeed," I responded. "You were great, better than Gertrude Lawrence in the 1950 movie."

"Thank you," she said, smiling. "Would you like to come backstage for a short visit?"

"I would love to," I responded.

"Give me about five minutes," she said as the applause died down. She took her final bow with the rest of the four-person cast.

I waited the five minutes and hurried backstage. Anne was alone in a small, cramped, disheveled room.

"Have a seat," she directed as I headed toward a small chair beside her small makeup stand.

I introduced myself and told her about my interest in films and the stage. I was still two years away from having a one-act play of my own entitled *An Evening's Entertainment* (1964) produced onstage by the Market Playhouse in the Georgetown section of Washington, D.C.

"I have followed your career and know you won the Academy Award for *National Velvet* and played the mother of the characters of a number of major stars," I remarked.

"I have had that good fortune," Anne responded. "What did you like about my acting?"

"I remember you vividly in two small parts that I thought were terrific," I elaborated. "The first was the way you lovingly handed Cary Grant's newborn baby over to him in *The Howards of Virginia* [1940] and as the mother of Montgomery Clift's character in *A Place in the Sun* [1951]. The look of mournful sorrow and regret on your face was a great job of acting. Simple but very effective."

I spent a few more minutes with Anne as she quickly prepared to leave the theater with a few friends. She wished me good luck and I left the theater, never to see her again. It was another very brief but welcome interlude I had with a celebrity. I later learned that Anne Revere died in December 1990, at the age of eighty-seven in Locust Valley, New York.

Mikhail Soloviev

In the Fall of 1966, I was living in the swanky Georgetown section of Washington, D.C. Danny Cunningham, a friend, called me at my subterranean apartment a short walk from Georgetown University. He wanted me to meet at a nearby restaurant a man whom he described as "a truly remarkable individual" and good friend. He said I should bring along my copy of the book *When the Gods Are Silent* (1952). It is a novel about a Russian dissident's fight against both the Nazis in World War II and the MGB—the Soviet Foreign Secret Police—after the global conflict.

"Why should I bring the book?" I asked.

"Because you are about to meet the author," Danny responded.

Enough said. The novel by Mikhail Soloviev is a 506-page masterful chronicle largely based on the author's own story. I took the book from my well-stocked library and hurried to the restaurant where I met this remarkable man and urged him to tell his story. I gave him the book and he in-

Chapter Ten: Quick Takes: From Baltimore to Stockholm

scribed: *"To Mr. Gordon Lore, with many best wishes. Mikhail Soloviev, October 26, 1966, Washington, D.C."*

Over drinks, this distinguished-looking man who was still wearing a fur-laced overcoat, sketched out the story of his life in near-perfect English:

> *I was born in the cold Russian steppes in 1908. Following the Russian Revolution in 1917, I was a student at Moscow University where I majored in writing... After that, I became an editor with Izvestia, the government newspaper.*

> *After World War II broke out in 1939, I was drafted into the Soviet Army and fought against the Germans when they invaded Russia. I was slightly wounded and taken prisoner. With a few other men, I managed to escape.*

Soloviev sipped his drink while Danny and I sat transfixed. Mikhail continued with his story:

> *With other Russian soldiers, I fought behind the German lines with one overwhelming thought: we would eventually break our beloved Russia out of the stranglehold that Adolph Hitler and Joseph Stalin had on the good people of both the Soviet Union and Germany. Stalin may have been a hero to some, but, to us, he was a dictator who had to be deposed. Even then, Russian prisons were being filled with anyone who spoke against the Soviet government and its leaders.*

"What about after the war?" I asked. "How did you remain free?" Soloviev continued his story. Danny had heard it before, but I was transfixed:

> *Shortly after the war ended in 1945, the MGB began hunting for me and some of the other compatriots. Fortunately, I was saved from being repatriated by a prominent American official in Austria as well as*

by the assistance of some friendly American officers who hid me in a centuries-old jail. It was while I was in this jail that I managed to get some writing material and began my novel.

In 1948, while I was living in Salzburg, Austria, the Soviet government again demanded that I be arrested and returned to Russia. Fortunately, however, U.S. Senator Arthur Vandenberg, along with the U.S. Commander-in-Chief in Austria, were able to keep me from being sent back to my homeland. Following that, I published my own anti-Communist newspaper I called The Flames. *In 1951, I came to the United States and continued my writing.*

Soloviev told us that no words could really accurately depict the horrors of war—of seeing dead and wounded soldiers lying in the cold snow—and the struggle of the good soldiers and others to fight and survive it. We finished our drinks while Mikhail said he had someone else he had to meet. We shook hands while I thanked him for relating his remarkable story. I never saw him again, but I still have my weathered autographed copy of his great book. It tells the story of a band of soldiers and others who tried to break the stranglehold that Communism had on not only Mother Russia, but much of other parts of the world as well.

Mikhail Soloviev wrote and published a few others books, including *Notes of a Russian War Correspondent* (1954). It is *When the Gods Are Silent*, however, that is the *magnum opus* for which he will be remembered.

In the White House

It was well-known that, like her feisty colleague, Helen Thomas, long-time White House Press Corps member Sarah McClendon has often been described as "the bane of Presidents." Neither of these no-nonsense women

Chapter Ten: Quick Takes: From Baltimore to Stockholm

would back down if they thought the President or White House Press Secretary Pierre Salinger was trying to pull the wool over their eyes.

I got to know Sarah when I first came to the White house with my press card in 1971. I was an Associate Editor with *Public Utilities Fortnightly* Magazine in Washington, D.C. The magazine was then the premier journal in the public utilities and environmental arenas. It was read every two weeks by the President, members of his cabinet, and many Congressional representatives. I was also a member of the U.S. Senate and House of Representatives Press Gallery.

During my first or second visit to the White House, I sat down next to Sarah. I introduced myself to her and asked if she knew someone who could sponsor me for membership in the National Press Club. As other reporters were finding seats waiting for Pierre Salinger to appear, McClendon grabbed my hand, motioning for me to rise.

"I'll be happy to sponsor you, Gordon," she remarked, "but you'll need two sponsors. I've got just the person."

Like a mother leading her child, Sarah quickly walked me over to someone standing beside some large photo bags. I immediately recognized Dan Rather. He still had some time to go before becoming one of the Big Three in television news reporting.

Dan held out his hand for a firm handshake and welcomed me to the White House. He readily agreed to be my co-sponsor.

"Watch out for this lady, Gordon," Rather remarked, smiling. "She doesn't take crap from anybody."

I thanked Dan for agreeing to be my co-sponsor and returned with Sarah to our seats. We still had a few minutes so I asked her to tell me a little about herself.

Sarah said she was born in the little town of Tyler, Texas, in 1910 as the youngest of nine children. In 1931, she graduated from the University of Missouri's School of Journalism. After working with several small-town newspapers, McClendon enlisted in the Women's Army Auxiliary Corps in 1942 during World War II.

Sarah didn't tell me much else herself since the press conference was about to begin. I later discovered that she made history as the first Army officer to give birth to a baby in a military healthcare setting, Walter Reed Army Hospital in Bethesda, Maryland. Following the war, she went on to bigger and better things. After establishing her own agency, the McClendon News Service, she regularly attended White House Press conferences asking her pointed, no-nonsense questions. She later wrote a book about her fifty years as a White House correspondent.

Dan Rather still had a way to go before he hit it big-time. For twenty-four years (1981-2005), he was the *CBS Evening News* anchor. With Tom Brokaw at *NBC News* and Peter Jennings at *ABC News*, Dan was one of the "Big Three" news anchors.

It was during my first few months as a White House press representative that I had the opportunity of joining Sarah, Dan and others in the Oval Office with President Richard M. Nixon and Environmental Protection Agency (EPA) Administrator William Ruckelshaus. The occasion was for the signing of a special initiative to help improve the quality of the air and water within the confines of the United States.

Even today, I am still somewhat reluctant to admit that, when I entered the Oval Office, I had not yet been cleared to do so. There was confusion among those jockeying to get in after Pierre Salinger announced that those who had the credentials to enter the Oval Office could do so. There was scrambling among the reporters for a good vantage point as we streamed through the small entranceway to the heart of the most famous house in America. I followed the crowd of reporters and found myself standing only a few feet from the President while Ruckelshaus and a few others were positioning themselves behind Nixon seated at his desk.

I then made what I later considered an incredibly stupid move. I impulsively stepped away from my place with the other reporters and walked straight up to the President's desk. I could hear a soft gasp from my colleagues. Out of the corner of my eye, I saw one of the Secret Service men lining the walls begin to move his hand inside his dress coat.

Jeeeezzz, I thought, a little shaken. *Is the son-of-a-bitch going to shoot me?*

But the President wasn't worried. He made an up-and-down calming motion with his right hand toward the agent, who quickly relaxed. Nixon gazed up at me and smiled. He didn't seem to be the slightest bit flummoxed. I also had the feeling that he knew who I was.

"Blue skies and blue water," he said, still looking straight at me. "That's our motto for this year."

Then he picked up the pen and signed the initiative. Back in my office later that day, I quickly typed an article with that motto, which was published in the next edition of *Public Utilities Fortnightly.* Hopefully, the President, Sarah, and Dan read the article.

I returned to the Oval Office one more time in a more subdued position at the back for another initiative I don't now remember. It was my time with my then friend and short-time mentor, Sarah McClendon, however, that I still remember with no small degree of fondness.

Joseph Cotten and Sal Mineo

In 1974, my wife, Marty, stepson, Jay Triche, and I moved from Maryland to Los Angeles, California. Our first residence was in an apartment on Horn Avenue above the famed Sunset Strip. There was an upscale neighboring apartment building next to us where actors Joseph Cotten and Sal Mineo lived. It was Cotten whom I had the opportunity of interacting with, although I did see Sal Mineo on several occasions outside his apartment building.

I was particularly interested in meeting Joseph Cotten. As a delivery boy for a local liquor company, my stepson, Jay Triche, had already met the actor. I had always enjoyed Cotten's work beginning with his major supporting role in Orson Welles' cinematic masterpiece, *Citizen Kane* (1941). He and Welles remained good friends until the *wunderkind* director's death. They starred together again in two more Welles-directed films, *The Magnificent Andersons* (1942) and *Journey Into Fear* (1943).

I ran into Cotten on two occasions as we were both taking our nightly walks. During our second visit, he invited me to sit with him at a table in the outdoor patio of his apartment building. I told him I most enjoyed him starring with Jennifer Jones and Gregory Peck in *Duel in the Sun* (1946). He informed me that Jones and his wife had been good friends. He also worked with Jennifer in *Since You Went Away* (1946).

"How did you get along with the great Orson Welles?" I asked.

"Fine," he answered. "Orson was real young when he was working on that film in 1940 and 1941 . . . Just twenty-two, I think. He was a real boy genius. People have said he was difficult to work with, but I didn't find him that way. He was easy-going with me, patient while leading me through my first movie role. He was awe-inspiring."

"I know the film was loosely based on newspaper mogul William Randolph Hearst, who tried to sabotage the film," I related.

"You're right there," Cotten replied. "Hearst did everything he could to kill it before it was even completed. He directed all his reviewers not to critique or even mention it. He dominated the country's press with his powerful newspapers and he forbade even mentioning the film. Heaven help any of his reporters or reviewers if they did. This was probably the main reason it wasn't a big box office success."

Citizen Kane may not have been a financial success, but it did remain their pick as the greatest movie ever made by a list of international critics for over forty years.

When I met Cotten, he was still in demand for smaller parts in Universal International films. I remembered seeing him in *The Abominable Dr. Phibes* (1971) with Vincent Price and *Solyent Green* (1973) starring Charlton Heston and Edward G. Robinson. After obtaining a part in Michael Cimino's *Heaven's Gate* (1980)—a box office bomb but what I thought was a highly underrated film which came to life for me in its extended uncut four-hour version—he turned his back on Hollywood. On February 6, 1994, Joseph Cotten died of pneumonia in Los Angeles.

I never directly interacted with Sal Mineo, but did see him on two different occasions outside his apartment building and during one of my nightly walks. He was with other people at the time.

I was never a big Mineo fan overall, but did admire his work as James Dean's friend in *Rebel Without a Cause* (1955) and in *Exodus* (1960) with Paul Newman and Eva Marie Saint. He was nominated for a Best Supporting Actor Oscar in both films.

Only a few months after we moved into our new home in the Hollywood Hills, Sal Mineo met an untimely end. On the evening of April 12, 1976, he was stabbed to death by a demented pizza deliveryman.

Susan Strasberg

In 1977 or 1978, my wife, Marty, worked for a public relations firm that represented the City of Hope, a world leader in the research and treatment of cancer, located in Duarte, California. I had the opportunity of accompanying her to one of the medical center's annual fund drives. Numerous celebrities were expected to attend.

Great food and an abundance of drinks were served in the large banquet room. I ordered a rum and coke and wandered off on my own as Marty talked with some of the guests. Then I saw one of my favorite actresses, the beautiful Susan Strasberg, standing alone beside a wall looking somewhat forlorn. I walked over, introduced myself and offered to freshen her drink. She gratefully accepted. As a fan, I had been in love with her since seeing her first two films, both released in 1955, *The Cobweb* and *Picnic*. Her performance as the frisky teenager in *Picnic* blew me away.

"Susan, it is such a pleasure meeting you," I gushed.

"Thank, you, Gordon," she replied. "What do you do?"

"I work as the Editor of the employee newspaper at Rockwell International in Canoga Park," I remarked.

"Oh, yes, I know about Rockwell," Susan retorted.

"I am also a big movie fan and you have been one of my favorite actresses since I first saw you in *The Cobweb* and *Picnic*," I continued, sipping my drink. "I also thought you gave a great performance in *Kapo* [1959]. You were wonderful in *Scream of Fear* [1961] and *Adventures of a Young Man* [1962], based on the younger years of Ernest Hemingway. I know you are the daughter of Lee Strasberg at the Actors Studio in New York and that you were a good friend of Marilyn Monroe."

"That's right," Susan replied, smiling. "I loved Marilyn and I miss her dearly. She was my best friend at the time and a much better actress than most people gave her credit for. She was great in *Bus Stop* [1958] and *Some Like It Hot* [1959]. She could drive you crazy sometimes, but she was still a beautiful soul with a spiritual knowledge few people knew about."

I took Susan's glass and replenished her drink as I reflected on her career. In 1955, she hit it big on her own by winning the title role in the Broadway production of *The Diary of Anne Frank*. She was nominated for a Tony Award at the young age of eighteen. She was also the youngest actress on Broadway to have her name above the marquee title. Later that same year, she graced the covers of both *Newsweek* and *Life*.

Following my third trip to the bar to refill Susan's drink (I believe it was Scotch and water), she was approached by several others, including the actor Bo Svenson, which ended my being alone with her. I waved goodbye to her as Marty and I left and she waved back.

Dear Marty. She was pissed. She had seen me mooning over Susan like a teeange boy. She didn't speak to me for a week. Bless her.

Later, Susan wrote two best-selling books. These included *Bittersweet* (1980) in which she described her tumultuous relationship with her parents, particularly her father. She also discussed her equally rocky love affairs with Richard Burton and Christopher Jones, whom she later married. Her other book was *Marilyn and Me: Sisters, Rivals, Friends* (1992). She called Monroe a "surrogate sister" in that tome.

Susan was also instrumental in producing two 1982 documentary films on her friend: *Remembering Marilyn* and *Marilyn Monroe: Beyond the Legend*. Prior to her marriage, she reportedly had love affairs with Cary Grant, Richard Burton, and Warren Beatty.

I also had my own unrequited love affair with Susan Strasberg. I just wasn't as lucky as Grant, Burton, or Beatty.

Years later, I was saddened to learn that Susan died on January 21, 1999, in New York, of breast cancer, a fate that also ended the life of my wife Marty.

Sam Iacobellis and the Cold War Gamble

Sam Iacobellis. The name itself conjured up a man in both the United States and Russia who was described as gregarious, charming, and energetic with unflappable aplomb.

As President of the Energy Systems Group at Rockwell International in

Canoga Park, California, Sam was my upstairs boss. I was the editor of the *Rockwell News*, a bi-weekly newspaper that went to thousands of employees engaged in critical work ranging from the Space Shuttle, the B-1 bomber, rockets, and nuclear energy.

Iacopbellis was tireless, known for working nearly twenty-four hours a day on critical projects with little or no sleep. He got jobs done with lightning speed.

I remember that, around 1980, a small delegation of four Japanese officials toured the facilities at the Energy Systems Group. As part of my duties at the group's public relations department, I was chosen to greet and host these visitors. Iacobellis was also keeping an eye on me.

Sam was a live wire and occasionally watched as I feted the visitors, who were grateful for my meticulous attention. They were lavished with the best food and drinks. They moved slowly and gracefully and I tried to do the same. Iacobellis, however, became frustrated. Things just weren't happening fast enough for the tireless, fast-paced chief.

Sam complained to my immediate boss and I was reprimanded. That quickly changed, however, when the gentlemen from Japan told Iacobellis that they thought I was an excellent host who did what he could to accommodate their needs. I was even given several small gifts, including handsome figures and elaborately decorated cards. *Whew!* I was out of the doghouse.

Sam called me into his office and graciously apologized to me. He also cleared the decks with my immediate supervisor.

Not long after this, in mid-1981, I left Rockwell and moved to begin a new spiritual life in Taos, New Mexico. Only a month or so later, the first Space Shuttle flew and safely landed, putting Rockwell squarely into the center ring of Washington politicians.

Meanwhile, Sam Iacobellis was quickly hitting it big. His name and expertise were quickly spreading through the political corridors of the nation's capitol. Shortly after I left Rockwell, newly-elected President Ronald Reagan tapped Sam Iacobellis to head a nationwide team of experts in the creation of 100 B-1 bombers in record time. Sam quickly accepted the challenge.

"We felt this was a national emergency program," he remarked. "We worked like we were on the front line of the Cold War."

From my home in New Mexico, I read that Sam intended to deliver 100 of the bombers to the nation's military arsenal. I had seen the prototype B-1 at Rockwell's Southern California headquarters. It was a sleek, pure black wonder that could put any other plane to shame. Producing 100 of them in a relatively short period of time would be a gigantic task. Iacobellis, however, was up to the challenge.

The overall project would require an expenditure of $20.5 billion and was considered "a cornerstone of Reagan's strategy to end the Cold War by engaging the Soviets in a costly arms race that would threaten them with bankruptcy."

It was a bold and dangerous move. The idea was to show the Soviets that such a fleet of highly technical aircraft would serve to deter war, not start it. American intelligence officials knew the Russians couldn't match it and would fear they were in real danger if war was declared. It was the ultimate effort to ensure peace with the buildup of a mighty aerial arsenal. It was also a huge improvement over the older B-52 fleet of aircraft.

At a price tag of $220 million each, the B-1 could fly only 200 feet off the ground, surge ahead at speeds up to 900 miles per hour, carry twenty-two cruise missiles, fly without refueling for eleven hours at a stretch, and quickly surge ahead from a standstill on the ground to an altitude of 10,000 feet in less than two minutes. Sam Iacobellis also flew the B-1 himself—twice.

Not long after word got out about the B-1 fleet, several Russian astronauts and generals shared their thoughts with Robert Cattoi, a former Rockwell chief engineer.

"One of them asked me, 'Do you know Sam Iacobellis?'" Cattoi related to the *Los Angeles Times*. "If you see him, tell him he was far more responsible for ending the Cold War than he might realize. We didn't have the resources to match [the B-1 program]. It was the straw that broke the camel's back."

Following the fall of the Berlin Wall and the ending of the Cold War in 1989, Sam Iacobellis and General Pyotr Deinekin, former commander of the Russian air force, traded models of the B-1 and a Soviet imitation of the aircraft. Deinekin wrote to Iacobellis: "We both should be pleased that our airplanes did not have to see each other in combat."

Sam retired after forty-three years at Rockwell. He was one of three corporate operating officers responsible for such high-priority projects as the company's rocket, aircraft, and spacecraft operations, which included the space shuttle. Later, Boeing bought Rockwell's aerospace and military business.

Less than a month before writing this account, I was saddened to learn that Sam Iacobellis died on September 3, 2016, from complications of a stroke.

Nathaniel Branden and Ayn Rand

In January 1985, my wife, Marty, and I were living in Hollywood, California. We were having marital problems and were looking for what we called "a quick fix" to resolve them. We had read the two main works of Ayn Rand, the controversial author of *The Fountainhead* (1946) and, particularly, *Atlas Shrugged* (1957).

We also knew that Rand had dedicated her *magnum opus*, *Atlas Shrugged* (the mammoth novel that a team of international reviewers voted as the most influential book of the twentieth century) to Nathaniel Branden. Nathaniel was a well-known psychologist who had been Rand's lover and chief promoter of her philosophy of objectivism.

Nathaniel and his wife, Devers, announced that they were holding a

Chapter Ten: Quick Takes: From Baltimore to Stockholm

weekend therapy session at a swanky hotel in Los Angeles. We quickly called and made arrangements to attend.

Marty and I gathered together with about fifteen other couples in the hotel meeting room. It was there that Branden, in order to break the ice, immediately jumped into what he knew everyone wanted to know: his affair with Ayn Rand. It would still be a couple of years before he would publish his own book about his relationship with the controversial author, *Judgment Day: My Years with Ayn Rand* (1989). Everyone settled comfortably into their chairs as Branden began:

> Devers and I know what you came here to hear. Yes, I was Ayn Rand's lover and a defender of objectivism, the philosophy she so beautifully expounded in The Fountainhead and Atlas Shrugged. In 1950, I read *The Fountainhead* and was taken with the philosophy of the main character, Howard Roark. I began exchanging phone calls and letters with Ayn, which I also shared with my lover, Barbara Weidman.
>
> At Ayn's invitation, Barbara and I visited with her and her husband, Frank O'Conner, at their home here in Los Angeles. We immediately became good friends. We spent hours discussing our mutual interest in philosophy.
>
> In 1953, Barbara and I were married with Ayn and Frank at our side. Ayn was nearly thirty years older than me, but our mutual love of her books and philosophy spurred amorous feelings. With Barbara and Frank's rather reluctant consent, Ayn and I began our affair in 1954. This lasted until 1957 with the publication of *Atlas Shrugged*. After that, Ayn became depressed and our affair ended.

"Why did Ayn become depressed?" someone asked.

Branden responded:

I think it may have been that she had invested so much of her own self and her philosophy into our affair. She had also worked so hard on Atlas Shrugged *that, at times, she became depressed, afraid that she would never finish it.*

Ayn spent a full two years working on the famous John Galt speech. She knew this would be the heart of the book and thought she would never be able to pull it off. She also had a fight with her editor, Bennett Cerf, who wanted her to leave it out because, as he put it: "What John Galt has to say is already in other parts of the book. It just bogs the reader down."

But Ayn held her ground. The speech comprises only fifty pages in the 1,000-page book, but it is the one part of the book that everyone talks about. So much for what even a famed editor like Bennett Cerf knows. . . .

At this point, I raised my hand and Branden pointed his finger at me.

"I was really taken by it," I said. "Having been an amateur actor and playwright in the 1960s, I actually carefully recorded it on reel-to-reel tape. It was three hours long. I have heard it three times, once with Marty. We became true Ayn Rand fans after that. We even shared it with some friends, all of whom had taken a shine to Rand's philosophy."

"That's interesting to hear, Gordon," Branden responded. "I'd like to hear it sometime."

That never happened, of course, but I kept the tape for many years, until it was lost during one of our many moves.

Branden continued his discourse:

In 1968, Ayn and I broke up. Then she wrote an article accusing me of several offenses. These included having an irrational attitude toward her philosophy and what she termed "unresolved psychological prob-

lems." I had no choice but to send out a letter to the members of the Nathaniel Branden Institute, which I had started in 1958, partly as a tribute to Ayn's dedicating Atlas Shrugged to me. I denied the accusations and offered my belief that Ayn had denounced me because of my unwillingness to continue our love affair.

This was an amazing discourse from a prominent psychologist. It was only the beginning of an intense weekend of marital problems put through the wringer of psychological cleansing. Both Marty, the love of my life who passed away from cancer in 2002, and I credited Nathaniel and Devers Branden's therapy with saving our marriage.

Branden had written several books during and after his relationship with Rand. These included *The Psychology of Self-Esteem* in 1959, followed by *How to Raise Your Self-Esteem* in 1987. It was his 1989 book *Judgment Day: My Years with Ayn Rand*, however, that became a top best-seller.

The one thing that I remember most about the weekend session was Branden's statement that a reason for his breakup with Rand centered on her failure to fully appreciate "the importance of kindness in human relationships." Rand had been a steel-like champion of objectivism with a self-centered heart that wouldn't bend. Nonetheless, she was still the author of two towering books in American literature.

I was saddened to learn that Nathaniel Branden had passed away on December 3, 2014, due to complications from Parkinson's disease. He was eighty-four.

Donald O'Connor

In 1992, as the Associate Editor of *Dimensional Stone* and *Tile & Decorative Surfaces* magazines, I made a trip to Seattle, Washington, to attend a trade show. As I began returning to Los Angeles inside the Seattle-Tacoma Airport, I saw Donald O'Connor sitting by himself in a small alcove. I sat down beside him and introduced myself. He said he was waiting for some ladies to pick him up for an appearance at one of their functions.

I had remembered O'Connor as the boyish actor who could dance his legs off. Very athletic. Boyish and charming. Bouncing. He more than proved that with Gene Kelly and Debbie Reynolds in *Singin' in the Rain* (1952), which some critics still rate as the best Hollywood musical. Donald won a Golden Globe for Best Performance by an Actor in a Comedy or Musical. His remarkable rendition of "Make 'Em Laugh" helped get him the Globe.

I told O'Connor that I had recently seen him in *I Love Melvin* (1954) with Debbie Reynolds and that I enjoyed his interaction with her even more than in *Singin' in the Rain*. He seemed to agree.

"Debbie was great in that," O'Connor told me. "I just love her. A real charmer and a great lady. Did you see her in *The Unsinkable Molly Brown* [1964]?"

"I did," I responded, but I didn't tell Donald that I wasn't particularly impressed by her performance in that film. I thought it was a bit overdone, even for her.

[On December 28, 2016, Debbie Reynolds died from the complications of a stroke at the age of eighty-four. Many pundits said that the feisty actress may have died from what they termed the "broken heart syndrome" only one day after her beloved daughter, Carrie Fisher, passed away from a heart attack following an eleven-hour flight from London to Los Angeles.]

I told Donald that I had read somewhere that one of his regrets was that he missed a chance to star as Bing Crosby's partner in *White Christmas* (1954). I asked him about that.

"It was that damned mule," he responded. "I was slated to play with Bing, but caught some kind of infectious disease from Francis. It was Danny Kaye who took my place. I can't complain, though. I've had a great career."

(In 1949, O'Connor began playing the lead role in a series of Francis the

Talking Mule films. One of these films was churned out every year until 1955.)

"I also thought you were great in *Call Me Madam* [1953] and *There's No Business Like Show Business* [1954] with Ethel Merman and Marilyn Monroe, among many others," I continued.

"Ethel was great," Donald said, smiling. "I loved her."

I was with O'Connor for less than fifteen minutes before he was whisked off for his engagement. On the plane back to Los Angeles, however, I reflected on his career.

Donald O'Connor began performing in films in 1937, appearing opposite Bing Crosby in *Sing You Sinners* when he was only twelve. From there, there was nowhere to go but up. He signed with Universal Pictures in 1941 and appeared in seven B-film musicals in a row, then graduated to A-films. On his eighteenth birthday in August 1943, during World War II, he was drafted into the U.S. Army.

After his release from the Army, Donald continued acting in films, television, and the stage up until about the time I met him. Two years before that, in 1990, he had quadruple heart bypass surgery. He also nearly died from complications of double pneumonia in 1998. He passed way from the effects of heart failure at seventy-eight on September 27, 2003, in Woodland Hills, California.

Ken Howard

One of the most enjoyable one-on-one interviews I had was with Ken Howard, the late President of the Screen Actors Guild/American Federation of

Television and Radio Artists (SAG-AFTRA), in 2005. I was the editor of two magazines in the kidney disease and renal transplantation arena. One of these journals was *For Patients Only*, the only magazine devoted strictly to those with kidney disease. The interview took place from my office in Woodland Hills, California.

At a tall six-feet-six, Ken was a towering figure with a pleasant smile and friendly personality. He was probably best known for his role as a basketball coach in the popular television series *The White Shadow* (1978-1981). It was partly based on his own experience as the only white player on an all-black high school basketball team.

Ken had also won a Tony Award for Best Supporting or Featured Actor in a Play in 1970 for *Child's Play*. I had remembered him best in the role of Thomas Jefferson in both the Broadway musical play and film *1776* (1969 and 1972). His co-star was Blythe Danner, the wife of Bruce Paltrow. Blythe and Bruce were the parents of Gwyenth Paltrow, Best Actress Oscar winner for *Shakespeare in Love* (1998), whom Ken considered as a surrogate daughter.

I asked Ken to outline the events leading to his diagnosis of kidney failure and beyond:

> *I was feeling lousy ... tired all the time. I checked it out with my doctor, who examined me and told me he could find nothing wrong. I believed that maybe I was working too hard, which caused me to not feel well, but it was being really fatigued most of the time that concerned me. Not a good thing as a serious working actor. I probably should have gotten a second opinion, but didn't at the time because I felt my doctor's diagnosis was correct.*
>
> *Finally, I did get a second opinion. It was bad news. The doctors discovered a blockage in my urinary tract that had been backing up, effectively dealing a potentially lethal blow to my kidneys. The docs*

Chapter Ten: Quick Takes: From Baltimore to Stockholm

discovered that my kidneys were working at only thirty percent of their function.

I had a procedure to remove the blockage, but my kidneys were so badly damaged that my doctors told me I would probably need a renal transplant in about five years. Sure enough, five years later my kidneys had failed to a point that another kidney became necessary. I was placed on the waiting list, but like many others waiting for a life-saving organ, it could take several years before one became available. I would have to find a live donor if I was going to live much longer.

My wife, Linda, volunteered to give me one of her kidneys, but, unfortunately, she was not a compatible donor. She did, however, discuss my condition with our dear friend, Jeannie Epper, a well-known stuntwoman who worked on such projects as the Wonder Woman *[1975-1979] TV series. As it turned out, she was a perfect match. I am forever indebted to her. She is a rare friend to whom the words 'thank you' just aren't enough for such a life-saving gift.*

At the time of our interview, Howard was a spokesperson for both the American Kidney Foundation and the American Association of Kidney Patients.

Howard told me he had recently finished his role in the film, *In Her Shoes* (2005), with Shirley MacLaine, Cameron Diaz, and Toni Collette. He said he had fun sparring with MacLaine when the Oscar winner (*Terms of Endearment* [1984]) discussed her involvement in spiritual and metaphysical matters, especially reincarnation. He said he loved Shirley but didn't believe in many of her views on the subject.

With his new kidney, Ken went on to be elected the National President of SAG in September 2009. He then led the fight to combine SAG with AFTRA. Two of his strongest supporters in this role were Academy Award winners Tom Hanks and George Clooney. The two unions finally merged and Ken Howard became the SAG-AFTRA President until his death on March 23, 2016, in Valencia, California, at the age of seventy-one.

I fondly remember my interview with this exceptional actor. He had even invited me to his lovely new home in the very upscale Toluca Lake section of Burbank, California (near the late Bob Hope's estate), but I could not make it because of a prior commitment.

This encounter with Ken Howard touched me deeply. He was one of the true dialysis and kidney transplant patients whose indomitable spirit enabled him to make a lasting contribution to the artistic, theatrical, and film communities and to inspire others with disabilities to achieve their highest goals.

My interview with Howard was a high point in my lifelong journey through the world of celebrity. Other highlights on this odyssey came through the good graces of those personalities in a wide variety of occupations. Their accomplishments, good graces, and willingness to share their thoughts about their lives helped make my own life more imbued with a genuine sense of gratitude that such enlightened, learned, spiritual, and giving individuals have graced my world . . . and now yours.

References

The Accused (1988 film). From *Wikipedia*, the free encyclopedia @ https://en.wikipedia.org/wiki/The_Accused_(1988_film).

Admin, The Truth About Betty Hill's Star Map, August 19, 2011.

An assassination attempt threatens President Harry S. Truman. November 1, 1950. History @ www.history.com/this-day-in-history/an-assassination-attempt-threatens-president-harry-s-truman.

Douglas and Barbara Anderson, *Chaco Canyon: Center of a Culture*, Southwest Parks and Monuments Association, Globe, Arizona, 1981.

Karla Araujo. James Cagney's Island Refuge. Martha's Vineyard @ www.nymagazine.com/news/2012/05/01/james-cagney%E2%80%99s-island-refuge.

Asmodeus. From *Wikipedia*, the free encyclopedia @ https://en.wikipedia.org/wiki/Asmodeus.

Astronotes. Armagh Planetarium's Stellar Blog! @ www.amaghplanet.com/blog/betty-hills-ufo-star-map-the-truth.html.

ATSabovetopsecret @ www.abovetopsecret.com/forum/thread1108871/pg1.

Danielle Bacher, Oliver Stone Looks Back at 'JFK.' The Oscar winning filmmaker on the legacy of the Kennedy assassination and the problems plaguing America today. *Rolling Stone*, November 4, 2013.

Alben W. Barkley. From *Wikipedia*, the free encyclopedia @ https://en.wikipedia.org/wiki/Alben_W_Barkley.

Alben W. Barkley, 35th Vice President (1949-1953). United States Senate. Senate History @ www.Senate.gov/artandhistory/history/common/Senate/VP_Alben-Barkley.htm.

W. Kamau Bell, The Star of the Original "Roots" explains Why The Remake Is Must-Watch Television. *Mother Jones*, May/June 2016.

Beverly Hot Springs @ www.beverlyhotsprings.com/about-us/water/.

Joan Blondell. From *Wikipedia*, the free encyclopedia @ https://en.wikipedia.org/wiki/Joan_Blondell.

Calabasas, California. From *Wikipedia*, the free encyclopedia @ https://en.wikipedia.org/wiki/Calabasas_California.

Claire Bloom. From *Wikipedia*, the free encyclopedia @ https://en.wikipedia.org/wiki/Claire_Bloom.

Hale Boggs. Check-Six.com. Offering Aviation History & Adventure First-Hand! @ www.check-six.com.

Hale Boggs. From *Wikipedia*, the free encyclopedia @ https://en.wikipedia.org/wiki/Hale_Boggs.

Gaddie Windage, #CollisionWithFame: Hale Boggs 1972, October 16, 2015 @ www.gaddiewindage.com/2015/10/collisionwithfame-hale-boggs-and-nick.htm/.

Boggs, Corinne Claiborne (Lindy), 1916-2013. History, Art & Archives, United States House of Representatives @ http://history.gov/People/Listing/B/BOGGS,Corinne-Claiborne-(Lindy)-(8000592)/.

Lindy Boggs. *Wikipedia*, the free encyclopedia @ https://en.wikipedia.org/wiki/Lindy_Boggs.

Lindy Boggs with Katherine Hatch, *Washington Through a Purple Veil: Memoirs of a Southern Woman*. Harcourt Brace & Company, New York, San Diego, London, 1994.

Thomas Hale Boggs, Jr. *Wikipedia*, the free encyclopedia @ https://en.wikipedia.org/wiki/Tommy_Boggs.

Adam Bernstein, Thomas H. Boggs, Jr., dead at 73. *The Washington Post*, September 15, 2014.

Thomas Hale Boggs Sr. Missing Veterans, October 16, 1972 @ www.missingveterans.com/1972/thomas-hale-boggs-sr/.

Bram Stoker's *Dracula* (1992). IMDb @ www.imdb.com/title/tto103874/.

References

Nathaniel Branden, *Judgment Day: My Years with Ayn Rand*. Houghton Mifflin Company, Boston, 1989.

Nathaniel Branden. *Wikipedia*, the free encyclopedia @ https://en.wikipedia.org/wiki/Nathaniel_Branden.

Nathaniel Branden-obituary, *The Telegraph* @ www.telegraph.co.ok/news/obituaries/113857724/Nathaniel-Branden-obituary.html.

Wernher von Braun. From *Wikipedia*, the free encyclopedia @ http://en.wikipedia.org/wiki/Wernher_von_Braun.

Dr. Wernher von Braun. MSFC History Office. Marshall Space Flight Center, Huntsville, Alabama @ http://history.msfc.nasa.gov/vonbraun/bio/html.

Wernher von Braun. V2 Rocket.com @ www.v2rocket.com/start/chapters/vonbraun.html.

Gary Brumburgh, Anne Revere. Biography. IMDb @ www.imbd.com/name/nm0720843/bio.

Mark Burns, War Returns to Solomons. Did you Miss World War II in Calvert County? *New Bay Times*, Volume VI, Number 31, August 6-12, 1998.

LeVar Burton. Celebrity. *TV Guide* @ www.tvguide.com/celebrities/levar-burton/162007/92804.

LeVar Burton. IMBd @ www.imbd.com/name/nm0000996/.

James Cagney Biography. IMBd @ www.imbd.com/name/nm0000010/bio.

James Cagney. From *Wikipedia*, the free encyclopedia @ https://en.wikipedia.org/wiki/James_Cagney.

James Cagney Photo. The Place. Celebrity Photos @ www.theplace2-ru/photos/James-Cagney.

James Cagney's Island Refuge, Martha's Vineyard @ www.mvmagazine.com/news/2011/05/01/james-cagney%E2%80%99s-island-refuge.

Chaco Canyon National Monument Things to Do. Virtual Tourist @ www.virtualtourist.com.

Pay Carney, 'Crossing Jordan' star deals with personal drama. CNN Headline News. CNN.com.

Chaco Culture National Historical Park. From *Wikipedia*, the free encyclopedia @ https://en.wikipedia.org/wiki/Chaco_Culture_National_Historical_Park.

Edward Champion, Richard Matheson: The Man and His Fiction. Reluctant Habits. Posted on June 24, 2013 @ www.edrants/richard-matheson-the-man-and-his-fiction/.

Sarah Churchill Dead in London; Daughter of Sir Winston was 67. *The New York Times*, September 25, 1982.

Sarah Churchill (1914-1982), IMDb @ www.imdb/name/nmo1614681.

City of Hope @ www.cityofhope.org.

John Cloud, Carol Bula, Greg Fulton, Alice Park, Elaine Shannon, and Dick Thompson, The Lure of Ecstasy. *Time*, June 5, 2000.

CNN Politics, Obama's last Medal of Freedom ceremony: The recipients, Posted on November 22, 2016 @ www.cnn.com/11/22/politics.obama-medal-of-freedom/.

The Colusa UFO Sightings—September 10th, 1976. AboveTopSecret, May 7, 2012 @ www.abovetopsecret.com/forum/thread838143/pg1.

Dr. Edward U. Condon, *Final Report of the Scientific Study of Unidentified Flying Objects*. Bantam Books: New York, Toronto, London, January 1969.

Corcoran Gallery of Art. From *Wikipedia*, the free encyclopedia @ https://en.wikipedia.org/wiki/Corcoran_Gallery_of_Art.

Miles Corwin, Psychiatrists Defend New Street Drug for Therapy. *Los Angeles Times*, May 27, 1985.

Miles Corwin, U.S. to Ban Use of Drug MDMA. Street Abuse Cited: Used by Psychiatrists. *Los Angeles Times*, May 31, 1985.

Joseph Cotton. IMDb Mini Biography @ www.imdd.com/name/nm0001072/bio?ref_=nm_ov_bio_sm.

Volker Boehm and Mo and William McPeak, Joseph Cotton. IMDb Mini Biography @ www.imdd.com/name/nm0001072/bio?ref_=nm_ov_bio_sm.

Gerry Cunningham, Burl Ives Flicker "Sparrow." *Small Boat Journal* #55, July 1987 @ www.widgetssailor/sbjournal/bi/index/html.

Gerry Cunningham, Buccaneer or Balladeer? *Small Boat Journal* #55, July 1987 @ http://council.home.mindspring.com/sbjournal/sbjindex.htm.

Dalai Lama Visits the Laogai Museum, 2009. Laogai Research Foundation @ www.laogai.org/news/dalai_lama_visits_laogai_museum.

Mike D'Angelo, *White Heat* has an all-time great ending, even if it seems to come out of nowhere. A.V. Club @ www.avclub.com/article/white-heat-has-an-all-time-great-ending-even-if-100822.

Daphnis et Chloe. From *Wikipedia*, the free encyclopedia @ https: wikipedia.org/wiki/Daphnis_et_Chloe%3%A9.

Rev. Charles R. Daugherty, *Gordon Ira Rupert Lore: Mission Man*. Baybank on the Patuxent, Lexington Park, Maryland, August 1979.

Ruth Dean, Her Uncle Peter Was Tchaikovsky. *The Sunday Star*, Washington, D.C., October 9, 1960.

Mike Devlin. Where in the SCV? (Episode One: The Saugus Café). SantaClarita.com @ www.santaclarita.com/blog/view.php?blog_entity_id=21768.

Joe DiMaggio. From *Wikipedia*, the free encyclopedia @ https://en.wikipedia.org/wiki/Joe_DiMaggio.

Jeane Dixon. From *Wikipedia*, the free encyclopedia @ https://en.wikipedia.org/wiki/Jeane_Dixon.

Doshna, Alan. UFOs Over Hollywood! Reel vs. Real Flying Saucers. An Interview with UFO Writer & Researcher Gordon Lore. *FILMFAX*, The Magazine of Unusual Film, Television, & Retro Pop Culture, Summer 2015.

Claudia Glenn Dowling, The Trouble with Ecstasy. *Life*, August 1985.

Dracula (1979 film). From *Wikipedia*, the free encyclopedia @ https://en.wikipedia.org/wiki/Dracula_1979_film).

Roger Ebert, *Dracula* (1978). IMDb @ www.imdb.com/title/tto103874/.

Mamie Eisenhower. From *Wikipedia*, the free encyclopedia @ https://en.wikipedia.org/wiki/Mamie_Eisenhower.

Why Mamie Eisenhower loved pink-more insight from the Eisenhower National Historic Site, July 4, 2009. Save the Pink Bathrooms @ https://savethepinkbathrooms.com/why-mamie-eisenhower-loved-pink-more-insight-from-the-eisenhower-national-historic-site/.

Explore James Jimmy Cagney, Vineyard 1955, and more! Pinterest, the world's catalog of ideas @ www.pinterest.com/pin/5708313215267906/.

Jodie Foster. From *Wikipedia*, the free encyclopedia @ https://en.wikipedia.org/wiki/Jodie_Foster.

Gene Fowler, Speaking of Texas: Sarah McClendon. *Texas Highways,* the Travel Magazine of Texas @ https://texashighways.com/eat/item/165-speaking-of-texas-sarah-mcclendon.

Frank Freidel and Hugh Sidey, *The Presidents of the United States of America.* Copyright 2006 by the White House Historical Association.

Frank Gehry-Architect. E-Architect @ www.e-architect.co.uk/architects/frank-gehry.

Frank Gehry's Golden Fish Sculpture. Bacelona Lowdown @ www.barcelonalowdown.com/frank-gehrys-golden-fish-sculpture/.

Frank Gehry. From *Wikipedia*, the free encyclopedia @ https://en.wikipedia.org/wiki/Frank_Gehry.

Associated Press. Obama to honor Scully, Gehry. City & State. *Los Angeles Times,* November 17, 2016.

CTV News, Canadian Lorne Michaels, Frank Gehry receives Presidential Medal of Freedom. Posted on Novembe 22, 2016 @ www.ctvews.ca/.

David Sokol, 28 Spectacular Buildings by Frank Gehry. Architecture + Design. *Architectural Digest*, October 2014.

Katherine Skiba, Stars honored as Obama awards presidential medals. *Los Angeles Times*, November 23, 2016.

Jessica Gelt, 50 Moments in Music Center History. *The Los Angeles Times*, November 14, 2014.

Peter Gerstenzang, Joe Franklin Made Boredom Beatific. *The Village Voice*, January 25, 2015.

References

Megan Gibson, *Big* Remake Heading to the Small Screen. *Time*, October 1, 2014.

George Gobel. From *Wikipedia*, the free encyclopedia @ https://en.wikipedia.org/wiki/George_Gobel.

Shirley Griffith and Steve Ember, Burl Ives, 1909-1995; Actor, Singer Recorded Hundreds of Songs. Learning English @ http://learningenglish.voanews.com/114683.html.

General Leslie Groves. Atomic Archive.com @ www.atomicarchive.com/Bios/Groves.shtml.

Leslie R. Groves. Manhatan Project Director, Washington, DC. Atomic Heritage Foundation @ www.atomicheritage.org/profile/leslie-r-groves.

Mel Gussow, Susan Strasberg, 60, Actress Lauded in 'Anne Frank,' Dies. *The New York Times*, January 23, 1999.

Gustaf VI Adolf of Sweden. From *Wikipedia*, the free encyclopedia @ https://en/wikipedia/org/wiki/Gustav_VI_Adolf_of-Sweden.

Richard Hall Additional Sources: Richard Hall, NICAP's Former Director Donald E. Keyhoe. A Tribute. National Investigations Committee on Aerial Phenomena @ www.nicap.org/tribute.htm.

Stephanie Hanes, Lindy Boggs dies; Congresswoman and Democratic Leader, *The Washington Post*, July 27, 2013.

List of Tom Hanks performances. From *Wikipedia*, the free encyclopedia @ https://en.wikipedia.org/wiki/List_of_Tom_Hanks_Performances.

Daryl Hannah. From *Wikipedia*, the free encyclopedia @ https://en.wikipedia.org/wiki/Daryl_Hannah.

Rob Hart, Richard Matheson's 'I Am Legend' Named Vampire Novel of the Century. Posted on April 5, 2012. Lit Reactor @ https://litreactor.com/news/richard-mathesons-I-am-legend-named-vampire-novel-of-the-century.

Celia Hatton, Harry Wu: Chinese human rights campaigner dies at 79. BBC News. April 27, 2016.

Christopher Hawtree, Richard Matheson obituary, June 25, 2013. *The Guardian* @ www.theguardian.com/books/2013/jun/25/richard-matheson-I-am-legend.

Rita Hayworth. From *Wikipedia*, the free encyclopedia @ https://en.wikipedia.org/wiki/Rita_Hayworth.

Brain Herrera, Creative Common. Lesley Ann Warren. Archive of Supporting Actresses. StinkyLulu @ http://stinkylulu/blogspot.com.

High Beam Research @ www.highbeam.com/doc/LP2-27319106.html.

The History of Taos. Art + History @ http://taos.org/art/history.

History of the Solomons Area. Calvert Marine Museum @ www.calvertmarinemuseum.com/history.htm.

Ken Howard. From *Wikipedia*, the free encyclopedia @ https://en.wikipedia.org/wiki/Ken_Howard.

I Aim at the Stars. From *Wikipedia*, the free encyclopedia @ https://en.wikipedia.org/wiki/I_Aim_at_the_Stars.

I Aim at the Stars. Movie Poster Shop @ www.moviepostershop.com/iaim-at-the-stars-movie-poster/1960.

I Am Legend (novel). From *Wikipedia*, the free encyclopedia @ https://en.wikipedia.org/wiki/I_Am_Legend_(novel).

Burl Ives. Biography. IMDb @www.imdb.com/name/nm0412322/bio.

Burl Ives. From *Wikipedia*, the free encyclopedia @ https://en.wikipedia.org/wiki/Burl_Ives.

Burl Ives (1909-1995). IMDb @ www.imdb.com/name/.

Johns Hopkins Peabody Institute @ www.peabody.jhu.edu/conservatory/finances.html.

MacKinlay Kantor, American Author, by the Editors of *Encyclopedia Britannica* @ www.britannica.com/biography/MacKinlay-Kantor.

MacKinlay Kantor. From *Wikipedia*, the free encyclopedia @ https://en.wikipedia.org/wiki/MacKinlay_Kantor.

Papers of MacKinlay Kantor. MsC635. Iowa Author. Manuscript Register. Collection Dates: 1950-1958. Special Collections Department, University of Iowa Libraries @ www.lib.uiowa.edu/scva/tomsc650/msc635/kantor.html.

References

Donald Keyhoe. From *Wikipedia*, the free encyclopedia @ https://en.wikipedia.org/wiki/Donald_Keyhoe.

Major Donald E. Keyhoe, NICAP Breaks With Colorado Project: New Evaluation System, Expanded Network To Offset Project Failure. *The U.F.O. Investigator*, published by the National Investigations Committee on Aerial Phenomena, Vol IV, No 6, May-June 1968.

Donald E. Keyhoe (1897-1988). Who's Who in UFOLOGY @ www.hallrichard.com/keyhoe.htm.

NICAP's Former Director Donald E. Keyhoe. A Tribute. National Investigations Committee on Aerial Phenomena @ www.nicap.org/tribute.htm.

Alvin Krebs, Rita Hayworth, Movie Legend, Dies. On This Day. The *New York Times*, May 16 1987.

LA PHIL. About Walt Disney Concert Hall. Gustavo Dudamel @ www.laphil.com.

Laogai Research Foundation. About Us. Harry Wu, Founder @ www.laogai.org/About-Us#HarryWu.

Frank Langella. From *Wikipedia*, the free encyclopedia @ https://en.wikipedia.org/wiki/Frank_Langella.

Elyssa Lee, LeVar Burton Q&A. *Sactown Magazine* @ www.sactownmag.com/February-March-2012/LeVar-Burton-Q-A/.

Letter from Alexander and Ann Shulgin, Lafayette, California, to Gordon and Marty Lore, Taos, New Mexico, July 10, 1984.

Ryan Lewellen, Daryl Hannah. *The Archivist* Volume XII: Where My Tribe At? *The Clan of the Cave Bear* (1985) and *Greystoke* (1983), February 16, 2015 @ www.cinapse.co/tag/daryl-hannah/.

List of *Star Trek: The Next Generation* Cast Members. *WikipediA* The Free Encyclopedia @ https://en.wikipedia.org/wiki/List_of_Star_Trek_The_Next_Generation_cast_members.

G.I. Rupert Lore, Sr. Geni @ www.geni.com/people/G-I-Rupert-Lore/.

G.I. Rupert Lore & Sons. Lore Oysters. Facebook at www.facebook.com/Loreoysters/photos.

Gordon Lore, Witnesses Observe UFO Electrical Blackout, *UFO Research Newsletter*, Vol. V, No. 3, December 1976-January 1977.

Letters from Gordon Lore, Taos, New Mexico, to Alexander Shulgin, Lafayette, California, June 15 and July 5, 1984.

J.C. Lore & Sons Oyster House. Files: Lore Plaque. *Wikipedia*, the free encyclopedia @ https://en.wikipedia.org/wiki/File:Lore_plaque_Dec_08.jpg.

J.C. Lore & Sons Oyster House. PropTal. Chesapeake Bay. Spinsheet Publishing Company, Annapolis, Maryland @ www.proptalk.com/j-c-lore-oyster-house/.

Jesse Levine. "A Musical Feast. Musician Bios" @ www.amusicalfeast.com/bios.htm/.

New York Violist. Remembering Jesse Levine, Dec. 19, 2008 @ http://nyviolist.blogspot.com/2008/12/remembering-jesse-levine.html.

Life Stinks. From *Wikipedia*, the free encyclopedia @ https://en.wikipedia.org/wiki/Life_Stinks.

Huey Long, The Man, His Mission, And Legacy @ www.hueylong.com/legacy/index.php.

G.I. Rupert Lore, Sr. Geni @ www.geni.com/people/G-I-Rupert-Lore/6000000005427491989.

Gordon Lore, Disney Concert Hall: Space Age Alliance of Computer Technology and Stone. *Dimensional Stone* Magazine, April 1993.

Gordon Lore, Shocking Claims That China Secretly Uses Condemned Prisoners For Their Organs Are Presented in Congressional Testimony. *Contemporary Dialysis & Nephrology*, August 1995.

Gordon Lore, UFO Scorches Highway. *The U.F.O. Investigator*, Published by the National Investigations Committee on Aerial Phenomena, Vol. III, No. 12, March-April 1967.

J.C. Lore Oyster House. From *Wikipedia*, the free encyclopedia @ https://en.wikipedia.org/wiki/J._C._Lore_Oyster_House.

Tina Louise. Famous Birthdays @ www.famousbirthdays.com/people/tina-louise.html.

References

Tina Louise. From *Wikipedia*, the free encyclopedia @ https://en.wikipedia.org/wiki/Tina_Louise.

Catherine Mann. From *Wikipedia*, the free encyclopedia @ https://en.wikipedia.org/wiki/Catherine_Mann.

Catherine Mann. Obituary. *Los Angeles Times*, May 12, 2006.

Daniel Mann. From *Wikipedia*, the free encyclopedia @ https://en.wikipedia.org/wiki/Daniel_Mann.

Daniel Mann (November 21, 1991). Netcemetery @ www.netcemetery/org/letter.?.8=d.

Michael Barson, Daniel Mann, American director. *Encyclopedia Britannica* @ www.britannica.com/biography/Daniel-Mann.

Linda Marsa, Special to The Times, Ecstasy's good side. The much-maligned drug may ease the anxieties of the terminally ill. *Los Angeles Times*, April 11, 2005.

Richard Matheson. From *Wikipedia*, the free encyclopedia @ http://en.wikipedia.org/wiki/Richard_Matheson.

Richard Matheson. Amazon @ www.amazon.com/Richard-Matheson/e/8000A9285E.

Richard Matheson. CinemaRETRO @ www.cinemarctro.com/index.php?/categories/8-Book-NewsReviews/P3.html.

Sarah McClendon. From *Wikipedia*, the free encyclopedia @ http://en.wikipedia.org/wiki/Sarah_McClendon.

Sarah McClendon Papers. Category Archives. Uttylervase. Posted on August 30, 2013.

Grand Dames of the Press Corps: Sarah McClendon and Helen Thomas @ https://uttylervase.wordpress.com/category/Sarah-McClendon-papers/.

Theodore McKeldin. From *Wikipedia*, the free encyclopedia @ https://en.wikipedia.org/wiki/Theodore_McKeldin.

Theodore R. McKeldin (1900-197 4). MSA SC 3520-1484. Archives of Maryland (Biographical Series). Maryland State Archives.

Theodore R. McKeldin papers. University of Maryland. University Libraries @ http://digital.lib.umd.edu/archives.uml.

Theodore R. McKeldin modernized Maryland. Governor and mayor: Baltimorean envisioned today's airport and Inner Harbor, practiced racial equality. Marylanders Of The Century. *The Baltimore Sun*, August 31, 1999.

William McNamara. From *Wikipedia*, the free encyclopedia @ https://en.wikipedia.org/wiki/William_McNamara.

William McNamara, Kathy Naab, October 1988). "You Asked...". *Milwaukee Journal*. Retrieved 20 January 2016.

William McNamara. Morning Wood. Kenneth in the (212) @ www.kenneth-inthe212.com/2006/02/morning-wood-william-mcnamara.html.

MDMA. From *Wikipedia*, the free encyclopedia @ https://en.wikipedia.org/wiki/MDMA.

Edwin Meese. From *Wikipedia*, the free encyclopedia @ https://en.wikipedia.org/wiki/Edwin_Meese.

Felix Mendelssohn. From *Wikipedia*, the free encyclopedia @

https://en.wikipedia.org/wiki/Felix_Mendelssohn.

Felix Mendelssohn, Pianist, Conductor, Composer (1809-1847). Bio @ www.biography.com/people/felix-mendelssohn-40373.

Felix Robert Mendelssohn, Universitat Hamburg @ www.uni-hamburg.de.

Mendelssohn's Nephew Dies, May 13, 1951. *Pittsburgh Post-Gazette*, May 16, 1951.

Interview: James A. Michener, Pulitzer Prize-Winning Novelist. January 10, 1991. St. Petersburg, Florida. Academy of Achievement @ www.achievement.org/autodoc/printmember/micOint-1.

James A. Michener. BookFans @ http://bookfans.net/james-a-michener/.

James A. Michener. From *Wikipedia*, the free encyclopedia @ https://en.wikipedia.org/wiki/James_A._Michener.

Joshua Rhett Miller, Body of man who hunted 'Lost Dutchman's' gold mine believed found in Arizona mountains. FoxNews.com, November 29, 2012.

References

Sal Mineo. Sal Mineo website @ www.salmineo.com/picgallery.html. Sal Mineo. From *Wikipedia*, the free encyclopedia @ https://en.wikipedia.org/wiki/Sal_Mineo.

Miss Sadie Thompson (1953). IMDb @ www.imbd.com/title/tt0046076/.

Robert Mitchum. Movies & TV. *The New York Times*, Feb. 14, 2016 @ www.nytimes.com/movies/person/49738/Robert-Mitchum/biography.

Robert Mitchum. From *Wikipedia*, the free encyclopedia @ https://en.wikipedia.org/wiki/Robert_Mitchum.

Robert Mitchum, 79, Dies: Actor With Rugged Dignity, July 2, 1997. *The New York Times* @ www.nytimes.com/1997/07/02/movies/robert-mitchum-79-dies-actor-with-rugged-dignity.html.

The Playlist Staff, The 10 Most Essential Robert Mitchum Movies, April 29, 2015. Indie Wire @ www.indiewire.com/2015/04/the-10-most-essential-robert-mitchum-movies-264579/#.

Robert Mitchum. Turner Classic Movies @ www.tcm.com/tcmdb/person/133126%7C132297/Robert-Mitchum/.

Sun Myung Moon. The Reverend Sun Myung Moon, founder of the Unification church, died on September 3rd, aged 92. From the print edition of *The Economist*, September 8, 2012.

The Rev. Sun Myung Moon. *The Telegraph* @ www.telegraph.co.uk/news/obituaries/95/7193/the-Rev-Sun-Myung-Moon.html.

Rev. Sun Myung Moon, A Life of Love for God and Humanity @ www.reverendsunmyungmoon.org.

Reverend Sun Myung Moon. From *Wikipedia*, the free encyclopedia @ http://en.wikipedia.org/wiki/Sun_Myung_Moon.

The Moonies. Everything you wanted to know about Sun Myung Moon and the Unification Church @ www.perkel.com/politics/moonies/.

Robin Munro. Frontline Interview @ www.pbs.org.

Sam Neil. From *Wikipedia*, the free encyclopedia @ https://en.wikipedia.org/wiki/Sam_Neill.

John Neville. From *Wikipedia*, the free encyclopedia @ https://en.wikipedia.org/wiki/John_Neville.

Sarah Newcomb McClendon (1910-2003). The State Historical Society of Missouri @ http://shs.unsystem.edu.

Sam Neill, Biblio. *Evil Angels/A Cry in the Dark* @ www.biblio.org/samneill/pictures/actd/.

Nixon Presidential Library & Museum. Nixon Photo Gallery @ www.nixonlibrary.gov/virtuallibrary/gallery12.php.

Richard Nixon. Whitehouse.gov @ www.whitehouse.gov/1600/presidents/richard nixon.

Simon Oakland. From *Wikipedia*, the free encyclopedia @ http://en.wikipedia.org/wiki/Simon_Oakland.

Simon Oakland (1915-1983). IMDb @ www.imdb.com/name/nm0643000/.

Donald O'Connor. From *Wikipedia*, the free encyclopedia @ http://en.wikipedia.org/wiki/Donald_09%02TConnor.

Donald O'Connor, IMDb @ www.imdb.com/name/nm0640307/.

Mark Olsen, Actor and Hollywood union chief, Ken Howard, dies at 66. Obituaries. *Los Angeles Times*, March 24, 2016.

Thomas P. ("Tip") O'Neill and William Novak, *Man of the House: The Life and Political Memoirs of Speaker Tip O'Neill*. Random House, New York, 1987.

110 in the Shade (1963). *WilkipediA* The Free encyclopedia @ https://wikipedia.org/wiki/110_in_the_Shade.

Organ Donation and Transplantation Statistics. National Kidney Foundation @ www.kidney.org.

Organ Transplantation in China. From *Wikipedia*, the free encyclopedia @ https://en.wikipedia.org/wiki/Organ_transplantation_in_China.

Andrew X. Pham, Making Waves: Chinese dissident and human rights activist Harry Wu continues his fight to expose China's injustice system. Metroactive@ www.metroactive.com/papers/metro/11.27.96/harry_wu_9648.html.

References

Mike Power, Alexander Shulgin obituary, June 3, 2014. *The Guardian* @ www.theguardian.com/science/2014/jun/03/alexander-shulgin.

Alexander Poznansky, Pyotr Ilyich Tchaikovsky, Russian Composer. *Encyclopedia Britannica* @ www.britannica.com/biography/Pyotr-Ilyich-Tchaikovsky.

The Queen of Spades (opera). From *Wikipedia*, the free encyclopedia @ https://wikipedia.org/wiki/The_Queen_of_Spades_(opera).

Joan Quigley. From *Wikipedia*, the free encyclopedia @ https://en.wikipedia.org/wiki/Joan_Quigley.

Dan Rather. From *Wikipedia*, the free encyclopedia @ https://en.wikipedia.org/wiki/Dan_Rather.

Jerry Reynolds, Tales of the Saugus Café @ www.scvhistory.com.

About Cokie Roberts. Texas Tech University. Office of the President @ www.ttu.edu/administration/president/lectureseries/cokieroberts.php.

Cokie Roberts. Commentator, Morning edition @ www.npr.org/people/2101090/cokie-roberts.

Cokie Roberts. From *Wikipedia*, the free encyclopedia @ https://en.wikipedia.org/wiki/Cokie_Roberts.

Cokie Roberts. History, Art & Archives. United States House of Representatives @ http://history.house.gov/Oral-History/People/Cokie-Roberts/.

Sam Roberts, Sam Iacobellis, Whose B-1 Bomber Recast the Cold War, Dies at 87. *The New York Times*, September 8, 2016.

Stephen V. Roberts, White House Confirms Reagans Follow Astrology, Up to a Point. *The New York Times*, May 4, 1988.

Rockwell International. From *Wikipedia*, the free encyclopedia @ https://en/wikipedia.org/wiki/Rockwell_International.

Dennis Romero, High Time. *Los Angeles Times*, September 1, 1995.

Josh Rosenfield, Criterion Discovery. *The Night of the Hunter*. Audiences Everywhere. Posted on November 11, 2014 @ www.audienceseverywhere.net/criterion-discovery-night-hunter/.

Ethan Sacks and Nancy Dillon, Golden Globe Awards 2013: Jodie Foster says she's not retiring from acting despite confusion over acceptance speech for Cecil B. De Mille Lifetime Achievement Award. *Daily News*, January 15, 2013.

Self-Realization Fellowship Lake Shrine @ http://lakeshrine/about-lake-shrine/visiting.

Self-Realization Fellowship Lake Shrine Temple. Yelp @ www.yelp.com/biz/self-realization-fellowship-lake-shrine-temple-pacific-palisades.

Jack Shafer, MDMA: Psychedelic Drug Faces Regulation. *Psychology Today*, May 1985.

Ann Shank, Sarasota Authors Gathered Weekly. Sarasota History Alive! Sarasota County History Center @ www.sarasotahistoryalive.com/history/articles/sarasota-authors-gathered-weekly/.

Ann and Alexander "Sasha" Shulgen, the "godfather of MDMA" need our help. Drugs and Other Things, March 5, 2013 @ https://drugsandotherthings.wordpress.com.

Alexander Shulgin. From *Wikipedia*, the free encyclopedia @ https//en.wikipedia.org/wiki/Alxander_Shulgin.

Alexander Shulgin and Ann Shulgin, *PiHKAL* and *TiHKAL* @ http://mdma.net/alexander_shulgin/shulgins.html.

Alexander Shulgin Research Institute @ www.shulginresearch.org/home.

Barbara Boggs Sigmund. From *Wikipedia*, the free encyclopedia @ https://en.wikipedia.org/wiki/Barbara_Boggs_Sigmund.

Barbara Boggs Sigmund, Mayor of Princeton and Ex-Teacher, 51. *The New York Times* @ www.nytimes.com/…./barbara-boggs-sigmund/mayor-of-Princeton-and-ex-teacher-51.html.

Barbara Boggs Sigmund. NJWH. New Jersey Women's History @ www.womenshistory.org/discover/biographies/barbara-boggs-sigmund/.

Chris Smith, Ecstasy may become an FDA-approved medical treatment in five years. April 5, 2016 @ http://tgr.com/2016/04/05/ecstasy-treatment-ptsd-anxiety/#.

References

Solomons Business Association. History @ www.solomonsmaryland.com/history/.

Solomons Island, Maryland. BayDreaming.com @ www.baydreaming/destinations/solomons-island-maryland/.

Solomons, Maryland. From *Wikipedia*, the free encyclopedia @ https://en.wikipedia.org/wiki/Solomons,_Maryland.

Mikhail Soloviev, *When the Gods Are Silent*. David McKay and Company, Inc., New York, 1952.

Mark Sommer. Jesse Levine, principal violist, music director and professor, Feb. 21, 1940-Nov. 11, 2008 @ www.amusicfeast.com/Jesse_Levine_FOR_Web.doc.

Jeff Stafford, Two Peas in a Pod—Blondell and Cagney in *Blonde Crazy*. Posted on August 21, 2011. Movie Morlocks @ http://moviemorlocks/com/2011/08/two-peas-in-a-pod-blondell-and-cagney-in-blonde-crazy/.

Bob Stage, Oliver Stone Biography. IMDb @ www/imdb.com/name/nm0000231/bio?ref_=nm_ov_bio.

Star Trek: The Next Generation. IMDb @ www.imdb.com/title/tt0092455/.

List of *Star Trek: The Next Generation* Cast Members. *WikipediA* The Free Encyclopedia @ https://en.wikipedia.org/wiki/List_of_Star_Trek:_The_Next_Generation_cast_members.

Rod Steiger. From *Wikipedia*, the free encyclopedia @ https://en.wikipedia.org/wiki/Rod_Steiger.

Rod Steiger. *In the Heat of the Night*. Yankee Gospel Girl. Old Movies, New Eyes @ https://yankeegospelgirl.com/201/07/21/old-movies-new-eyes-in-the-heat-of-the-night/.

Rod Steiger. Obituary. BBC News World Edition @ http://news/bbc.co.uk/2/h/entertainment/1056105.stm/.

Scott Adams, Rod Steiger. Biography @ www.imbd.com/name/nm0001768/bio.

Patrick Stewart Network. The Official Patrick Stewart Fan Club Website @ www.patrickstewart.org/.

Patrick Stewart. From *Wikipedia*, the free encyclopedia @ http://en.wikipedia.org/wiki/Patrick_Stewart.

Stockhom Palace. From *Wikipedia*, the free encyclopedia, @ https://en.wikipedia.org/wiki/Stockholm_Palace.

Oliver Stone. From *Wikipedia*, the free encyclopedia @ https://en.wikipedia.org/wiki/Oliver_Stone.

Picture of Susan Strasberg. Listal @ www.listal.com/viewimage/5903494.

Susan Strasberg. From *Wikipedia*, the free encyclopedia @ https://en.wikipedia.org/wiki/Susan_Strasberg.

Tony Subia, Superstition Mountain (at Apache Junction, Arizona). Arizona Vacation Guide @ www.arizona.com/superstition_mountain.html.

Superstition Mountains. From *Wikipedia*, the free encyclopedia @ https://en.wikipedia.org/wiki/Superstition_Mountains.

Pyotr Ilyich Tchaikovsky. Biography. Composer (1840-1893 @ www.biography/com/people/pyotr-ilyich-tchaikovsky-9503375.

Larry Torres, Land, Light and Legend of Taos: Taos Mountain sacred to all. *The Taos News*, July 7, 2011.

Anastasia Toufexis and Patricia Delaney, A Crackdown on Ecstasy. *Time*, June 10, 1985.

Harry S. Truman. From *Wikipedia*, the free encyclopedia @ https://en.wikipedia.org/wiki/Harry_S._Truman.

Harry S. Truman Library & Museum @ www.trumanlibrary.org.

Manuvera, President Harry S. Truman. "I am Cyrus," August 17, 2010. The official website of Dr. Kaveh Farrokh @ https://kavehfarrokh.com/cyrus-the-great/president-harry-s-truman-I-am-cyrus/.

25th Academy Awards, From *Wikipedia*, the free encyclopedia @ https://en.wikipedia.org/wiki/25th_Academy_Awards.

The 2016 World Cup of Hockey Logos. Brands of the World @ www.brandsoftheworld.com/content/the-2016-world-cup-of-hockey-logos.

Arthur H. Vandenberg. From *Wikipedia*, the free encyclopedia @ https://en.wikipedia.org/wiki/Arthur_H._Vandenberg.

References

Ralph Vartabedian, Sam Iacobellis 1929-2016, Built B-1 bomber fleet, *Los Angeles Times*, September 7, 2016.

Lloyd Vries, Actor Rod Steiger Dies. CBS News. The Associated Press, July 9, 2002 @ www.cbsnews.com/news/actor-rod-steiger-dies/.

Walt Disney Concert Hall. From *Wikipedia*, the free encyclopedia @ http://en.wikipedia.org/wiki/Walt_Disney_Concert_Hall.

Lesley Ann Warren. Biography. IMDb @ www.imbd.com/nm0000690/bio?ref_=nm_ov_bio_sm.

The Washington Times. From *Wikipedia*, the free encyclopedia @ http://en.wikipedia.org/wiki/The_Washington_Times.

The Washington Times @ www.washingtontimes.com/.

Craig Webb. *Architect,* the Journal of the American Institute of Architects. Voices @www.architectmagazine.com/author/craig-webb.

The Lawrence Welk Show. From *Wikipedia*, the free encyclopedia @ https://en.wikipedia.org/wiki/The_Lawrence_Welk_Show.

Frank F. White, Jr., *The Governors of Maryland 1777-1970*. (Annapolis: The Hall of Records Commission, 1970), pp. 285-291.

William B. Tennison on Cruises. Sunset Supper History Cruise. Calvert Marine Museum @ www.calvertmarinemuseum.com/237/Wm-B-Tennison-Cruises.

Kenneth Turan, Joan Blondell gets top billing at film festival. *Los Angeles Times*, October 30, 2016.

Rhys Williams (Welsh-American actor). *WikipediA* The Free encyclopedia @ https://en.wikipedia.org/wiki/Rhys_Williams_(Welsh-American_actor).

Duke of Windsor, From *Wikipedia*, the free encyclopedia @ https://en.wikipedia.org/wiki/Duke_of_Windsor.

Duke & Duchess of Windsor @ www.royalty.nu/Europe/England/Windsor/EdwardVIII.html.

Windsor Castle. Royal Collection Trust @ www.royalcollection.org.uk/visit/windsorcastle.

World War II Database @ www.ww2db.com.

China human rights campaigner Harry Wu dies. Associated Press. Daily Mail.com @ www.dailymail.co.uk/wires/ap/article-3560781/China-human-rights-campaigner-Harry-Wu-dies.html.

Harry Wu. From *Wikipedia*, the free encyclopedia @ https://en.wikipedia.org/wiki/Harry_Wu.

The Story of Harry Wu. Political Prisoners.eu @ www.politicalprisoners.eu/harry-wu.html.

Tomas Bouska, Interview with Mr. Harry Wu. The Story of Harry Wu. Political Prisoners.eu @ www.politicalprisoners.eu/harry-wu.html.

William Yardley, Frederick I. Ordway III Dies at 87; NASA Official Helped Shape 'Space Odyssey.' *New York Times*, July 13, 2014.

William Yardley, Nathaniel Branden, a Partner in Love and Business with Ayn Rand, Dies at 84. The *New York Times*, December 8, 2014.

Index

Numbers in **bold** indicate photographs

A
Accused, The (1988) 145, 146
Adolf, King Gustaf VI 192-194
Adventures of Robin Hood, The (1946) 51
Arant, Gayle 91
Arant, Les 91
Armstrong, Louis ("Satchmo") 92
Arnold, Kenneth 63, 67
Asmodeus **118**, 129
Astaire, Fred 34
Atlas Shrugged (1957) 208, 209, 210, 211

B
Baltimore Symphony Orchestra 179, 180
Bantam Books 75
Begich, Congressman Nick 7, 9
Benedictine School for Exceptional Children 72
Berliner, Donald ("Don") 73
Beverly Hot Springs 135-155
Bibb, Professor Frank Leon 184-185
Big Country, The (1958) 55
Blondell, Joan 29
Bloom, Claire 134, 182-184
Boggs, Barbara see Sigmund, Barbara Boggs
Boggs, Cokie see Roberts, Cokie
Boggs, Marie ("Lindy") 1, 2, 3, 6, 7, 8-9, 10-13, 14, 15-16, **108**
Boggs, Thomas ("Tommy") Hale, Jr. 1, 2, 16, 18-19, **108**
Boggs, Thomas Hale, Sr. 1, 2, 3-7, 8-9, 10, 15, 18, 43, **108**
Booth, Shirley 136, 137
Branden, Devers 208-209
Branden, Nathaniel 208-211
Braun, Dr. Wernher von 68, 187-189
Breaux, Senator John 19
Brown, Townsend 65
Bryan, Colonel Joseph 79, 80, 82, 83, 84-85
Burge, Brad 106
Burton, LeVar 138-140
BUtterfield 8 136, 137

C
Cagney, James 28-31, **109**
Calvert Independent, The 4
Canby, Vincent 38
Cape Fear 36
Catia 3-D 158-159, 161, 162, 163
Cat on a Hot Tin Roof (1958) 55, 137
Central Intelligence Agency (CIA) 79-80, 83-87, 128, 150
Cerf, Bennett 210
Cerny, Paul 88, 90
Chaplin, Charles ("Charlie") 183
China Daily 177
Churchill, Sarah 12
Citizen Kane (1941) 202, 203
Clarke, Arthur C. 68, 69
Condon, Dr. Edward U. 75, 80
Contemporary Dialysis & Nephrology 169

Corea Times, The 136
Cotten, Joseph 34, **123**, 201-203
Coulon, Candy 16
Coulon, Charles ("Charlie") 1, 2, 3, 5, 16
Coulon, Elizabeth 1, 2, 3, 5, 16
Crosby, Bing 29, 212, 213
Crowder, Clifford N. 73
Cry in the Dark, A 154
Cunningham, Danny 196-197

D
Danner, Blythe 214
Daphnis and Chloe 165
Day, Doris 28
Deal, Borden 53
Dean, James xxv, 49-50, 52, 203
DeBoy, Annie ix, 4, 34, 45
DeBoy, Frank ix, 45
Deneault, Harold H., Jr. 67, **115**
Desire Under the Elms (1958) 55
Deinekin, General Pyotr 208
Diary of Anne Frank, The (1955) 204-205
DiMaggio, Joe 155
Dimensional Stone Magazine 158, 211
Disney, Lillian 157, 164
Disney, Walt 157
Down to the Sea in Ships record album 47-49, **111**
Dracula (1931) 152
Dracula (1979) 151-152
"Dress of White Silk, A" 33
Druffel, Ann 76, 77, 78, 92
Duel (1971) 32
Duel in the Sun (1946) 202
Duke of Windsor, The 189-191
Dulles, CIA Chief Allen 150

E
Earle, Captain Guy ix-x
Earle Family of Newfoundland and Labrador, The (2015) x, xxiv, 253-254

Earle, Neil xxiv
East of Eden (1955) xxv, 49-50
Ebert, Roger 143, 151
Eisenhower, First Lady Mamie 187, 188
Eisenhower, President Dwight D 24, 25, 187
Ellis, Paula 133-134
Energy Systems Group 205-206
Epper, Jeannie 215
Evans, Leroy 179
Evening's Entertainment, An 195
Exorcism **118**, 125, 129

F
Face the Nation 6
Falk, James 72
Farley, Walter 54
Federal Bureau of Investigation (FBI) 6-7, 85, 146,
Final Report on the Scientific Study of Unidentified Flying Objects 75-76
Firestorm: Dr. James E. McDonald's Fight for UFO Science (2003) 76, 78
Flames, The 198
Fleishmann, Ernest 165
Flying Saucer Conspiracy, The (1955) 63
Flying Saucers: A Modern Myth of Things Seen in the Skies (1958) 65
Flying Saucers Are Real, The (1950) 63, 64
Flying Saucers from Outer Space (1953) 63
Flying with Lindberg (1928) 64, 67, **114**
"Foggy Dew" 55
Follow the Sun (1951) 16
For Patients Only Magazine xxi, xxiv, 214
Foster, Jodie **120**, 145-146
Fountainhead, The (1946) 208, 209
Fournet, Dewey 79, 80-81, 82
Francis the Talking Mule 212-213
Franklin, Joe 69-71
Fuller, John G. 69-70

Index

G
Galt, John 210
Gandhi, Mahatma 138
Garrison, Jim 150
Gehry, Frank O. xxiv, 157-168
Giant (1956) xxv, 49, 52
Gilligan's Island (1964-1967) 141
G.I. Rupert Lore & Sons Marina 21, 33, 43, **108**
Glass Menagerie, The (1945) 194, 195
Going Home (1971) 38
Goldstein, Louis 43
Gore, Vice President Al 15
Grant, Cary 196, 205
Grant, Richard 135
Gravitz, Dr. Melvin 128
Groves, General Leslie R. 187, 188

H
Hall, Richard ("Dick") H. xxii, 66, 74, 78, 81, 82, 83, 87, 88
Halpern, Dr. John H. 95
Halsey, Admiral Bull xx
Hanks, Tom **121**, 143, 153-154, 167, 216
Hannah, Daryl 142-144
Haupt, Charles 186
Hayworth, Rita 33-34, **110**
Hearst, William Randolph 202
Heaven's Gate (1980) 203
Helms, Senator Jesse 169-170
Herald-Tribune, The 53
Heritage Auctions 194
Hill, Barney 70-71
Hill, Betty 70-71
Hillenkoetter, Admiral Roscoe 79, 84
Hinckley, Jr., John W. 145
Hitler, Adolf 180, 197
Hoover, J. Edgar 6
Hope, Bob 29, 216
Howard, Ken 213-216
Howards of Virginia, The (1940) 196

Huh, Dr. 136, 141
Hynek, Dr. J. Allen 73, 74, 76-77, 92, **116**

I
Iacobellis, Sam 205-208
I Aim at the Stars (1960) **113**, 186-189
I Love Melvin (1954) 212
In the Heat of the Night (1967) 133, 134
Interrupted Journey, The: Two Hours "Aboard a Flying Saucer" (1966) 70
Ives, Burl 35-36, 38, 45-59, **110, 111**
Ives, Helen 36, 47, 48, 52, 56, 66-67

J
Jackson, General Andrew 11-12
Jack Was Every Inch a Sailor 48-49, 58, 59
Jett, Dr. Page 50, 51
JFK (1991) 149-150
Johnson, President Lyndon B. 6, 15
Jonathan Livingston Seagull xii-xiii
Jones, Jennifer 194, 202
Jonz, Don 7
Judgment Day: My Years with Ayn Rand (1989) 209, 211
Jung, Dr. Carl 65-66
Jurgens, Curt 188

K
Kaeburn, Dr. Leslie 69
Kantor, MacKinlay 53-54
Katchen, Leon 73, **116**
Kazan, Elia 52
Kennedy, John F. 6, 10, 15, 17, 43, 149-150
Kennedy, John F., Jr. 143, 144
Kennedy, Robert F. 10, 43
Keyhoe, Major Donald E. 63-67, 69, 74, 75, 79-85, 87-88, 92, **112, 114**
King Edward VIII see Duke of Windsor
Koushnareff, Jessie 38, 40, 41
Kubrick, Stanley 68-69, 152

L

Lafitte, Jean 11
Langella, Frank 151-152
Laogai: The Chinese Gulag (1992) 174
Laughton, Charles 35
Lawrence, Gertrude 195
Leary, Anne xi-xii
Leary, Lt. Commander Joseph xi-xii
Levine, Jesse 185-186
Life Stinks! (1991) 147
Lindberg, Charles 64
Lolita (1997) 152
Lombardo, Guy 5
Long, Governor Huey 3-4
Lore, Dora Frances Deboy x, xiv, xv, xvi-xvii, xxiii-xv, 5, 6, 10-11, 12, 14, 22, 23-24, 25, 26-27, 43, 45, 50-51, 54, 58, 179, 180, 181, 182
Lore, Faye 35
Lore, Gordon Ira Rupert ("Dick"), Sr. x, xiv, xv, xvi-xvii, xxiii-xv, 3, 5, 6, 8, 10-11, 12, 14, 21, 22, 23-24, 25, 26-27, 41, 42, 43, 45, 50-51, 54, 58, 179, 180, 181, 182
Lore, Jon Shaw x, 42, 179, 180
Lore, Martha ("Marty") DeGroat xxii-xxiii, xxv-xxvi, 77-78, 88, 93, 94, 95, 97, 98, 99-100, 102, 103, 104, 106-107, 125, 128, 144, 201, 203-204, 205, 208, 209, 210, 211
Loren, Sophia 55
Los Angeles Times Magazine 165
Louise, Tina **119**, 140-141, 142
Love Me or Leave Me (1955) 28
Lucky Stars (1995) 38
Lugosi, Bela 151-152

M

MacIntyre, William 79
MacLaine, Shirley 38, 215
Magnani, Anna 136, 137
Malone, John 11
Maltzen, Michael 164
Mann, Cathy 136-138
Mann, Daniel 136-138
Marilyn and Me: Sisters, Rivals, Friends (1992) 205
Marilyn Monroe: Beyond the Legend (1982) 205
Martin, Norman 73
Massey, Raymond 49-50
Matheson, Richard 31-33
McClendon, Sarah 198-201
McDonald, Dr. James E. 74, 76-78, 88, 92
McDonald, John 54
McGowen, Elaine 91
McGowen, Fred 91
McKeldin, Theodore Roosevelt 24-28
McNamara, William ("Billy") 145, 146-147
Meese, Edwin 131, 132
Mendelssohn, Felix Robert 179-182
Merman, Ethel 213
Metzger, George R. 159-162
Michener, James A. xvii-xxi
Mineo, Sal 201, 202, 203
Mishtowt, Madam Illarion 38-41
Miss Sadie Thompson 33-34
Mitchum, Dorothy 35, 38
Mitchum, Robert 35-38, **111**, **112**
Monroe, Marilyn 143, 155, 204, 205, 213
Moon, Reverend Sun Myung 41-43
Morrison, Anita 14-15
Morrison, Mayor DeLesseps ("Chep") 14
"Mr. UFO" 63
Multidisciplinary Association for Psychedelic Studies (MAPS) 105-106
Munro, Robin 169
Mutual UFO Network (MUFON) 87, 90
Mysteries of the Skies: UFOs in Perspective 53, 67-68, 69-70, 82, **115**

Index

N
Nagata, Minoru 164
National Investigations Committee on Aerial Phenomena (NICAP) xxii, 63, 65-71, 73-88, **112**, **116**
National Law Journal 19
National Velvet 194, 195
Neill, Sam 154
Neville, John 182-184
Nevins, Dr. Allan xxvi
New York Times, The 38, 75-76
Nixon, Pat 187
Nixon, President Richard M. 6-7, 25, 41-42, 200-201, 254
Nixon, Stuart 79-80, 85, 86, 87

O
Oakland, Simon 70-71
O'Conner, Frank 209
O'Connor, Donald 211-213
"Ol' Man River" 57
Ordway, III, Dr. Frederick 68-69
Osborne, Robert 37
Oswald, Lee Harvey 6, 149-150

P
Pandora and the Flying Dutchman 2
Parisot, Aldo 186
Patton 37
Patton, General George xi, 37
Pawnbroker, The 133-134
Pecha, Bill 88-91
Pecha, Lenda 90
Peck, Gregory 36, 55, 194, 202
Picnic 204
Platoon 150
Pomeroy, James 72
Powers, William 73
Psychology of Self-Esteem, The 211
Public Utilities Fortnightly 199, 201

R
Raintree County 137
Rand, Ayn 164, 208-211
Rather, Dan 199, 200
Reading Rainbow 139
Reagan, Nancy 128, 130
Reagan, President Ronald 43, 128, 130, 145, 207
Remembering Marilyn 205
Research Analysis Corporation 72
Revere, Anne 194-196
Revere, Paul 194
Rice, Anne 32, 33
Roberts, Cokie 1, 2, 4, 15, 16, 17-18, **108**
Robinson, Kris xxi
Rockwell News 206, 254
Roddenberry, Gene 140
Rodriguez, Dr. Antonia ("Toni") **117**, 128-133
Rogers, Ginger 34
Romero, George A. 32-33
Roosevelt, President Theodore xxiv
Roots 139
Roots: The Gift 139
Rose Tattoo, The 136
Roush, J. Edward 74
Roxanne 143
Ruckelshaus, William 200-201
Russian Revolution 40, 197
Ryan's Daughter 37

S
Sagan, Dr. Carl 74
Salinger, Pierre 199, 200
Salonen, Esa-Pekka 165-166
Sandburg, Carl 54
Saturday Review 70
Scarface (1984) 149
Schulz, William F. 170-171
Scott, George C. 37, 184

Seven Little Foys, The 29
Seven Year Itch, The 143
1776 214
Shakespeare, William xvi, 182, 184, 185
Shirer, William 54
Shulgin, Alexander ("Sasha") 95-107
Sigmund, Barbara Boggs 1-2, 4-5, 7, 15-17, **108**
Sigmund, Professor Paul 17
Silence of the Lambs, The 146
Simon, Dr. Benjamin 70
Simpson, Wallis 191
Singin' in the Rain 212
Sing You Sinners 213
Smith, Richard S. 162-164
Soloviev, Mikhail 196-198
Somewhere in Time 32
South Pacific xviii, xxi
Spiner, Brent xxiii, 138, 139-140
Stalin, Joseph 197
Star Trek: The Next Generation 138-140
Stealing Home 145, 146
Steiger, Michael 134
Steiger, Rod 133-134, 184
Stewart, Patrick xxiii, 138, 140
Stoker, Bram 151
Stone, Oliver xxiii, 149-150
Story of G.I. Joe, The 36
Strange Effects From UFOs 68, 85, 253
Strasberg, Lee 140, 144, 147, 148, 149, 204
Strasberg, Susan 144, 203-205
Streep, Meryl 154
Streetcar Named Desire, A 184
Suddenly Last Summer 137
Suez 14
Sullivan, Walter 75-76
Svenson, Bo 20

T
Tawes, Governor Millard 43
Taxi Driver 145
Taylor, Elizabeth xxv, 49, 136, 137, 194
There's No Business Like Show Business 213
This is the Army 55
Thomas, Julia 56
Torresola, Griselio 22, 23
Troublemaker 175
True Magazine 63
Truman, Bess 22
Truman, President Harry S. 13, 22-24, **109**
Turner Classic Movies' *Private Screenings* 37
Twain, Mark xix
2001: A Space Odyssey 68-69
Two for the Seesaw 38
Tydings, Senator Joseph 43

U
UFO Investigator, The 71, 253
UFO Research Newsletter 83, 88
Unsinkable Molly Brown, The 212
U.S. News & World Report 66

V
Vallée, Dr. Jacques 76-77, 92, **116**
Vandenberg, Senator Arthur 198
Vanity Fair 166

W
Walt Disney Concert Hall **122**, 157-168
Waltz, Jacob 56
Warren, Chief Justice Earl 150
Warren, Lesley Ann 147-149
Warren, Margo 148
Washington Through a Purple Veil: Memoirs of a Southern Woman 16
Wayfaring Stranger, The 54
Webb, Craig 160
Weidman, Barbara 209

Index

Welles, Orson 31, 34, 202
When the Gods Are Silent 196, 198
White Christmas 212
White Heat 29
White Shadow, The 214
Williams, Justin xvii-xviii
Williams, Rhys xvii-xviii
Wilson, Rita 153
Wind Across the Everglades 36, 52-53, 55
Wolfson, Dr. Philip 105

Wonder Woman 215
Wood, Marie 72
Wu, Harry xxiv, 169-170, 172-178

Y

Yankee Doodle Dandy 29
Yogananda, Swami Paramahansa 138

Z

Zahniser, Sarah Jane 192

About the Author

Gordon Lore began his professional writing/editing career as Vice President/Secretary-Treasurer of the National Investigations Committee on Aerial Phenomena (NICAP, then the world's largest UFO organization) in the mid-1960s. He was responsible for heading a large scientific network of subcommittees and their members who lent their expertise toward solving one of the primary mysteries of the twentieth century and beyond. He played a prominent role in the first-ever Congressional day-long hearing on UFOs in September 1968. Lore was an uncredited scientific advisor to the late director Stanley Kubrick on his seminal science fiction film, *2001: A Space Odyssey*, in 1967. He is also the senior author of *Mysteries of the Skies: UFOs in Perspective* (Prentice-Hall, Inc., 1968), the first-ever book based entirely on the early history of UFOs, and the sole author of *Strange Effects From UFOs* (NICAP. 1969). He edited *UFOs: A New Look,* the *UFO Investigator* and the *UFO Research Newsletter.* He wrote and edited hundreds of published articles on one of the most mysterious scientific puzzles of all time. His latest book, *The Earle Family of NEWFOUNDLAND and the Birth of a Canadian Atlantic Province*, is now available as a Nook Book on the Barnes & Noble website. This work, with the title *The Earle Family of Newfoundland and Labrador,*

was also published in book form on July 1, 2015, by DRC Publishing in St. John's, Newfoundland and Labrador. Gordon is also in the process of uploading his new book entitled *The Priest of Kali: A Novelized Biography Based on the Life and Spiritual Ecstasies of Sri Ramakrishna* on the Barnes & Noble or Amazon Nook Book site.

Gordon also became a writer-editor in the public utilities field in which he became a White House and Congressional Senate/House Gallery correspondent. He was in the Oval Office of the White House in 1972 when President Richard M. Nixon signed Environmental Protection Agency legislation to improve air and water quality within the United States and its territories. In 1975, Lore became the Editor of *The Rockwell News*, Rockwell International's employee newspaper, and wrote about numerous topics ranging from the Apollo program to the Space Shuttle and nuclear energy. From 1992 to 2012, he was a prominent writer-editor in the kidney disease and renal transplantation arena. His hundreds of published articles on this topic led to his being recognized as a nominee for the prestigious first Medal of Excellence (known as the Nobel Prize of the renal care field) from the American Association of Kidney Patients (AAKP). One of the articles he solicited resulted in the formation of a dialysis clinic in the only hospital on the island country of Belize, leading to his AAKP recognition.

Lore has also written and published on a number of other issues, including the spiritual, the occult, and the early history of aviation. He is particularly known among his colleagues as never having missed an editorial deadline in his entire half-a-century career.

Gordon may be reached at (661) 255-7155, Gordon.lore@gmail.com and at his personal website at www.gordonlore.com.

www.ingramcontent.com/pod-product-compliance
Lightning Source LLC
Chambersburg PA
CBHW071703160426
43195CB00012B/1559